Office of Population Censuses and Surveys
Social Survey Division

Private renting in England 1993/94

A report of the 1993/94 Survey of English Housing
carried out by Social Survey Division of OPCS
on behalf of the Department of Environment

Siobhán Carey

London: HMSO

Contents

Contents *continued*

Acknowledgements

Any large scale survey involves the co-operation and collaboration of a large number of people. First mention should go to all those who gave up their time to be interviewed, their co-operation was particularly appreciated. I would also like to thank the interviewers who worked on the survey and my colleagues in OPCS who contributed to the study, in particular the Survey of English Housing team. I would particularly like to thank Denis Down (Department of the Environment) for his unfailing support and interest in this study and for his insightful comments on drafts of this report.

Notes to tables

1. The following conventions have been used in tables:

Thousands	0	No cases
	[]	Number of cases less than 30
	..	Data not available
Percentages -	-	No cases
	*	Percentage not shown because the base is small (under 30)
	0	Less than 0.5%
	..	data not available

2. The tables exclude households for whom information is missing for the items analysed. This means that the number of cases in a category may vary slightly from table to table.

3. Unless otherwise stated, changes and differences mentioned in the text are statistically significant at the 95% confidence level.

Introduction

The size and composition of the private rented sector has changed beyond all recognition since the start of the century when it was the most common form of housing tenure. Although the private rented sector now only represents a small proportion, 9.7%, of the total housing market, it has been growing over the last few years and plays an important role in meeting the housing demands of a number of groups: young people setting up home for the first time, households in the process of relocation and new households forming as the result of divorce or separation.

This report describes the main characteristics of the private rented sector in 1993 and makes comparisons with previous private renters surveys. The report is based on information collected as part of the 1993/4 Survey of English Housing (SEH), the first in a new series of annual housing surveys. The SEH is a continuous multi-purpose housing survey carried out by the Social Survey Division (SSD) of OPCS for the Department of Environment (DoE), the government department responsible for housing policy in England. Part of the survey focuses specifically on the private rented sector because, unlike the other sectors, there is very little information available on private tenants from administrative sources or regular statistical returns.

A separate volume reports the results from the SEH for 1993/94 for other sectors.[1]

Previous surveys of private renters

Since the late 1970s a series of surveys of the private rented sector have been carried out on behalf of the Department of the Environment by OPCS. These surveys have monitored changes in the characteristics of private tenants and their households, the kinds of accommodation rented, the rents paid and the type of agreement under which tenants rent their accommodation.

The first of these surveys of privately renting households was carried out in 1978[2] and provided a benchmark for the series. More recent private renters surveys in 1988 and 1990[3] have looked at the effects of legislative changes on the sector over the recent past.

The 1988 and 1990 private renters surveys straddled the 1988 Housing Act which introduced major changes to the types of tenancies available, allowing private landlords to charge market rents and making it easier for them to regain possession of their property. The 1990 survey was carried out some 18 months after the legislation was implemented. A year later a study was carried out in five local authorities to examine how the effects of deregulation varied in areas with different types of housing markets.[4] A summary of legislation relating to private renters is given in Appendix E.

As far as possible, the SEH used the same questions and definitions as the previous surveys. Any differences which are likely to affect comparability are noted in the text.

Design of previous surveys

Previous surveys of private renters were designed as follow-up surveys to the OPCS Labour Force Survey. Interviewing private renters as part of the SEH has a number of advantages. Apart from reducing the number of stages at which non-response can occur, the SEH was able to identify tenants who rent within owner occupier or social renting households, that is, where the head of household is not renting privately. This small group of private renters were not included in previous surveys.

The sample

The SEH sample was designed to yield a representative sample of 20,000 households in England each year. The sample was selected in two stages: first, a sample of postcode sectors was selected from the Postcode Address File (PAF); then, a sample of addresses was selected within the sampled sectors. The design provides a nationally representative sample in each quarter of the year. A fuller description of the sample design is given in Appendix B.

Response to the survey

The sample consisted of about 29,000 addresses which yielded about 25,000 households eligible for interview. Interviews were achieved with 80%. A total of 1,714 privately renting households was identified and a further 93 non-privately renting households were found to contain private tenants. These households contained 1,958 tenancy groups (defined in the section 'Units of analysis and definitions' below) and interviews were carried out with 95%. (See Appendix B)

Weighting and grossing

The data presented in this report are weighted and grossed to give estimates for the whole population of England. Comparisons of the SEH with the Labour Force Survey suggest that the 1993/4 SEH may have underestimated the proportion of privately renting households by 0.9 percentage points. The SEH data have therefore been weighted to compensate for this under-estimation. A description of the weighting and grossing method is given in Appendix C.

Units of analysis and definitions

Estimates of the size of the private rented sector (Chapter 1) are based on households but for the most part of this report the unit of analysis is the tenancy group.

A household is defined as a group of people living regularly at the same address, who either share at least one meal a day or share a living room.

The term 'tenancy' is used to describe the renting agreement whereby tenants rent the accommodation or occupy it free of charge.[5] The different types of letting agreements are described in Chapter 2 and Appendix A.

The term 'tenancy group' refers to everyone covered by the same renting agreement. Members of a tenancy group share the legal status conferred by the agreement and their accommodation is paid for by a single rent. Households which consist of a single family unit (see Appendix A for definition) will contain only one tenancy group. Some households, flat sharers for example, may contain more than one tenancy group depending on the composition of the household and on the letting arrangements with the landlord.

The tenant or partner in each tenancy group was interviewed. The tenant is defined as the person in whose name the accommodation is rented unless that person is a married or cohabiting woman. In such cases it is the woman's husband or partner who is defined as the tenant in the same way that the definition of head of household gives priority, by statistical convention, to the male partner.

Data presentation and interpretation

Data collected through a survey are subject to sampling error; the sampling errors for the key variables are given in Appendix D. Most tables show both percentages and the estimated total number (rounded to the nearest thousand) of tenancies or households for the groups being described. In many cases, this is a higher degree of precision than the sampling error would warrant, but it allows the user to add and subtract figures in tables without further loss of accuracy. Text references to the grossed figures are rounded to the nearest 10,000.

Key data are presented in charts and tables in the text. More detailed figures, including the source data for the charts, are given in Annex tables at the end of the report.

Unweighted sample bases for the main characteristics are given at the beginning of the Annex tables. However, since approximately one in a thousand households was sampled, the unweighted base for a percentage is generally similar to the corresponding number of thousands shown in the table.

Notes and references

1 Hazel Green and Jacqui Hansbro. *Housing in England 1993/94.* HMSO (London 1995).
2 J E Todd, M R Bone and I Noble. *The privately rented sector in 1978.* HMSO (London 1982).
3 Tricia Dodd. *Private renting in 1988.* HMSO (London 1990).
4 Irene Rauta and Ann Pickering. *Private renting in England 1990.* HMSO (London 1992).
   Margaret Bone and Errol Walker. *Private renting in five localities.* HMSO (London 1994).
5 Some of the arrangements between landlord and tenant are informal and are not strictly legal tenancies, though we refer to them collectively by this term.

1 The privately rented sector in 1993

SUMMARY

- The number of households renting privately fell from 1.91 million in 1981 to 1.7 million in 1988. Towards the end of the 1980s the number of households renting privately started to increase and by 1993 1.93 million rented privately. In percentage terms, that was 11% of households in 1981, 9% in 1988 and 10% in 1993

- Over half of all lettings in 1993 (56%) were assured or assured shorthold lettings and 19% were regulated lettings; the proportion of tenancy groups with assured or assured shorthold lettings has doubled since 1990 (28%)

- The proportion of tenants renting from an individual (rather than corporate) landlord increased from 53% in 1988 to 60% in 1990 to 67% in 1993 (These figures do not include lettings by a resident landlord, who are necessarily individuals).

- Fewer tenancies in 1993 were renting from an employer (13%) than in 1990 (21%).

- Over a quarter of tenants (560 thousand) were living in converted flats and 12% (260 thousand) were living in purpose-built flats. Higher proportions of tenancy groups in London were living in converted or purpose-built flats (39% and 25% respectively) than in other regions.

- Over half of all tenancy groups in 1993 (1.1 million) consisted of one adult, 37% aged 16-59 and 14% aged 60 or over.

This chapter looks at the place of private renting in the overall housing market and outlines some of the main characteristics of the sector and how they vary across region.

1.1 Background

At the beginning of the century private renting was the most common form of housing tenure (an estimated 90% of all dwellings). Since then enormous changes have taken place. Since the Second World War the combined effect of the growth of home ownership, slum clearance and restriction of rents has resulted in a decrease in the size of the private rented sector. By 1972, only 18% of households in England rented privately and by the start of 1978 this had dropped to 12%.[1]

The size of the sector remained broadly stable during the quiet housing market of the early 1980s then declined again in the period when there was most activity in the owner-occupied market and rising house prices. At the low point in early 1989 there were 15% fewer privately renting households than in 1981. After 1989 there was a sustained increase so that by 1993 the number had recovered to about the same level as in 1981. Both the deregulation of new lettings and the downturn in the owner-occupied market made renting more attractive relative to owner occupation. The provisions of the 1988 Housing Act which affected the private rented sector came into effect in January 1989. They allowed landlords to charge a market rent on lettings starting after that date and introduced a new form of tenancy agreement, the Assured Shorthold, which gave the landlord repossession of the accommodation at the end of the agreed term. Difficulties in selling, combined with the greater ease of repossession, encouraged some owner occupiers to let their property rather than leave it vacant. Other measures which probably contributed to the increase were the extension of the Business Expansion Scheme tax concessions to the private rented housing sector between April 1988 and December 1993 and the temporary letting of property by moving owner occupiers who could not sell in a depressed housing market.

1.2 Trends in other sectors

The increase in owner occupation and social renting in the post war period was matched by a decline in the private rented sector. The increase in home ownership was stimulated by a number of measures such as favourable tax treatment[2] and then, in the 1980s, the 'Right-to-buy' legislation. The number of households owning their homes increased from 9.9 million (57%) in 1981 to 13.5 million (68%) in 1993.[3] The social rented sector has also seen a number of changes. After the Second World War local authority housing provision expanded quickly and, by the beginning of the 1980s, 5.1 million households in England (30%) rented from a local authority. Following the 'Right-to-buy' legislation, the number of households renting from a local authority decreased steadily and, by 1993, 3.7 million households (19%) were local authority tenants.

The 1988 Housing Act provided a new financial structure for house building by housing associations and allowed for transfers of local authority housing stocks to housing associations ('large scale voluntary transfers'). In addition, an increasing proportion of the finance for new housing association accommodation was raised from private sources and it was government policy for housing associations to replace local authorities as the providers of new subsidised housing for rent. Both measures - the legislation and private sector funding - have increased the housing associations' role in providing subsidised rented housing. Between 1981 and 1993 the number of households renting from a housing association doubled from 360 thousand households (2%) to 730 thousand households (4%).

Looking at trends in the social rented sector as a whole, Figure 1.1 shows that the number of such households decreased from 5.5 million (32%) in 1981

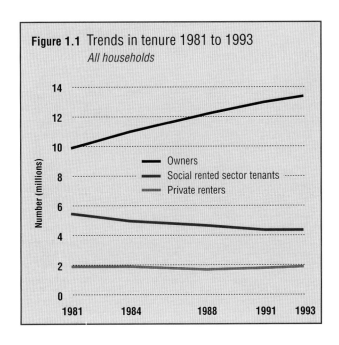

Figure 1.1 Trends in tenure 1981 to 1993
All households

Owners
Social rented sector tenants
Private renters

Number (millions)

to 4.4 million (23%) in 1991 but did not change between 1991 and 1993. The decrease in the number of households renting from a local authority was accompanied by a compensating increase in the number of households renting from a housing association. (Figure 1.1)

1.3 The size of the sector

Estimates from the SEH show that there were 1.93 million households in England (9.7% of all households) renting privately in 1993. This is an increase on the estimated numbers of privately renting households and on the proportion of all households who rent privately since the 1991 and 1989 Labour Force Surveys.[4]

Year	Number of households	% of all households
1981	1,910,000	11.1
1984	1,920,000	10.7
1989	1,610,000	8.6
1991	1,820,000	9.4
1993	1,930,000	9.7

1.4 Types of letting agreements

The letting agreement, or tenancy, refers to the arrangement between the landlord and tenant under which the tenant occupies the accommodation.[5] The analysis of letting agreements is therefore based on tenancies rather than households. For the purposes of analysis, letting agreements are grouped into eight categories:

- Assured
- Assured Shorthold
- Regulated - rent registered
- Regulated - rent not registered
- Lettings not accessible to the public - rent free
- Lettings not accessible to the public - rent paid
- Resident landlord lettings
- No security lettings

See Chapter 2 and Appendix A for a description of the different types of letting agreements. The classification of letting agreements is slightly different to that used in the 1988 and 1990 private renters reports and reflects changes in the range of tenancies available.

As mentioned in the Introduction, the SEH includes tenants who live in non-privately renting households. Less than 1% of non-privately renting households were found to incorporate private tenants. Four per cent of all tenancy groups were in non-privately renting households, almost all in owner-occupied households. The characteristics of these tenancies and their host households are described in Chapter 2.

The most common form of letting agreements found in 1993 were Assured and Assured Shorthold lettings. There were an estimated 830 thousand tenancies with assured shorthold lettings in 1993 and a further 380 thousand had assured lettings. These two types of lettings accounted for 56% of all lettings in 1993, almost three times as many as regulated lettings (19%) or lettings not accessible to the public (17%). (Figure 1.2)

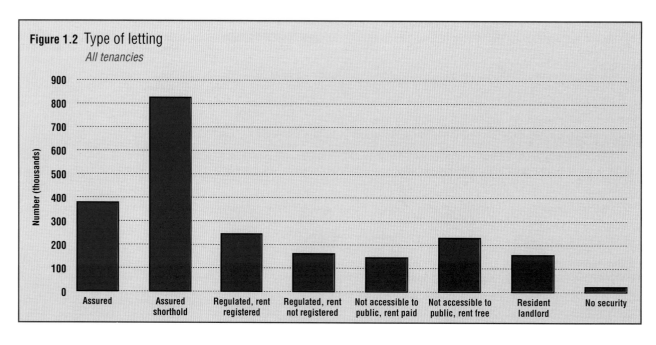

Figure 1.2 Type of letting
All tenancies

The proportion of tenancies (in privately renting households[6]) with assured or assured shorthold lettings has more than doubled since 1990, from 28% to 58%. Because all new lettings since 1989 are deregulated, the regulated sector has decreased in size with the largest reduction occurring in lettings whose rent was not registered, the proportion falling from 33% in 1988 to only 8% in 1993. (Figure 1.3)

1.5 Types of landlord

The majority of tenancies in 1993 were lettings by non-resident individual landlords, (1.4 million or 67%).

When tenancies in non-privately renting households are excluded, the proportion of tenancies in 1993 renting from a private individual is 70%. This is an increase on the proportion found in previous surveys, 53% in 1988 and 60% in 1990. The second half of the 1980s was a period of rapid house price inflation with house prices reaching a peak in 1989. The fall in house prices since 1989 and difficulties in selling, or unwillingness to sell for a lower price than was paid for the property, led many owners to let their property instead. Research among letting agents in 1993 found that almost one fifth (18%) of landlords they acted for were private individuals who were unable to sell their properties.[7]

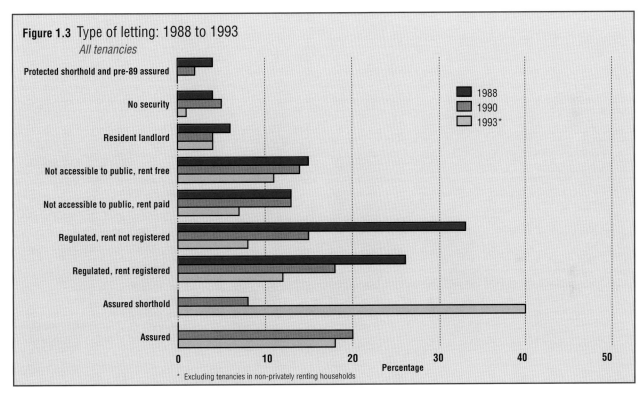

Figure 1.3 Type of letting: 1988 to 1993

All tenancies

* Excluding tenancies in non-privately renting households

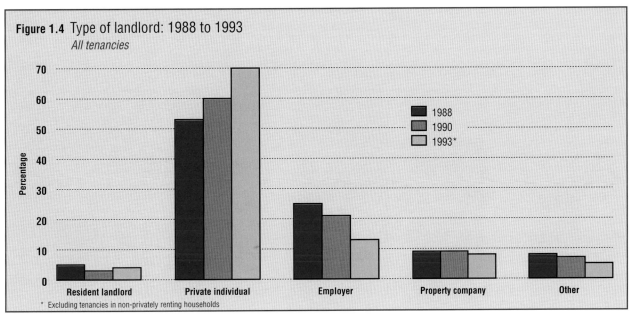

Figure 1.4 Type of landlord: 1988 to 1993

All tenancies

* Excluding tenancies in non-privately renting households

The proportion of tenants renting accommodation from their employer decreased from 21% in 1990 to 13% in the 1993 survey. (Figure 1.4)

1.6 Type of accommodation

An estimated 560 thousand tenancies (26%) were living in converted flats and a further 260 thousand (12%) were living in purpose-built flats. Over half of all tenancy groups, 1.25 million (58%) were living in houses as opposed to flats or other types of accommodation. (Figure 1.5)

The proportion of tenancy groups living in converted flats increased from 17% in 1990 to 26% in 1993 (27% when private renters in non-privately renting households are excluded). There is anecdotal

evidence that converted flats were more difficult to sell over the last few years and are therefore more likely to be let when the owner wanted to move. (Figure 1.6)

1.7 Length of tenancy

In terms of the length of the tenancy[8] the private rented sector is more polarised than other sectors. The majority of tenancies were recent: one third (710 thousand) had started in 1993 or 1994 and a further 29% (630 thousand) started in 1991 or 1992. Thus, almost two thirds of all tenancies (1.34 million) dated from 1991 or later. Although most tenancies are fairly recent there is a still a considerable number of tenants who have been resident for a very long time. Just over one in ten tenancies (210 thousand) started before 1969. These older tenancies are mainly in regulated tenancies and

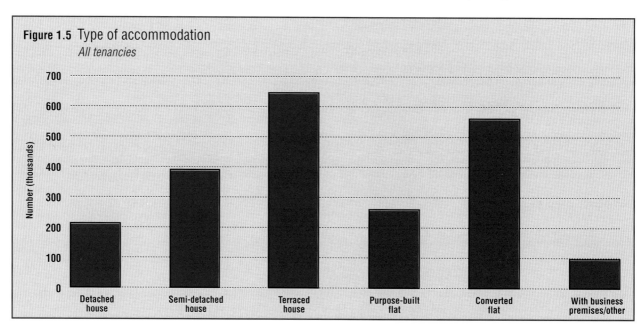

Figure 1.5 Type of accommodation
All tenancies

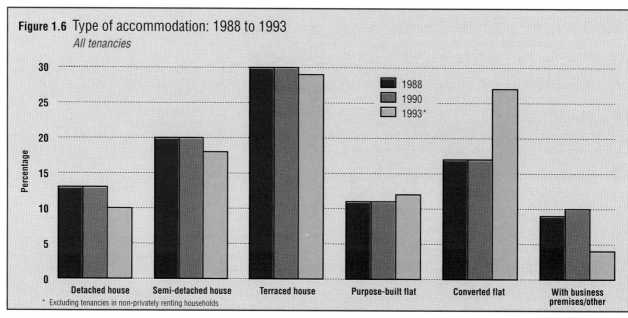

Figure 1.6 Type of accommodation: 1988 to 1993
All tenancies

* Excluding tenancies in non-privately renting households

would face a sharp increase in rent as well as, probably, the loss of security of tenure if they moved. The relative brevity of lettings accounts for a large part of the redistribution of letting types and, in particular, for the increase in the proportion of assured and assured shorthold tenancies since their introduction. (Figure 1.7)

1.8 Composition of tenancy group

Over half of all tenancy groups in 1993 (1.1 million) consisted of one adult, 37% (800 thousand) aged 16-59 and 14% (300 thousand) aged 60 or over. Just under a quarter of tenancies (500 thousand) contained two adults and the majority of these consisted of people under 60. Lone parents with dependent children accounted for just 5% of tenancy groups (110 thousand). (Figure 1.8)

Figure 1.9 shows trends in tenancy group composition between 1988 and 1993. For comparability with previous surveys tenancies in non-privately renting households are excluded from the 1993 data. Over this period, the proportion of tenancy groups consisting of one adult aged 16 to 59 has increased while the proportion consisting of older people has decreased. In 1988, 25% of tenancies consisted of one adult aged 16-59; this had increased to 28% of tenancies in 1990, and 35% in 1993 (37% including tenancies in non-privately renting households).

Although the proportions of tenancies in the different groups changed between 1988 and 1993, the only tenancy group that declined in actual size was older two-person tenancy groups. In 1990 there were estimated to be 200 thousand such tenancy groups and the estimated

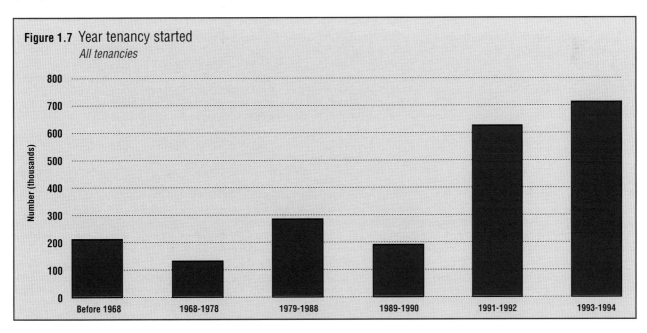

Figure 1.7 Year tenancy started
All tenancies

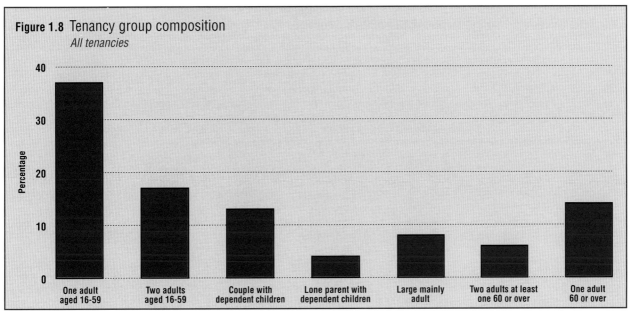

Figure 1.8 Tenancy group composition
All tenancies

number in 1993 was 130 thousand tenancies. Tenancy groups comprising older people tend to be in long-standing regulated tenancies. The proportion of tenancies containing one person aged 60 or over decreased by one percentage point but the estimated number of such tenancies increased from 260 thousand to almost 300 thousand. The change in balance between one and two person tenancy groups is probably due to the death of a partner in what was originally a couple household. Because of the steadily declining numbers of tenancies with regulated lettings there is relatively little replenishment from younger age cohorts. (Figure 1.9)

1.9 Regional variations in private renting

The proportion of households who rent privately varies by region. Private rented accommodation tends to be concentrated in large cities and university towns which have young, mobile populations. Greater London and the South West had the highest proportions of privately renting households (14%). The South West has a combination of a large student population and a high proportion of households in tied accommodation, mainly Armed Services personnel in Ministry of Defence property. Other regions with higher than average proportions of private renters may have one of these factors, for example, East Midlands has a large student population and East Anglia has a relatively large number of agricultural workers in tied accommodation, but it is the presence of both factors which probably explains the high proportion in the South West. The northern regions had relatively low proportions of privately renting households (6% - 8%). (Figure 1.10)

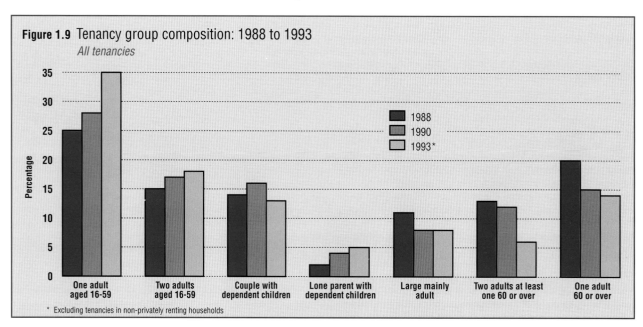

Figure 1.9 Tenancy group composition: 1988 to 1993
All tenancies

* Excluding tenancies in non-privately renting households

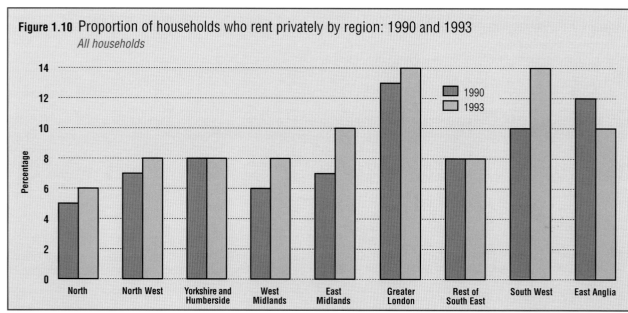

Figure 1.10 Proportion of households who rent privately by region: 1990 and 1993
All households

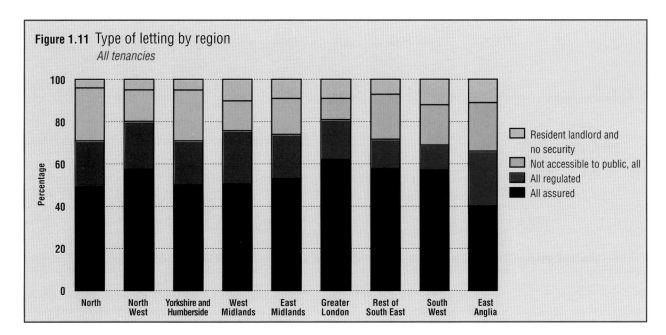

Figure 1.11 Type of letting by region
All tenancies

Variations in the proportion of households who rent privately and the greater concentration of population in the South means that 60% of all privately renting households were in the South.

Figure 1.11 shows type of letting analysed by region. Greater London had the highest proportion of assured and assured shorthold tenancies (62%) while East Anglia had the lowest proportion of such lettings (40%). It has already been noted that East Anglia had a high proportion of agricultural workers in tied accommodation. It also had a high proportion of older tenancies compared with other regions. Forty one per cent of tenancies in East Anglia started before 1988 compared with 28% of tenancies in Greater London, 26% of tenancies in the South West and 30% of tenancies in the East Midlands for example. This

means that there has not been the same opportunity for the redistribution of tenancies into the newer lettings types as there was in other regions which had a higher proportion of recent lettings. (Figure 1.11)

The majority of lettings in all regions were lettings by non-resident individual landlords. Lettings by property companies were most common in the Greater London area (14%) and in the North West (12%) while the proportion of lettings by employers were lower in both these areas than in England as a whole. (Figure 1.12)

Tenancies in Greater London were much more likely to be living in purpose-built or converted flats than tenancies in other regions. Almost two thirds of tenancies in London were living in flats (39% in

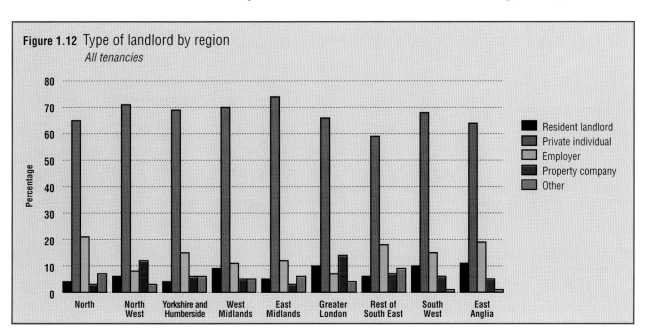

Figure 1.12 Type of landlord by region
All tenancies

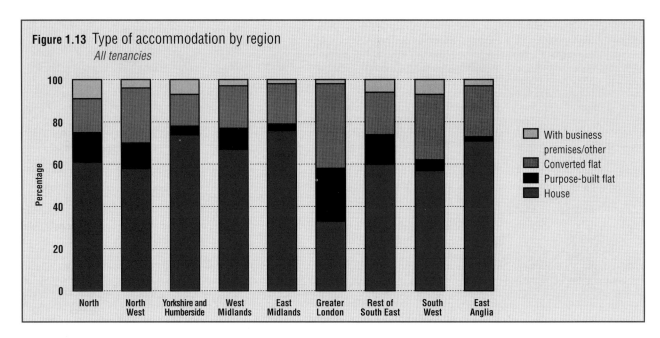

Figure 1.13 Type of accommodation by region
All tenancies

Legend:
- With business premises/other
- Converted flat
- Purpose-built flat
- House

Regions (x-axis): North, North West, Yorkshire and Humberside, West Midlands, East Midlands, Greater London, Rest of South East, South West, East Anglia

converted flats and 25% in purpose-built flats), compared with 36% of tenancies in the South West and just 20% of tenancies in Yorkshire and Humberside. (Figure 1.13)

1.10 Differences between urban and rural areas

Figure 1.14 shows the distribution of letting types by whether the local authority district is mostly urban or mostly rural in character. The classification of urban and rural is not very precise, there are substantial rural areas in the 'urban' local authority districts and most of the 'rural' districts include some medium sized towns. Lettings not accessible to the public were twice as common in rural areas (27%) as in urban areas (14%). Most of such tenancies in rural areas were renting accommodation which went with a job, 88% compared with 56% in urban areas. (Figures 1.14 and 1.15)

Notes and references

1   *General Household Survey 1972.* HMSO (London 1978).
2   Mortgage interest relief plus the equivalent for owner occupiers with incomes too low to pay much tax, the end of Schedule A in 1963 and the sole or main residence exemption from capital gains tax.
3   Department of the Environment. *Housing Trailers to the 1981 and 1984 Labour Force Surveys.* HMSO (London 1988).
    Department of the Environment. *Housing in England: Housing Trailers to the 1988 and 1991 Labour Force Surveys.* HMSO (London 1993).
4   The SEH was weighted and grossed to provide estimates for England. See Appendix C for a description of the grossing method used and differences from previous methods. Estimates are based on households and do not include tenancies in non-privately renting households.
5   See units of analysis and definitions in Introduction and Appendix A.
6   To maintain comparability with previous surveys, tenancies in non-privately renting households have been excluded from the 1993 data.
7   Joseph Rowntree Foundation. *Housing research findings No. 90* (May 1993).
8   The definition of tenant gives priority, by statistical convention, to men, as does the definition of head of household. In a few cases the tenant's partner may have been renting the accommodation before him. In these cases the start of tenancy is taken as the date he moved in even though she may have been there longer.

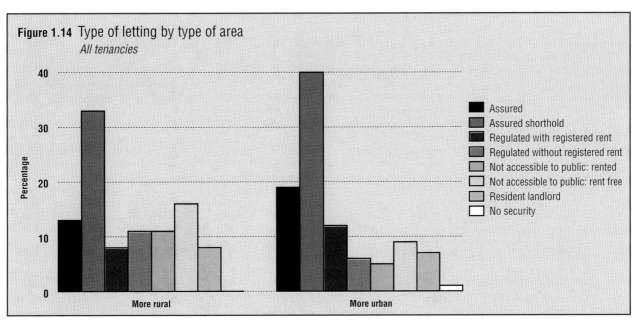

Figure 1.14 Type of letting by type of area
All tenancies

Legend:
- Assured
- Assured shorthold
- Regulated with registered rent
- Regulated without registered rent
- Not accessible to public: rented
- Not accessible to public: rent free
- Resident landlord
- No security

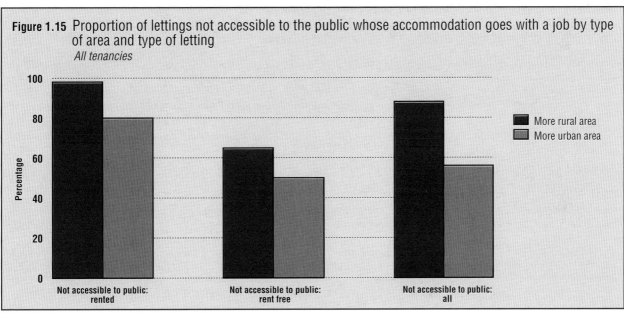

Figure 1.15 Proportion of lettings not accessible to the public whose accommodation goes with a job by type of area and type of letting
All tenancies

Legend:
- More rural area
- More urban area

2 Characteristics of different letting types

SUMMARY

- Assured and assured shorthold lettings were the most common form of letting type in 1993, accounting for 1.2 million lettings (56%). Tenants with this type of letting agreement tended to be young people in employment. Most rented from a private individual (85%) and only 14% rented from a corporate landlord.

- Regulated lettings accounted for 19% of all lettings in 1993, about 400 thousand lettings. All regulated lettings necessarily started before 1989, and tended to be of long duration. They were held predominantly by older people and the accommodation tended to be older, nearly all rented unfurnished.

- Seventeen per cent of lettings in 1993 were not accessible to the public (380 thousand). Tenancy groups with this type of tenancy were quite diverse in composition; 26% were married or cohabiting couples with dependent children and 39% contained one or two adults of working age. Over two thirds of tenants were renting from an employer.

- Resident landlord and no security lettings made up just 8% of all lettings, 160 thousand resident landlord lettings and 20 thousand no security lettings. Typically these were fairly recent lettings to one young tenant living in furnished accommodation with a resident landlord. Over a third of tenants were living in converted flats (39%) and a relatively high proportion (20%) shared part of their accommodation with another household.

- There were 90 thousand tenancy groups in non-privately renting households and as a group they were fairly homogenous. Typically, the tenants were young unmarried men living in a household where the head of household was also young and unmarried. Most were renting from someone who was buying their home with a mortgage.

This chapter provides profiles of the tenancy groups in each of the four main letting types, describing both the main features of the tenants and of the accommodation in which they were living.1 The last part of the chapter looks at the characteristics of private renters in non-privately renting households, a group not covered by the earlier surveys.

2.1 Types of letting

Tenancies were classified into one of eight different letting types depending on the type of agreement tenants had with their landlord. For most analyses in this report the tenancies are grouped into four broad categories. Figure 1.2 showed the overall distribution of different types of lettings and the Annex tables to this chapter give a more detailed breakdown for all eight categories. The different types of letting are:

Assured lettings
- assured lettings
- assured shorthold lettings

Regulated lettings
- regulated lettings with registered rent
- regulated lettings in which the rent is not registered

Lettings not accessible to the public
- tenancies who rent from an employer
- rent free lettings

Other lettings
- no security lettings
- lettings in which there is a resident landlord.

The next four sections summarise the main features of tenants in each of the four main letting types so as to create a profile of the different groups. The aim of the text is to provide a pen picture rather than a comparative analysis. The accompanying charts (Figures 2.1 to 2.13) however, present the information in a different way; they each show the characteristics of tenants in all four letting types, so that comparisons between letting types can be made.

2.2 Assured and assured shorthold lettings

All tenancies starting after 14th January 1989 are Assured, unless there is a written notice that they are Assured Shorthold or they fall into one of the excluded categories, for example, business lettings or lettings by resident landlords. Tenants with assured lettings have security of tenure and the landlord can seek possession only on one of the grounds specified, such as where the tenant has not been paying the rent regularly or where the landlord wishes to use the property as his/her main residence. Rents are agreed at the beginning of the tenancy, with provision for review. Tenancies starting on 15th January 1989 or later could be Assured Shorthold. The landlord must give written notice at the outset that the tenancy is an Assured Shorthold. Assured Shorthold lettings are for a fixed term of at least six months and tenants have security of tenure, as for Assured tenancies, during the fixed term, at the end of which the landlord is entitled to possession. Rents are agreed between landlord and tenant.

Assured and assured shorthold lettings were by far the most common type of letting and between them

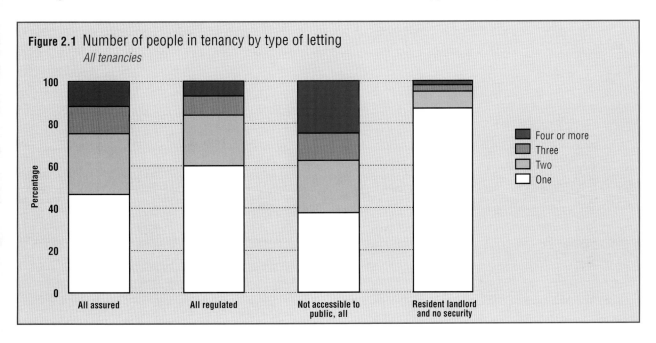

Figure 2.1 Number of people in tenancy by type of letting
All tenancies

accounted for more than half of all lettings (56%). This represents about 1.2 million lettings, 800 thousand assured shorthold and 400 thousand assured. They were also the most diverse group both in terms of the characteristics of the tenants and in terms of the accommodation they rented.

Tenants tended to be young people in employment and drawn from all socio-economic groups. The majority of tenancy groups consisted of one or two adults of working age:

- 68% contained one or two persons aged under 60
- 25% consisted of 3 or more people
- 55% of tenants were aged under 30
- 50% of tenants were working full time
- the mean disposable tenancy group income was

slightly higher than average (£200 compared with £190 a week)[2]

- most tenants (87%) had started their current letting agreement in 1991 or later

The accommodation occupied by assured and assured shorthold tenancy groups was fairly evenly divided between furnished and unfurnished[3] accommodation. Most rented their accommodation from a private individual rather than a corporate landlord.

- 32% lived in converted flats
- Similar proportions were renting furnished (51%) and unfurnished (49%) accommodation
- 42% were living in accommodation that was above the bedroom standard[4]
- Over half were renting accommodation valued in

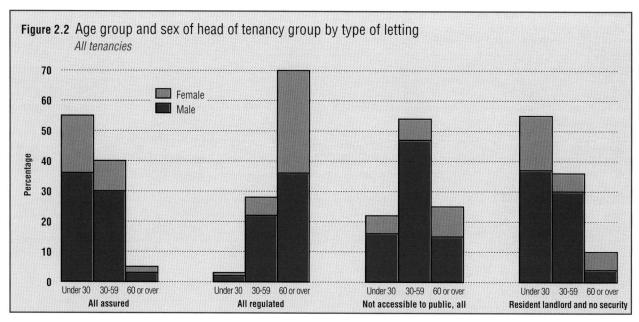

Figure 2.2 Age group and sex of head of tenancy group by type of letting
All tenancies

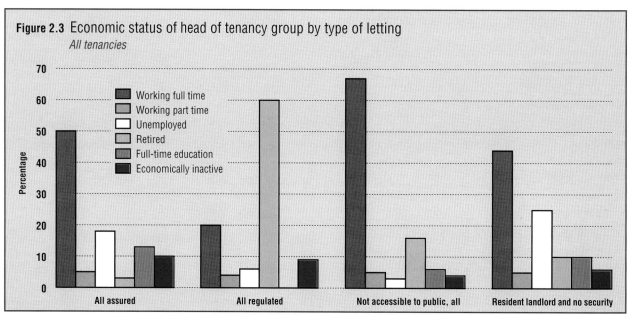

Figure 2.3 Economic status of head of tenancy group by type of letting
All tenancies

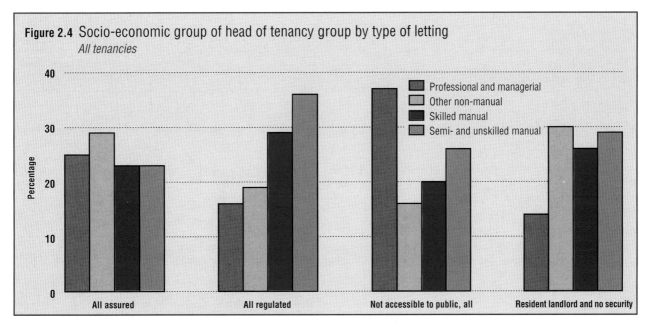

Figure 2.4 Socio-economic group of head of tenancy group by type of letting
All tenancies

Legend:
- Professional and managerial
- Other non-manual
- Skilled manual
- Semi- and unskilled manual

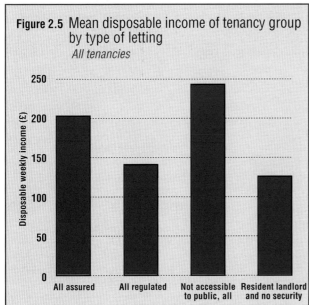

Figure 2.5 Mean disposable income of tenancy group by type of letting
All tenancies

the two lower council tax bands (£52 thousand or less)

- 86% rented their accommodation from a private individual

2.3 **Regulated lettings**

Most private lettings by non-resident private landlords which began before 15th January 1989 are Regulated tenancies unless they fall into one of the excluded categories (for example, lettings not accessible to the public and no security lettings). No new Regulated tenancies could be created from that date but the status of regulated tenancies in existence at that time remains unchanged. Tenants have full security of tenure and the landlord can gain possession only on fairly narrowly specified grounds. Either the landlord or the tenant can apply to the rent officer for registration of a fair rent, which becomes the maximum the landlord can charge. Not all regulated lettings have registered rents but the possibility of registration probably affects the rent charged.

Regulated lettings accounted for 19% of all lettings in 1993, about 400 thousand lettings. All regulated lettings necessarily started before 1989, and tend to be of long duration. They were held predominantly by older people and the accommodation also tended to be older, nearly all rented unfurnished.

- 46% of tenancies consisted of one person aged 60 or over; a further 20% contained 2 adults, one or both aged 60 or over
- 60% were one-person tenancies
- 70% of tenants were aged 60 or over
- 60% were retired
- the mean disposable income of the tenancy group was lower than average (£140)
- almost two third of tenants (64%) started their current agreement before 1979

Tenants with regulated lettings tended to live in old unfurnished houses which sometimes lacked amenities:

- 70% lived in houses rather than flats
- 95% rented unfurnished accommodation
- 58% lived in accommodation built before 1919
- 70% rented accommodation that was above the bedroom standard
- 13% were sharing or lacking a kitchen or at least one amenity
- 71% rented from a private individual

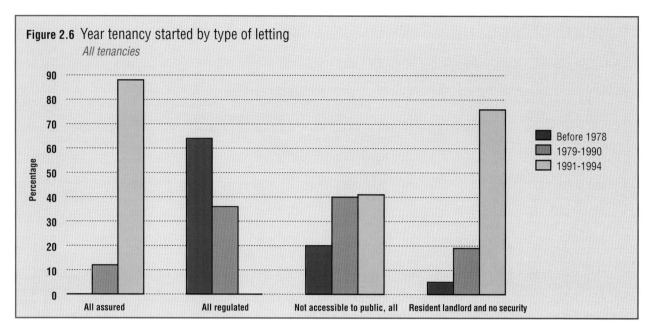

Figure 2.6 Year tenancy started by type of letting
All tenancies

Legend:
- Before 1978
- 1979-1990
- 1991-1994

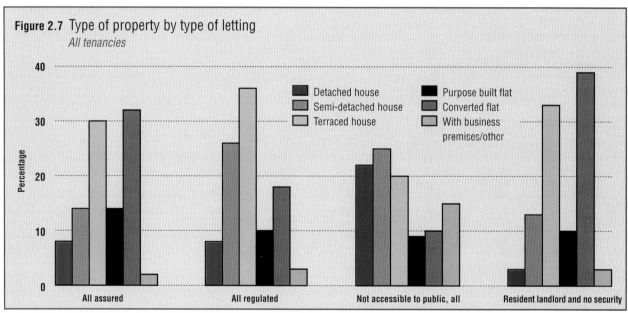

Figure 2.7 Type of property by type of letting
All tenancies

Legend:
- Detached house
- Semi-detached house
- Terraced house
- Purpose built flat
- Converted flat
- With business premises/other

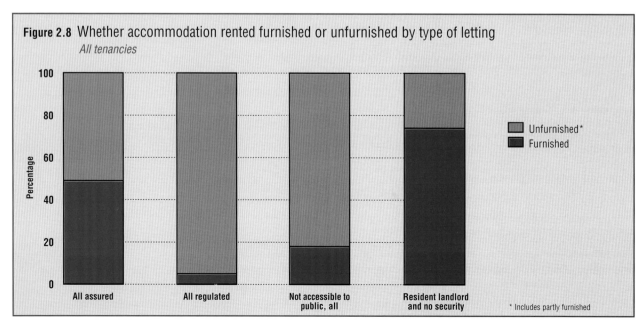

Figure 2.8 Whether accommodation rented furnished or unfurnished by type of letting
All tenancies

Legend:
- Unfurnished*
- Furnished

* Includes partly furnished

2.4 **Lettings not accessible to the public**

Lettings not accessible to the public are mostly lettings by employers to their employees and rent-free lettings to friends or relatives of the landlord. They also include lettings by universities and colleges to their students. Being inaccessible to the public, is not, as such, a legal category but all the groups listed are outside the Rents Act as regards security of tenure.

Letting not accessible to the public accounted for 17% of lettings in 1993. This equates to some 380 thousand lettings, 150 thousand rent paying (7%) and 230 thousand rent free lettings (11%).

The tenancy groups who were renting under this type of agreement tended to consist of families with children or one person of working age in professional or managerial occupations:

- 26% were married or cohabiting couples with dependent children and 39% contained one or two adults aged under 60
- 38% contained 3 or more people
- 54% of tenants were aged 30 - 59
- two thirds (67%) of tenants were in full time employment
- 37% of tenants were in professional or managerial occupations
- the mean disposable tenancy group income was higher than average (£240 per week)
- 41% of tenants started their current agreement in 1991 or later

Most tenants lived in unfurnished houses rented from an employer:

- Two thirds were renting houses (22% were detached houses)
- 82% rented the accommodation unfurnished
- Three quarters (74%) rented accommodation that was above the bedroom standard
- 17% rented accommodation valued in the higher council tax bands (bands F to H, more than £120,000)
- 68% rented from their employer

2.5 **Resident landlord and no security lettings**

Resident landlord lettings (where the landlord lives in the same building, and in the same flat in a purpose-built block) are normally outside the rules governing Regulated and Assured tenancies. The security of the tenant is limited and rents are generally agreed between landlord and tenant. No security lettings are lettings accessible to the public but outside the Rent Act. These include lettings where the landlord provides meals and a substantial amount of attendance, lettings for the purpose of a holiday and lettings where a licence to occupy and not a tenancy was granted to the occupant.

These types of letting made up just 8% of all lettings, almost 180 thousand lettings. The vast majority were resident landlord lettings, 160 thousand in all and the remaining 20 thousand were no security lettings. The resident landlord group includes 90 thousand lettings within households where the household as a whole does not rent privately. Such lettings occur when, for example, an owner occupier lets a room to a tenant who, in survey terms, forms part of the household because of the degree of sharing with the host. These

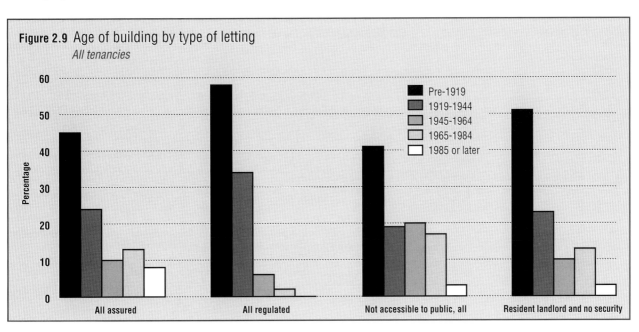

Figure 2.9 Age of building by type of letting

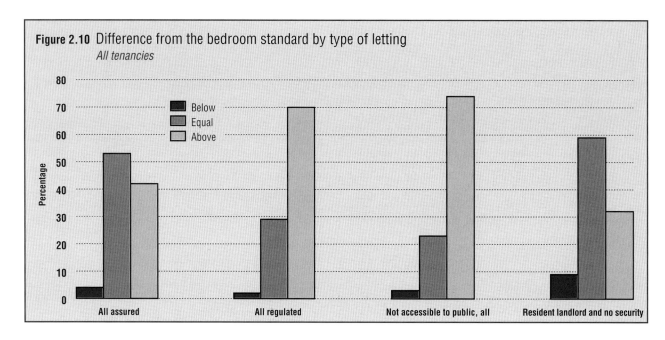

Figure 2.10 Difference from the bedroom standard by type of letting
All tenancies

lettings are described more fully in section 2.6 below. Resident landlord and no security lettings were typically fairly recent lettings to one young tenant living in furnished accommodation with a resident landlord. The characteristics of the tenancy groups are similar in some respects to those of people with assured and assured shorthold agreements:

- 8% of tenancy groups consisted of one person aged under 60
- 55% of tenants were aged under 30
- 28% were in households where there was more than one tenancy group (see table A2.2)
- 25% of tenants were unemployed
- the mean disposable weekly income of the tenancy group was the lowest of all letting types (£130)
- 13% of tenants were from an ethnic minority group

- 76% of tenants started their agreement in 1991 or later

Tenants with this type of letting agreement tended to live in furnished accommodation, particularly converted flats, and a relatively high proportion shared part of their accommodation with another houschold:

- 39% lived in converted flats
- 74% rented the accommodation furnished
- 20% lived in non-self contained accommodation (shared circulation space)
- About one third rented accommodation that was above the bedroom standard (32%)
- 85% were renting from a resident landlord

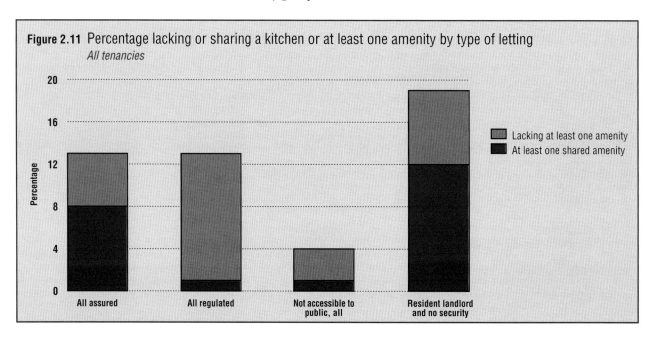

Figure 2.11 Percentage lacking or sharing a kitchen or at least one amenity by type of letting
All tenancies

2.6 **Private renters in non-privately renting households**

Lettings within households where the household did not itself rent privately were mentioned in the previous section. The SEH is the first survey to provide information on these tenancies, which were not covered in the previous private renters surveys. Although they were included in the profiles by letting type, because they are included in the survey for the first time it is worthwhile describing their main characteristics separately. There were some 90 thousand such tenancies in 1993 (4% of tenancies).

Where there was more than one person renting from the household head, the tenants tended to have separate agreements so that there was a high proportion

of one-person tenancies and a high proportion of the households contained more than one tenancy group.

Private renters in non-privately renting households were a fairly homogenous group. Typically they were young, unmarried men, living in a household headed by someone who was also young and unmarried. The main characteristics of the tenants and head of households are summarised below. Equivalent information about the characteristics of tenancies in privately renting households are quoted in parentheses for comparison (Table A2.15).

Characteristics of the tenants
- 94% of tenancies consisted of one person *(49%)*
- Over half of the tenants, 58%, were aged under 30 *(38%)*

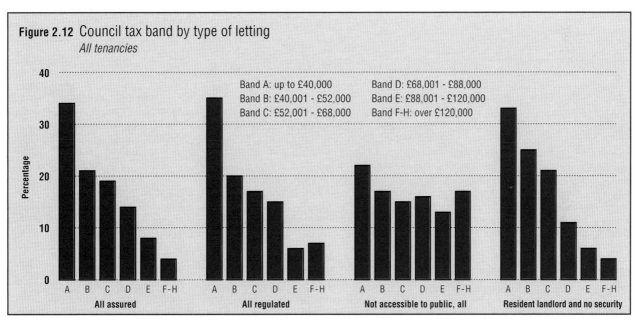

Figure 2.12 Council tax band by type of letting
All tenancies

Band A: up to £40,000
Band B: £40,001 - £52,000
Band C: £52,001 - £68,000
Band D: £68,001 - £88,000
Band E: £88,001 - £120,000
Band F-H: over £120,000

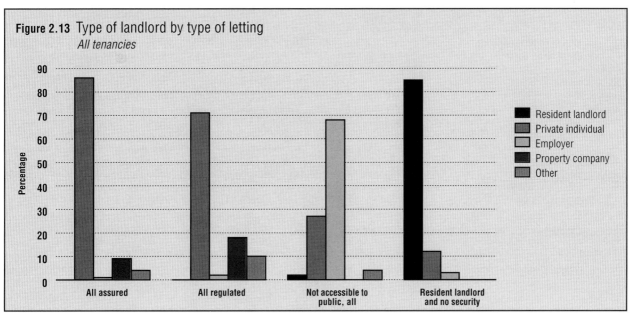

Figure 2.13 Type of landlord by type of letting
All tenancies

Resident landlord
Private individual
Employer
Property company
Other

Table 2.1 Composition of tenancy group by type of letting
All tenancies   *England*

Type of letting	Composition of tenancy group							
	One adult aged 16-59	Two adults aged 16-59	Couple with dependent child(ren)	Lone parent with dependent child(ren)	Large mainly adult	Two adults at least one 60 or over	One adult 60 or over	Total
								thousands
Assured	201	72	36	24	20	10	16	378
Assured shorthold	329	212	109	73	71	13	20	826
All assured	529	283	145	97	92	22	35	1 204
Regulated, rent registered	31	10	16	5	17	53	112	245
Regulated, rent not registered	24	7	13	1	15	27	76	162
All regulated	55	17	30	6	33	79	188	407
Not accessible to public, rent paid	43	26	51	3	15	4	4	146
Not accessible to public, rent free	40	37	47	4	24	23	54	230
Not accessible to public, all	83	63	98	7	39	27	58	375
Resident landlord	126	11	2	3	1	1	15	158
No security	[16]	[0]	[0]	[0]	[5]	[1]	[0]	[22]
Resident landlord and no security	141	11	2	3	6	2	15	180
All	809	374	274	113	170	130	297	2 166
								percentages
Assured	53	19	9	6	5	3	4	100
Assured shorthold	40	26	13	9	9	2	2	100
All assured	44	24	12	8	8	2	3	100
Regulated, rent registered	12	4	7	2	7	22	46	100
Regulated, rent not registered	15	4	8		9	16	46	100
All regulated	13	4	7	1	8	20	46	100
Not accessible to public, rent paid	30	18	35	2	10	3	3	100
Not accessible to public, rent free	17	16	20	2	11	10	23	100
Not accessible to public, all	22	17	26	2	10	7	15	100
Resident landlord	79	7	1	2	1		10	100
No security	*	*	*	*	*	*	*	*
Resident landlord and no security	78	6	1	2	4	1	9	100
All	37	17	13	5	8	6	14	100

- 82% were men *(68%)*
- 71% were single *(38%)*
- 30% were unemployed *(13%)*
- 35% were living in households containing more than one tenancy group *(8%)*

The majority of tenants in non-privately rented households had furnished rooms in a house:

- Three quarters were living in a house *(57%);* only 8% lived in converted flats *(27%)*
- 28% were living in accommodation built after 1964 *(16%)*
- 80% of tenancies started in 1991 or later *(61%)*

Characteristics of the head of household
The head of household was typically young, unmarried and working. Most were buying their accommodation with a mortgage. Equivalent information about the characteristics of head of household in privately renting households are quoted in parentheses for comparison.

- 42% were aged under 30 *(38%)*
- 54% were single *(37%)* and 26% were divorced or separated *(16%)*
- 70% were in full-time employment *(48%)*
- 83% were buying their home with a mortgage and only 9% were council or housing association tenants

Notes and references

1 References to the accommodation occupied by tenancy groups relates to the accommodation occupied by the household as a whole. Since over 90% of households contained only one tenancy group, this is equivalent to the tenancy group's accommodation in most cases.

2 See Chapter 6 for analysis of income.

3 Partly furnished accommodation is included in the unfurnished category.

4 'Bedroom standard' is the notional number of bedrooms considered necessary for a household given the age, sex and marital status of its members; a fuller definition is given in Appendix A.

3 Characteristics of private renters and their accommodation

SUMMARY

- The proportion of tenants aged under 30 has increased from 29% in 1988 to 35% in 1990 and to 39% in 1993 (38% excluding private renters in non-privately renting households)

- Since 1990 the proportion of tenants who are unemployed has increased from 5% to 14% (13% excluding private renters in non-privately renting households). An increase in unemployment among existing tenants can only be a partial explanation; a much increased proportion of new tenants who are unemployed must also have been a factor.

- There has been a corresponding decline in the proportion of tenants in full-time employment, from 59% in 1990 to under half (47%) in 1993, but an increase in those in full-time education, from 4% to 9%.

- Over a third of tenancies (37%) were renting their accommodation furnished. Nearly half of tenancy groups living in converted flats or purpose-built flats were renting the accommodation furnished compared with about a quarter of those in detached or semi-detached houses.

- Over half (52%) of tenancies living in converted flats were living in accommodation in the lowest council tax band, up to £40,000 (band A).

- Eleven per cent of tenancies were renting accommodation which was not self-contained. Tenancy groups living in converted flats were most likely to be in accommodation that was not self-contained (36%).

- One in seven tenancies (14%) were sharing (or lacking) a kitchen or at least one amenity (a shower or bath and inside WC). Tenants in converted flats were most likely to be lacking or sharing amenities (34%).

- The vast majority (96%) of tenancies were in accommodation which was either equal to or above the bedroom standard.

- Most tenants (78%) were satisfied with their accommodation. Those living in accommodation which was not self-contained or was below the bedroom standard were more likely to be dissatisfied than other groups.

This chapter examines the characteristics of private renters and some features of the accommodation in the private rented sector.

3.1 Characteristics of the tenant

Private renters are predominantly a young, mobile population and are becoming more so. The proportion of tenants[1] aged under 30 increased from 29% in 1988 to 35% in 1990 and 39% in 1993, while the percentage aged 30 to 59 remained stable and the percentage aged 60 or over decreased. A small part of the increase in the youngest age group is due to the inclusion of private renters in non-privately renting households. (see Chapter 2). However, the proportion of tenants aged under 30

remains high (38%) when these tenants are excluded. In numerical terms, the number of tenants in both younger age groups increased (from 520 thousand to 850 thousand for 16-29 year olds and from 650 thousand to 860 thousand for 30-59 year olds). The numbers decreased only in the oldest age group (from 580 thousand to 460 thousand). (Figure 3.1)

The proportion of tenants in full-time employment has decreased since the last private renters survey. Less than half of all tenants in 1993 (47%) were in full-time employment compared with 59% in the 1990 survey. Over the same period, the proportion of tenants who were in full-time education increased from 4% to 9%. In previous private renters surveys fieldwork was carried out between June and September, a time when some students might not have been available for interview while others might have been in summer employment or unemployed when interviewed. This may account for some of the redistribution. The increase in the proportion of younger tenants may also have contributed.

Since 1990 the proportion of tenants who are unemployed increased from 5% to 14% (13% when private renters in non-privately renting households are excluded) and this increase is supported by findings from the Labour Force Survey.[2] While this increase is probably associated with the increase in young tenants and the general increase in unemployment, there may be other contributing factors such as a possible increased proportion of unemployed people entering the private rented sector or rising unemployment in areas with a high

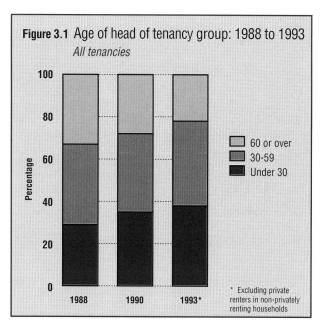

Figure 3.1 Age of head of tenancy group: 1988 to 1993
All tenancies

Legend: 60 or over; 30-59; Under 30

* Excluding private renters in non-privately renting households

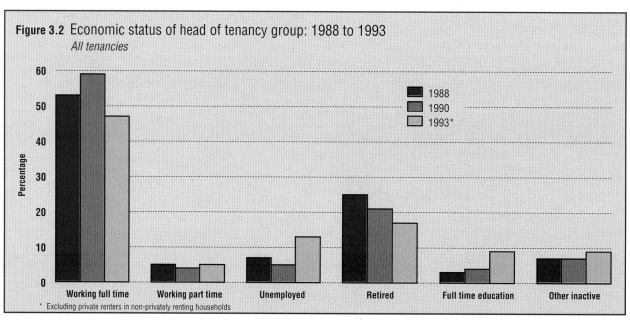

Figure 3.2 Economic status of head of tenancy group: 1988 to 1993
All tenancies

Legend: 1988; 1990; 1993*

* Excluding private renters in non-privately renting households level of private rented accommodation. (Figure 3.2) Unemployment was highest among tenancy groups consisting of one adult (17%) and lone parents and couples with dependent children (17% and 15%). When further broken down by age (Table A3.3), the economic status profile of other types of tenancy groups showed the expected variations with high proportions of the older groups consisting mainly of retired people (74% and 82%) and younger tenancy groups containing a majority of working tenants. (Figure 3.3, Table A3.3)

While private renters overall were evenly divided between the different socio-economic groups there were differences between different types of tenancy groups. Tenants in groups consisting of couples with dependent children were most likely to be in professional and managerial occupations. Lone parents with dependent children were most likely to be in other non-manual occupations (43%). (Figure 3.4)

3.2 **Privately rented accommodation**

The type of accommodation[3] occupied by private renters was commented on in Chapter 1 where it was noted that the proportion of tenancies in converted flats had increased since 1990 when the last private renters survey was carried out. In 1993 over a quarter of all tenancy groups (560 thousand) were living in converted flats and a further 12% (260 thousand) were living in purpose-built flats. Over half of all tenancies lived in houses. (See figure 1.5) Figures 3.5 to 3.8 look at the characteristics of the

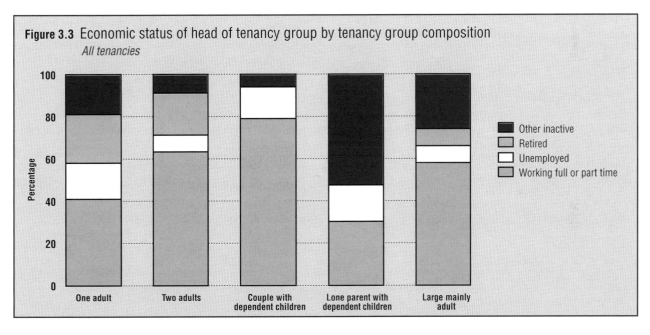

Figure 3.3 Economic status of head of tenancy group by tenancy group composition
All tenancies

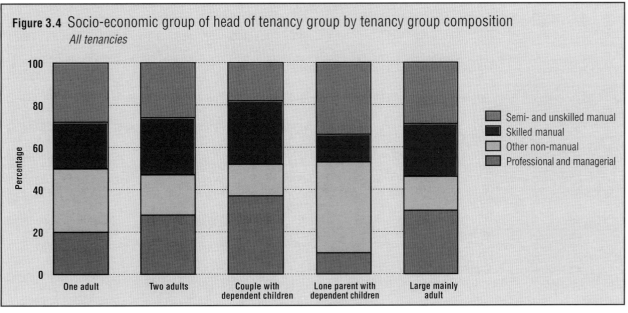

Figure 3.4 Socio-economic group of head of tenancy group by tenancy group composition
All tenancies

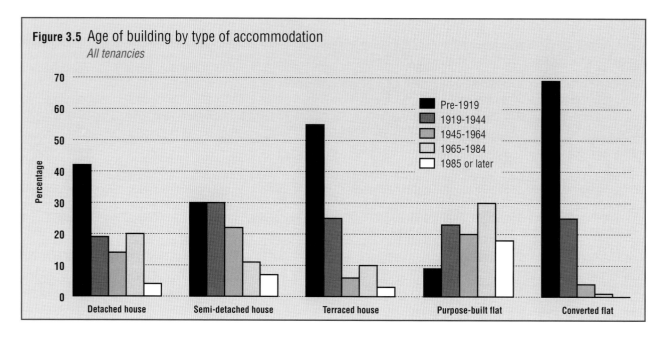

Figure 3.5 Age of building by type of accommodation
All tenancies

accommodation occupied by private renters by type of accommodation.

Converted flats and terraced houses tend to be in older buildings: 69% of tenancy groups renting converted flats were living in buildings constructed before 1919 as were 55% of tenancy groups living in terraced houses. Nearly half of tenancy groups living in purpose-built flats were living in buildings built after 1964 including 18% in property built after 1984. (Figure 3.5)

The proportion of tenancies renting their accommodation furnished has increased since the 1990 survey, 37% compared with 29% in 1990. This increase is due to the increase in the proportion of tenancies living in flats which are more likely than

houses to be rented furnished and the decline in the number of regulated lettings which usually provide unfurnished accommodation. Nearly half of tenancy groups living in converted flats or purpose-built flats were renting the accommodation furnished compared with about a quarter of those in detached or semi-detached houses. (Figure 3.6)

Figure 3.7 shows the proportion of tenancy groups renting from different types of landlord by accommodation type. The majority of tenancy groups were renting from individual landlords except for tenancy groups living in accommodation with business premises[4] (see Table A3.7). Tenants living in detached houses were more likely to rent from an employer than those in other types of accommodation. Almost a third of tenants (31%) in

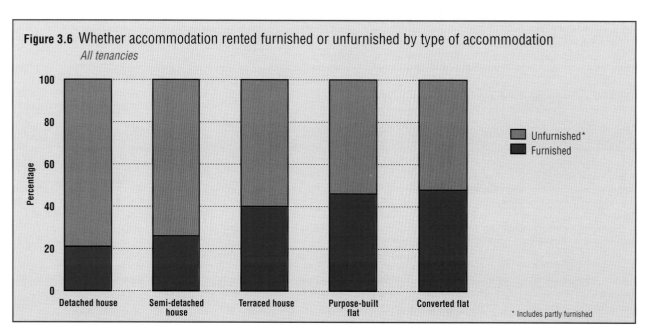

Figure 3.6 Whether accommodation rented furnished or unfurnished by type of accommodation
All tenancies

* Includes partly furnished

detached houses rented from an employer compared with 18% of those in semi-detached houses and less than one in ten of tenants in other types of accommodation. (Figure 3.7)

As might be expected there was a close association between the type of accommodation and its value as indicated by the council tax band. Over half (52%) of tenancies living in converted flats were living in accommodation in the lowest council tax band, up to £40,000 (band A). Detached houses tended to be valued in the higher council tax bands; a quarter of all tenancies in detached houses were living in accommodation valued at more than £120,000 (bands F to H). (Figure 3.8)

3.3 **Housing standards**

One measure of the standard of accommodation is access to various amenities. Amenities were defined as a separate kitchen, a shower or bath and an inside WC. One in eight tenancies (260 thousand or 12%) were sharing or lacking at least one of these amenities. Tenants in converted flats were most likely to be sharing or lacking amenities (26%), although most had cooking facilities. (Figure 3.9)

Another measure of housing standards is whether the accommodation is self-contained.[5] Just over 1 in 10 tenancies (11%) were renting accommodation which was not self-contained. Tenancy groups living in converted flats were most likely to be in non-self-contained accommodation (36%). (Figure 3.10)

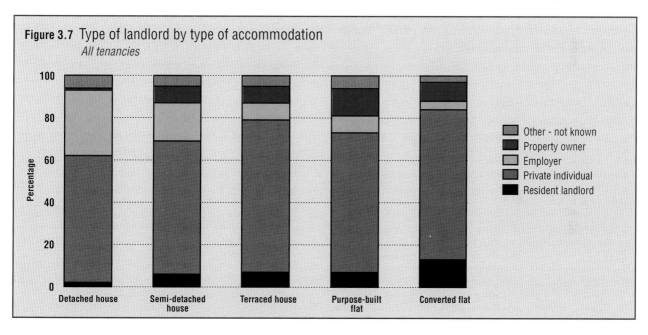

Figure 3.7 Type of landlord by type of accommodation
All tenancies

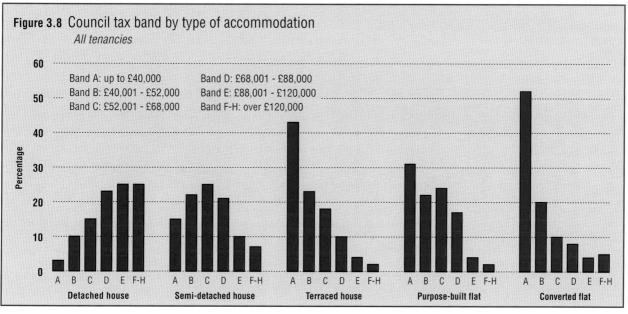

Figure 3.8 Council tax band by type of accommodation
All tenancies

Band A: up to £40,000
Band B: £40,001 - £52,000
Band C: £52,001 - £68,000
Band D: £68,001 - £88,000
Band E: £88,001 - £120,000
Band F-H: over £120,000

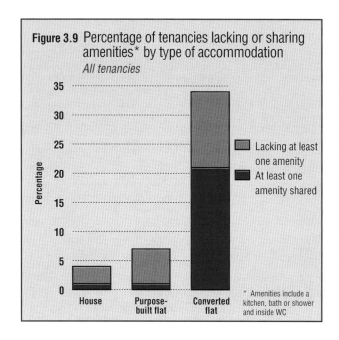

Figure 3.9 Percentage of tenancies lacking or sharing amenities* by type of accommodation
All tenancies

* Amenities include a kitchen, bath or shower and inside WC

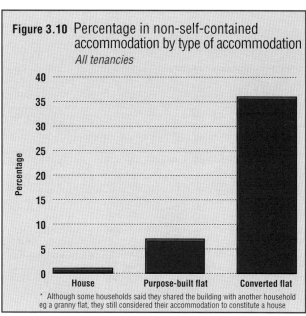

Figure 3.10 Percentage in non-self-contained accommodation by type of accommodation
All tenancies

* Although some households said they shared the building with another household eg a granny flat, they still considered their accommodation to constitute a house

3.4 Accommodation characteristics and tenancy group composition

So far this chapter has described the accommodation occupied by private renters without reference to the people who occupy it. Figure 3.11 shows the type of accommodation occupied by different types of tenancy groups. Relatively high proportions of tenancy groups consisting of one or two persons aged 16 to 59 were living in converted flats (41% and 28%) and about a half were living in houses. At least two thirds of tenants in other types of tenancy group lived in houses. (Figure 3.11)

Almost all older tenancy groups rented their accommodation unfurnished as did high proportions of couples and lone parents with dependent

children. Conversely, over a half of tenancies containing one person under 60 were living in furnished accommodation. Such tenancies were far more likely to be living in non-self-contained accommodation than other types of tenancy groups (22% and 8% or less). About a fifth were sharing or lacking amenities compared with 14% or less of other groups. (Figures 3.12 to 3.14)

There is a wide variety of accommodation available in the private sector. While the previous analyses give some indication of the standard of accommodation occupied by different groups a more direct measure is obtained by relating the size of the accommodation to the number of people who occupy it,- referred to as occupation density. Two separate but related measures of the adequacy of the

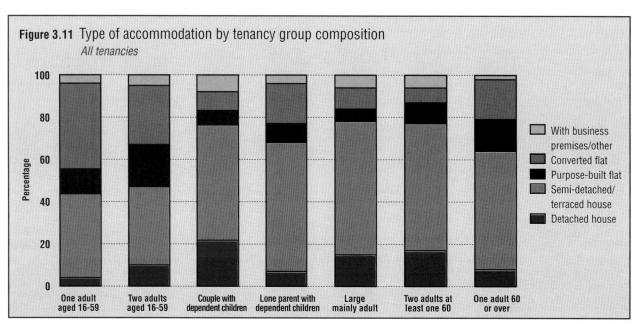

Figure 3.11 Type of accommodation by tenancy group composition
All tenancies

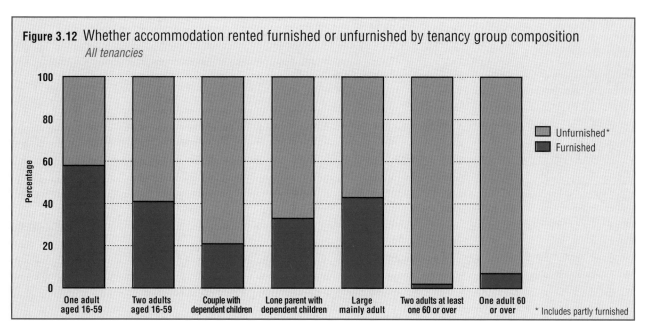

Figure 3.12 Whether accommodation rented furnished or unfurnished by tenancy group composition
All tenancies

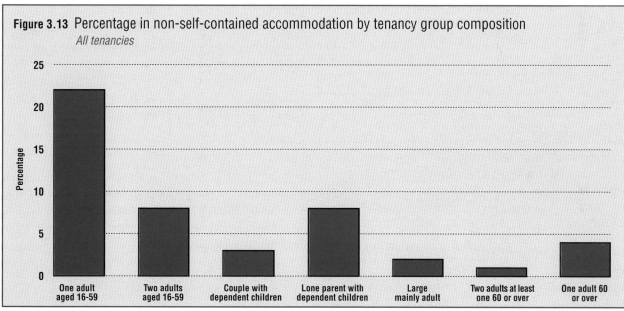

Figure 3.13 Percentage in non-self-contained accommodation by tenancy group composition
All tenancies

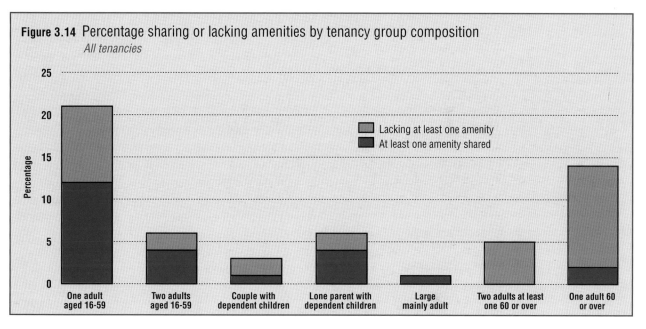

Figure 3.14 Percentage sharing or lacking amenities by tenancy group composition
All tenancies

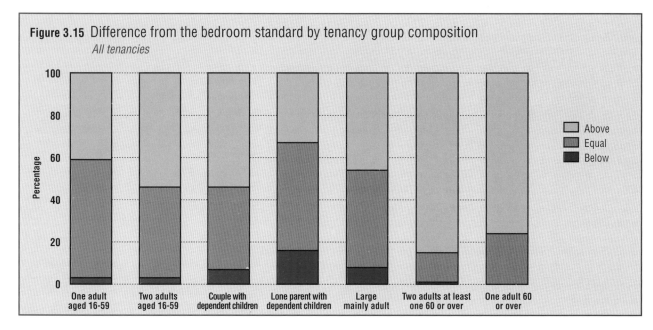

Figure 3.15 Difference from the bedroom standard by tenancy group composition
All tenancies

Legend: Above / Equal / Below

X-axis: One adult aged 16-59 | Two adults aged 16-59 | Couple with dependent children | Lone parent with dependent children | Large mainly adult | Two adults at least one 60 or over | One adult 60 or over

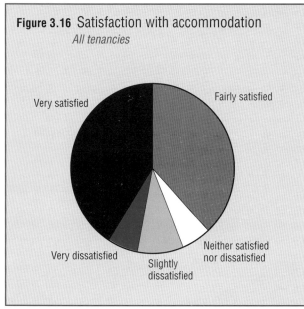

Figure 3.16 Satisfaction with accommodation
All tenancies

Very satisfied / Fairly satisfied / Neither satisfied nor dissatisfied / Slightly dissatisfied / Very dissatisfied

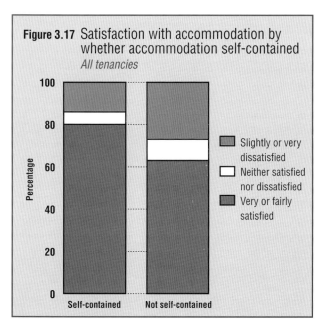

Figure 3.17 Satisfaction with accommodation by whether accommodation self-contained
All tenancies

Legend: Slightly or very dissatisfied / Neither satisfied nor dissatisfied / Very or fairly satisfied

X-axis: Self-contained | Not self-contained

accommodation for the household are used. One of the measures compares the number of bedrooms available against a calculated required minimum number of bedrooms based on the composition of the household in terms of age, sex, relationship and marital status. (See Appendix A for details of how the standard is calculated.) The second measure, rooms per person, relates the number of 'rooms' available to the number of people who live in the accommodation.[6]

The vast majority (96%) of tenancies were in accommodation which was either equal to or above the bedroom standard.

Lone parents with dependent children were more likely than other tenancy groups to occupy accommodation below the bedroom standard while older people were far more likely to be in accommodation above the bedroom standard. Sixteen per cent of lone parents with dependent children were in accommodation below the bedroom standard compared with 8% or less in other groups. On average, tenancy groups which contained one or two people had more rooms per person than other tenancy groups. Tenancy groups which consisted of couples or lone parents with dependent children and large mainly adult groups all had less than 2 rooms per person on average (1.5, 1.8 and 1.7) while tenancy groups consisting of one or two adults all had an average of 2 or more rooms per person. (Figure 3.15, Table A3.13)

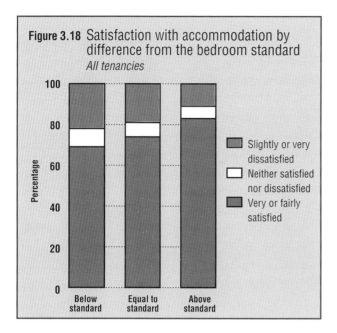

Figure 3.18 Satisfaction with accommodation by difference from the bedroom standard
All tenancies

Legend:
- Slightly or very dissatisfied
- Neither satisfied nor dissatisfied
- Very or fairly satisfied

3.5 **Satisfaction with accommodation**

The vast majority of tenants (78%) were satisfied with their accommodation. As might be expected those living in accommodation which was not self-contained or which was below the bedroom standard were more likely to be dissatisfied than other groups. Twenty seven per cent of tenancies in non-self-contained accommodation and 31% of those in accommodation below the bedroom standard were dissatisfied with their accommodation. (Figures 3.16 to 3.18)

Tenants satisfaction with their accommodation was also related to both the age and type of the accommodation they occupied. The proportion dissatisfied increased from 6% among tenants in accommodation built after 1984 to 18% among those in accommodation built before 1919. A quarter of tenants living in converted flats were either very dissatisfied or slightly dissatisfied with their accommodation. This type of accommodation was typically in older buildings and a relatively high proportion was not self-contained. Among tenants in self-contained accommodation, tenants in converted flats were more likely than those in other types of accommodation to be dissatisfied (not shown). (Figures 3.19 and 3.20)

Notes and references

1   The tenant is defined as the person in whose name the accommodation is rented unless that person is a married or cohabiting women. In such cases it is the woman's husband or partner who is defined as the tenant.

2   The proportion of privately renting households in the Labour Force Survey where the head of household was unemployed increased from 5.5% in Spring 1990 to 12% in Spring 1993 and Spring 1994.

3   References to the accommodation occupied by tenancy groups relates to the accommodation occupied by the household as a whole. Since over 90% of households contained only one tenancy group, this is equivalent to the tenancy group's accommodation in most cases.

4   Other accommodation includes caravans and boats of which there were a very small number. The vast majority of tenants in the other/business premises category were living in accommodation attached to business premises and over half were renting from an employer.

5   Non-self-contained accommodation was defined as sharing a bathroom, kitchen or toilet or sharing circulation space (that is, a passage, hall or stairway to get from one part of the household's accommodation to another).

6   Bathrooms, toilets, kitchens less than 6.5 feet wide, rooms which cannot be used, are shared with someone outside the household or are used solely for business purposes are excluded from the room count.

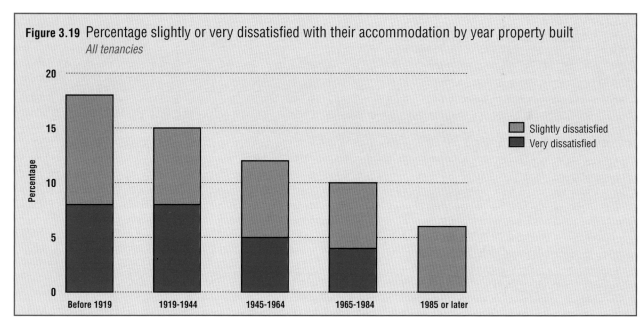

Figure 3.19 Percentage slightly or very dissatisfied with their accommodation by year property built
All tenancies

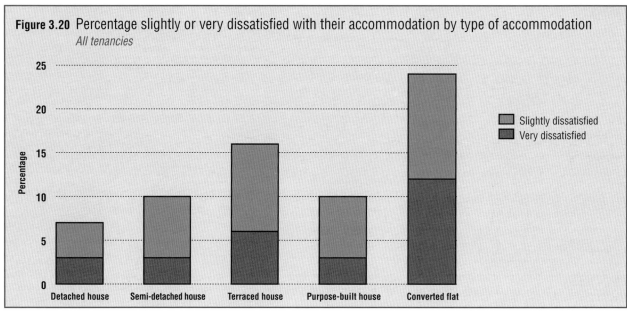

Figure 3.20 Percentage slightly or very dissatisfied with their accommodation by type of accommodation
All tenancies

4 Rent and Housing Benefit

SUMMARY

- Tenants were charged £60 per week on average for their accommodation. Average rents ranged from £31 among tenants in regulated lettings to £80 among those with assured shorthold agreements.

- Within each of the main tenancy types, Assured, Assured Shorthold and Regulated, the main factor affecting rent was the value of the property, as indicated by the council tax band.

- Average rents in London were twice as high as those in the north and one third more than those in the rest of the south.

- Newer tenancies had higher rents on average than older tenancies: mean weekly rent for tenancies which started in the period 1979-1988 was £36 but was £74 for tenancies which started in 1993 or 1994.

- Just over a half of all tenants thought that the rent they paid was about right for the accommodation and one third thought it very high or slightly high; the proportion considering their rent high was greatest, 43%, among tenants with assured shorthold agreements.

- At the time of interview, 100 thousand tenants (6%) were at least two weeks behind with their rent; a further 80 thousand (4%) had been in arrears in the previous year.

- 800 thousand tenants were estimated to be eligible for Housing Benefit, 47% of all tenants paying rent; 600 thousand were eligible for full benefit and 200 thousand were eligible for partial benefit.

- The proportion eligible for Housing Benefit ranged from 15% among tenants in lettings not accessible to the public to 62% among those in the regulated sector.

- 200 thousand tenancy groups, one quarter of those estimated to be eligible, did not receive Housing Benefit. This proportion rose to 58% among tenancy groups consisting of two adults under 60. However the survey probably over-estimates eligibility for Housing Benefit.

- An estimated 680 thousand tenancy groups included at least one person receiving Housing Benefit, 36% of all tenancies paying rent.

This chapter looks at the rents charged to private tenants and the factors which affect rent. It also looks at eligibility for Housing Benefit and take up of benefit by those eligible. As all the analyses in this chapter concern rent, tenants who occupy their accommodation free of charge are excluded. As differences in rent between assured and assured shorthold lettings are of interest they are presented as discrete classifications in this chapter.

4.1 Comparability of rents

Rent may be purely a charge for the accommodation or it may include additional charges for various services, for example, electricity or telephone usage. Simply comparing the amount of rent charged by the landlord to groups in different situations can therefore be misleading. In order to make rents comparable, adjustments have to be made to take account of what is included in the rent. In previous private renters surveys a 'comparable weekly rent' was calculated by subtracting from the rent the amounts paid for any services included. Water rates were treated differently to other services: if a tenant paid water rates separately from the rent, the amount paid was added to the rent so that all rents *included* water rates.

This approach was adopted because many people whose rent included water rates did not know how much they paid and so the amount could not be deducted. However, since comparable rent is intended to represent a basic rent which does not cover any extras and because Housing Benefit is not payable on water rates, it should ideally exclude water rates. For the SEH analysis, therefore, it was decided to treat water rates in a different way from previous surveys so as to construct a more satisfactory measure of comparable rent. An amount for water rates was imputed, using information from regional water authorities, and the imputed charge was deducted from the rent of tenants who paid water rates as part of the rent. The amount imputed varied according to the type of accommodation occupied.

Although this change improves the information on rents in the SEH, it reduces comparability of the rents presented in this report and those presented in the reports of previous surveys. However, the amount deducted for water rates was relatively small, about £2.80 per week on average.

4.2 Comparable rent levels

Figure 4.1 shows the estimated numbers of tenancies charged different levels of comparable weekly rent. The most common level of rent was between £30 and £40 per week, paid by 320 thousand tenancies (18%) and a further 260 thousand were paying rents between £20 and £30 per week. (Figure 4.1)

The mean rent charged to private tenants was £60 per week, a considerably higher amount than that for households in social rented sector accommodation, estimated from the main part of the survey to be £35.[1] Assured and assured shorthold tenancies had the highest mean rents, £60 and £80 respectively. Regulated lettings had the lowest mean rent, £31, and tenancies not accessible to the public and other letting

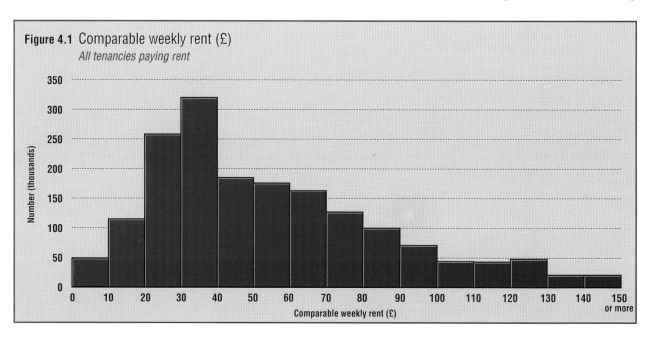

Figure 4.1 Comparable weekly rent (£)
All tenancies paying rent

types had broadly similar mean rent levels at around £40. Mean values, however, are sensitive to the presence of a few extreme values; medians, which divide the distribution in half, are less affected by extremes and so provide an alternative indicator of general levels of rent. As Figure 4.2 shows, the median rent was lower then the mean in all letting types indicating that some tenants had very high rents. (Figure 4.2)

Figure 4.3 shows the range of rents for each type of letting. The vertical lines represent the range of rents between the top and bottom deciles, that is the range of rents paid by most tenants excluding the 10% of tenants with the highest rents and the 10% with the lowest rents. Both types of assured lettings and lettings not accessible to the public had a very much wider range of rents than other groups. (Figure 4.3)

4.3 **Factors which determine rent**

Many factors will determine the amount of rent charged and some of these may be inter-related. By using a modelling analysis, multiple regression, it is possible to identify the factors that have the greatest impact on rent and those that have no significant impact once the main factors have been taken into account. Because the factors affecting rent levels within the different types of lettings are of interest, the rent modelling analysis was carried out separately for tenancies with different types of letting agreement. Rent modelling was not carried out on tenancies with no security and resident landlord lettings due to the relatively small number of cases (8% of lettings).

Rents within each type of letting have been modelled in terms of characteristics of the property. It would be possible, technically, to include the characteristics of the tenants, such as their income and whether they were receiving Housing Benefit. However, this would show what tenants could afford or were prepared to pay rather than what rent the property commanded.

The results of the models for each letting type are summarised in Table 4.1 which shows which characteristics were included in the model and the order in which they entered, the most important characteristics being entered first. As can be seen from the table, the characteristics which had most bearing on the amount of rent charged were quite different for tenancy groups in the different letting types. The value of the property, as indicated by the council tax band, was the most important determinant of the rent of tenants in all letting types except for lettings not accessible to the public.

For **assured shorthold lettings,** the factors which most affected rent, in order of importance, were:

- the council tax band
- whether the property was in London
- whether the property was in the South East (other than London)
- whether the property was built between 1965 and 1984
- the number of rooms
- whether the tenancy started in 1990 (associated with a low rent)
- whether the property was built after 1985

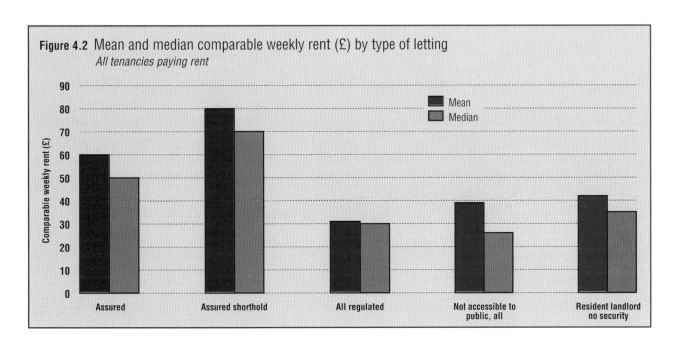

Figure 4.2 Mean and median comparable weekly rent (£) by type of letting
All tenancies paying rent

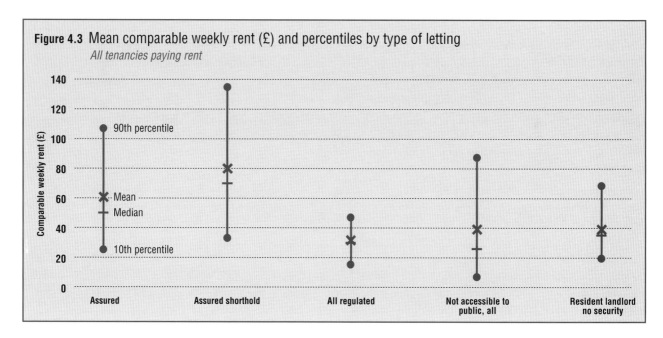

Figure 4.3 Mean comparable weekly rent (£) and percentiles by type of letting
All tenancies paying rent

Other variables included in the model but which did not contribute significantly to explaining variations in rent were: whether the property needed repairs, type of accommodation, whether the property was rented furnished, and which year after 1990 the tenancy started.[2]

For **assured lettings** the factors which most affected rent in order of importance were:

- the council tax band
- the age of the property
- whether the property was in need of repair
- whether the property was a converted flat
- whether the tenancy started in 1993, 1992 or 1991

The year the tenancy started was found to increase the rent for assured tenancies by a steady amount for each year between 1991 and 1993.

For **regulated lettings** a large number of factors were found to affect rent. In order of importance these were:

- the council tax band
- whether the property was in the South East (excluding London)
- whether the property was a converted flat
- the number of rooms
- whether the property was in London
- whether the tenancy started in 1985 or later
- whether the property was built between 1965 and 1984
- whether the tenancy started between 1965 and 1974
- whether the property was a purpose-built flat

For **lettings not accessible to the public** the following factors were found to affect rent:

- whether the accommodation was rented furnished
- whether the property was a converted flat
- the council tax band
- whether the accommodation was a detached house or bungalow
- whether the property was in the South East (excluding London)
- whether the accommodation was in need of repair

Whether the accommodation was rented furnished and whether the property was a converted flat were more important than council tax band in explaining variations in rent for these tenancies. Other things being equal, tenants in detached houses had lower rents than those in terrace houses indicating, perhaps, that rents for lettings not accessible to public in this type of property do not necessarily reflect the true market rent of the property.

The characteristics included in the model for tenancies not accessible to the public gave the 'best fit' and explained 63% of the variation in rents for this group. The models for the two assured tenancy types each explained 53% of the variation in rents and the model for the regulated sector explained 33% of the variation. Although the last model was not such a good fit as the others, the amount of variation explained by the other models was high for this type of analysis indicating that many of the major influences has been identified. (Table 4.1)

Table 4.1 Modelling rents - results of multiple regression analysis
All tenancies with Assured, Regulated or Not accessible to public lettings　　　　　　　　　　　　　*England*

Characteristic	Type of letting			
	Assured	Assured shorthold	All regulated	All not accessible to public
				coefficients £ per weeek +
Council tax band **	0.75 [1]	0.49 [1]	0.43 [1]	0.33 [3]
Region				
London		49.27 [2]	8.08 [5]	
Rest of South East		16.76 [3]	13.54 [2]	21.96 [5]
Rest of country	*	*	*	*
Furnished				40.77 [1]
un-furnished	*	*	*	*
Type of accommodation				
Detached house/bungalow				-27.76 [4]
Semi-detached				
Terraced house	*	*	*	*
Purpose built flat			5.69[9]	
Other flat	16.53 [4]		10.44 [3]	52.29 [2]
Age of property				
1985 or later	35.93 [2]	10.18 [7]		
1965-1984		13.89 [4]	13.32 [7]	
before 1965	*	*	*	*
Number of rooms		2.89 [5]	3.35 [4]	
Needs repair	-12.82 [3]			-16.49 [6]
Year tenancy started				
1994				
1993	24.19 [5]			
1992	20.95 [6]			
1991	16.76 [7]			
1990		-13.61 [6]		
pre 1990	*	*		
1985 or later			5.22 [6]	
1980-1984				
1975-1979				
1965-1974			-5.23 [8]	
before 1965			*	
1990 or later				
1985-1990				
1875-1984				
Before 1984				*
Constant	£10.17	£26.39	£7.70	£14.77
Percentage of variation explained by model	53%	53%	33%	63%

* Reference category for characteristic
** The value used was the mid point of band/1000: Band A=20, B=46, C =60, D= 78, E= 104, F=140, G=240, H= 250
+ The figures in brackets show the order in which the characteristics entered the model.

The model chosen is additive so that, for example, being in London adds £49.27 a week to the rent for an Assured Shorthold. An alternative form of modelling is multiplicative so that, to continue the example, being in London would increase the rent by a certain percentage. A multiplicative model is intuitively more plausible, in that one would expect being in London to add more to the rent, in absolute terms, for a high value property (as measured by the council tax band) than for a low value property. However, the additive model fitted the data rather better than the multiplicative models tested. It is possible that further work might result in a better version of the multiplicative model.

Modelling analyses can also be used to predict the amount of rent that will be charged for different types of accommodation. Each tenancy can be thought of as being charged a base rent ('constant' in Table 4.1) to which various amounts are added depending on the characteristics of the accommodation. The amount to be added is calculated by multiplying the value of the characteristic by the corresponding coefficient in Table 4.1. The value of the characteristic is one with the exception of number of rooms and council tax band.

For example, an assured shorthold tenancy in London in the lowest council tax band, in a house built between 1965 and 1984 with 4 rooms would be predicted to have a rent of £114:

£26.39   (base rent)
+ (£0.49 x 20) for the council tax band
+ £49.27 for London
+ £13.89 for the age of the property
+ (£2.89 x 4) for the number of rooms
= £114

While the model is useful for identifying the characteristics which have a significant bearing on the rent, it does not give an indication of the overall level of rent that is actually charged in different situations. This is examined in the following section.

4.4 Differences in rent

As might be expected there was enormous variation in the rents paid by tenancies in different regions. On average, tenants in London were charged twice as much in rent as those in the North and Midlands and one third more than those in the rest of the south (South East, South West and East Anglia). This pattern was repeated in all types of letting. Although there were only slight regional variations in the regulated sector, average rents in regulated lettings in the North and Midlands were significantly lower than in southern regions. (Figures 4.4 and 4.5)

Figure 4.6 shows the mean rents in each region and for England as a whole for all assured lettings and regulated lettings as these are of most interest. Regional variation in average rents was much more marked among assured lettings than regulated lettings. (Figure 4.6)

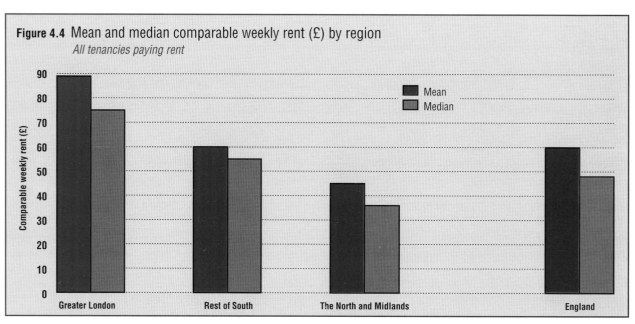

Figure 4.4 Mean and median comparable weekly rent (£) by region
All tenancies paying rent

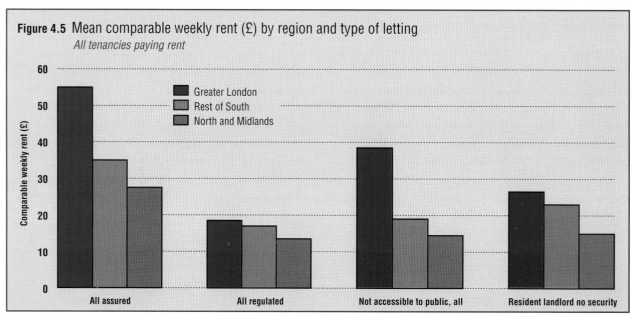

Figure 4.5 Mean comparable weekly rent (£) by region and type of letting
All tenancies paying rent

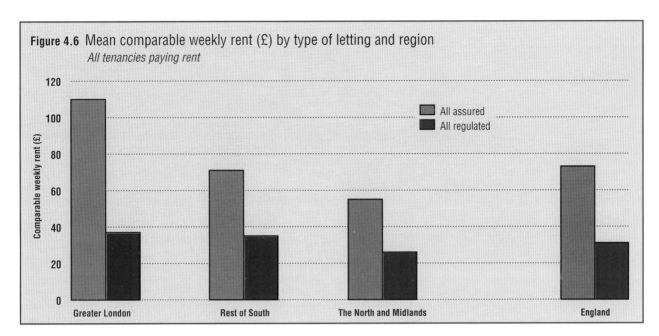

Figure 4.6 Mean comparable weekly rent (£) by type of letting and region
All tenancies paying rent

In the previous section, certain features of the accommodation were found to have a significant bearing on the amount of rent charged. The most important factor for three of the letting types was the value of the property as indicated by the council tax valuation band. As Figure 4.7 shows, mean rent increased with the value of the property, rising from £42 for properties in the lowest council tax band to £85 for properties valued at £88,000 to £119,000. The mean rent for properties valued at £120,000 or more was £111 but this group included some tenants with exceptionally high rents so the median value of £65 is probably a better measure of general rent level for these properties. (Figure 4.7)

Figure 4.8 shows the range of rents for properties in different council tax bands. As expected, the mean

rents and upper ranges increased with the value of the property but the value of the lowest decile did not vary greatly indicating that some households in high valued property were charged low rents. (Figure 4.8)

Newer tenancies had higher rents on average than older tenancies. The mean rent for tenancies which started in the period 1979 - 1988 was £36 while tenancies starting in 1993 or 1994 were charged, on average, £74. A high proportion of tenancies starting before 1989 are regulated lettings, the remainder being mainly lettings not accessible to the public and resident landlord lettings. No new regulated lettings could start after 15th January 1989, their place being taken by Assured and Assured Shorthold lettings. This accounts for the higher average rents for tenancies starting in 1989 or later. (Figure 4.9)

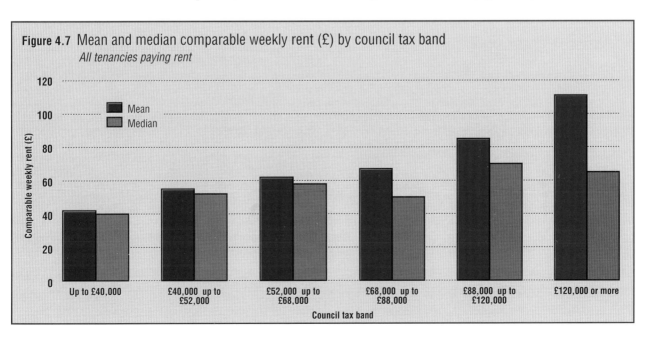

Figure 4.7 Mean and median comparable weekly rent (£) by council tax band
All tenancies paying rent

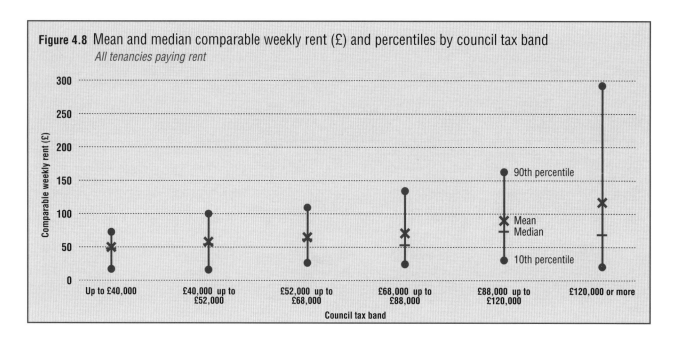

Figure 4.8 Mean and median comparable weekly rent (£) and percentiles by council tax band
All tenancies paying rent

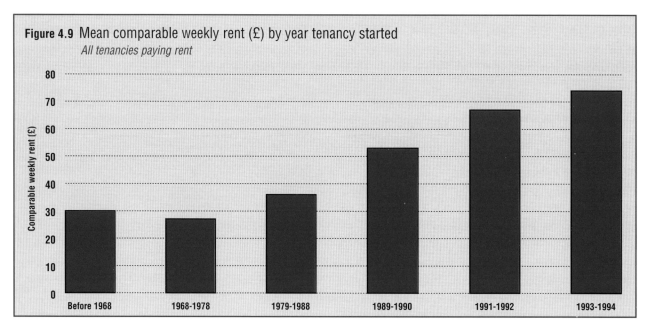

Figure 4.9 Mean comparable weekly rent (£) by year tenancy started
All tenancies paying rent

4.5 Opinion about rent

Just over a half of all tenants said that they thought that the rent they paid was about right for the accommodation and one third thought it very high or slightly high. Tenants in assured shorthold lettings were more likely than other groups to think their rent was high (43%). Within the resident landlord and no security letting category, a far higher proportion of tenants in lettings with no security thought their rent high, 37%, than did tenants with a resident landlord, 17% (see Table A4.4). (Figure 4.10)

Not surprisingly, people with relatively high rents were more likely to consider their rent very or slightly high than those with low rents. Almost half of tenants

paying £50 or more per week considered their rent high. The converse was also true: 44% of tenants who were charged under £15 per week thought that their rent was low. (Figure 4.11, Table A4.5)

4.6 Rent arrears

Tenants were asked whether they were up to date with their rent payments or whether any rent was owing for a fortnight or longer. At the time of interview, 100 thousand tenants (6%) said that they were at least two weeks behind with their rent and a further 80 thousand (4%) had been in arrears during the previous year. Detailed analysis of the characteristics of people who were in arrears cannot be carried out because the number of cases is small (152). Such

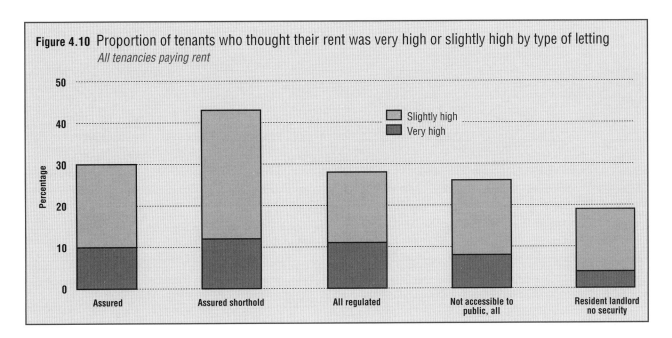

Figure 4.10 Proportion of tenants who thought their rent was very high or slightly high by type of letting
All tenancies paying rent

analysis may be possible for the 1994 Survey Report when data for two years can be combined.

4.7 Eligibility for Housing Benefit

Housing Benefit is intended to help people on low income to pay their rent. Eligibility for Housing Benefit depends on a number of factors such as the net income and savings of the tenants, the composition of the tenancy group and their circumstances. An 'applicable amount' is calculated which takes into account the circumstances of the applicant and this is compared with their income. Those whose income is at or below the level of the applicable amount are eligible for Housing Benefit which covers the whole of their rent. Tenants whose income exceeds the applicable amount may be eligible for partial benefit. Some categories of tenant are

not eligible for Housing Benefit regardless of their financial circumstances - for example, people with savings of more than £16,000.

Using the data collected in the SEH, it was possible to make an assessment of whether the tenancy group was eligible for Housing Benefit for most tenancies paying rent. Estimating eligibility for benefits from survey data is subject to error and some people may be estimated to be eligible for the benefit when the more complete information available to a Housing Benefit office would show them not to be eligible. Work carried out by the Department of Social Security (DSS) has established that assessments of eligibility based on household surveys such as the SEH tend to overstate eligibility.[3] The preferred source of data on benefit eligibility remains the one published by the DSS.[4] This does not distinguish

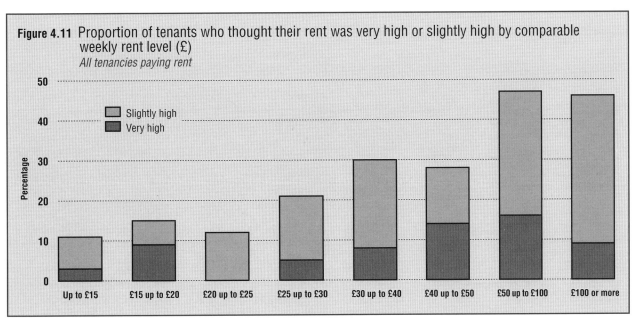

Figure 4.11 Proportion of tenants who thought their rent was very high or slightly high by comparable weekly rent level (£)
All tenancies paying rent

however between tenants of private landlords and housing associations.

The method of assessment used on the SEH data correctly identified as eligible 95% of those who were actually getting Housing Benefit.

Of the estimated total of 1.7 million rent paying tenancies, 800 thousand (47%) were estimated to be eligible for Housing Benefit, 600 thousand (34%) for full benefit and 200 thousand (13%) for partial benefit. This is an increase in the proportion of tenancies estimated to be eligible for Housing Benefit in the 1990 survey (500 thousand or 38%). The large increase in numbers eligible is made up of a 24% increase in the proportion eligible compounded with a 29% increase in the number of rent-paying tenants recorded in the survey. Part of the latter results from the inclusion for the first time in 1993/94 of lodgers forming part of a non-privately renting household (see Chapter 2, section 2.6).

Certain types of tenancy group were more likely than others to be eligible for Housing Benefit. A very high proportion of lone parents with dependent children were eligible (88% or 90 thousand tenancies) as were high proportions of tenancies containing older people. Just over three quarters of older people living alone (150 thousand) were eligible for either full or partial Housing Benefit as were 57% of tenancy groups comprising two adults one or both of whom was aged 60 or over (50 thousand). Although only 40% of younger one-person tenancy groups were estimated to be eligible for Housing Benefit, they accounted for the largest number of eligible tenancies, 330 thousand. (Figure 4.12)

Not surprisingly, high proportions of tenancy groups with low incomes were eligible for Housing Benefit while very few of those with incomes in the higher bands were eligible. Over 80% of tenancy groups with a net weekly income below £80 were eligible for Housing Benefit, and the majority of these were eligible for full benefit. Although 73% of those in the next income group (£80 to £119 per week) were eligible, they were more evenly distributed between those eligible for full (41%) and those eligible for partial benefit (32%). (Figure 4.13)

In three of the types of lettings - assured, assured shorthold and lettings with a resident landlord or no security - similar proportions of tenants were eligible for Housing Benefit (45% to 49%). The main difference was between those in regulated lettings and those in lettings not accessible to the public. Almost two thirds of tenants in regulated lettings were eligible for Housing Benefit, not surprising given the profile of the sector, described in Chapter 2, compared with only 15% of tenants in lettings not accessible to the public. Far higher proportions of tenancies paying less than £100 per week in rent were estimated to be eligible for Housing Benefit than tenancies with higher rents. Almost all tenancies paying less than £50 per week were estimated to be eligible (95%) as were 77% of tenancies paying between £50 and £100 per week. (Figures 4.14 and 4.15)

4.8 Numbers receiving Housing Benefit

An estimated 680 thousand tenancy groups were receiving Housing Benefit, 36% of tenancies paying rent (31% of all tenancies including rent-free). The

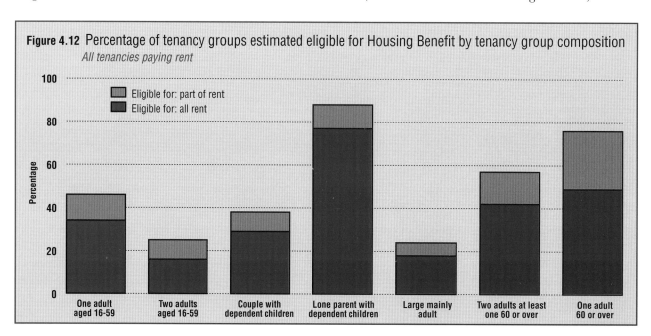

Figure 4.12 Percentage of tenancy groups estimated eligible for Housing Benefit by tenancy group composition

All tenancies paying rent

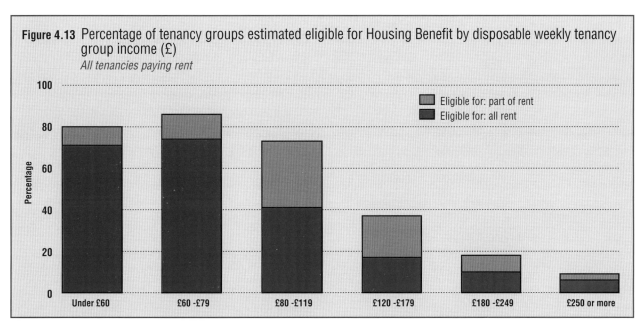

Figure 4.13 Percentage of tenancy groups estimated eligible for Housing Benefit by disposable weekly tenancy group income (£)

All tenancies paying rent

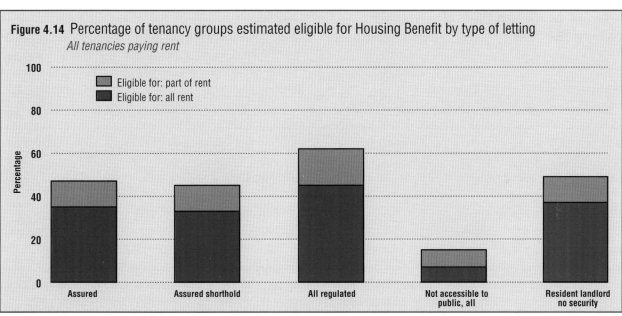

Figure 4.14 Percentage of tenancy groups estimated eligible for Housing Benefit by type of letting

All tenancies paying rent

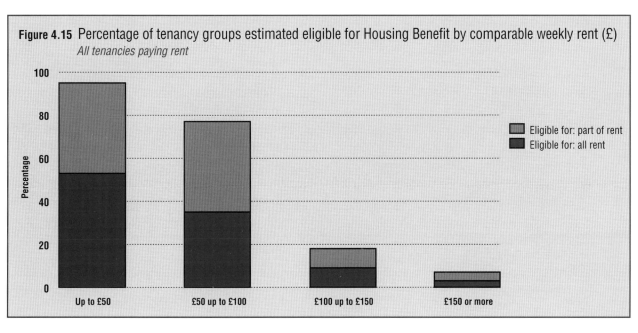

Figure 4.15 Percentage of tenancy groups estimated eligible for Housing Benefit by comparable weekly rent (£)

All tenancies paying rent

questions on Housing Benefit were in the income section of the survey, which was not completed for a proportion of tenancy groups, so it is unknown whether tenants were receiving Housing Benefit in 7.5% of rent-paying cases. The number of recipients quoted above includes a proportion of these unknowns; the same proportion are assumed to be receiving Housing Benefit as among those for whom it is known.

The SEH estimate of the proportion of rent-paying private tenants who receive Housing Benefit (36%) is in good agreement with the estimate of 33% for England from the 1993 Family Expenditure Survey (FES). However, the SEH total of 680 thousand recipients is well below the total of 990 thousand estimated by the DSS from administrative returns for November 1993, about the mid-point of the 1993/94 survey. This would represent 52% of rent-paying tenancies. There are a number of reasons why the two sources may differ:

Coverage
The DSS figures include recipients in hostels and bed-and-breakfast establishments, not included by the FES or SEH which cover people in private households only. The DSS give an upper limit of 90 thousand such recipients.

Multiple recipients
The DSS figures count each recipient separately; the survey figures are for the number of households (FES) or tenancies (SEH) with someone receiving Housing Benefit. Although the two people forming a couple, and other close relatives within a household, cannot claim Housing Benefit separately, there are some households with unrelated adults where more than one person may claim in respect of his or her share of the rent.

Survey under-reporting
Some Housing Benefit recipients may not know or remember that they are receiving it, possibly thinking of payment as part of their state retirement pension, for example. Although claiming Housing Benefit requires positive action for most private tenants, there is likely to be some element of under-reporting.

Non-response bias
It is possible that the proportion of Housing Benefit recipients is higher among households that did not give an interview (refusals and non-contacts) than among those that did. Whether this is in fact so is not known. The potential for non-response bias in the SEH is minimised by the high overall response rate of 80% but there is still likely to be some.

Allocation between housing association and private tenancies
The Housing Benefit administrative system is different for local authority tenants on the one hand, and housing associations and private tenants on the other. There is no difficulty in distinguishing between local authority and other recipients in the administrative returns, but housing associations and private tenant recipients cannot always be distinguished with certainty. The evidence from surveys is that at least some of the recipients coded from the administrative returns as private tenants are, in fact, housing association tenants.

Conclusion
The conclusion is that the higher estimate of private renters receiving Housing Benefit from administrative sources is the combined result of differences in coverage and definition, some degree of overstatement in the administration sources and understatement in surveys. The survey figures shown in the rest of this chapter are likely to understate the take-up of Housing Benefit, but by how much is not yet known.

4.9 Housing Benefit take-up rates

This section presents results on take-up rates, that is the numbers receiving Housing Benefit[5] as proportions of those estimated to be entitled to it. The overall rate estimated directly from the SEH is 75%. The combination of a degree of overestimation of entitlement to Housing Benefit and, possibly, understatement of receipt of Housing Benefit means that this will be an underestimate. The DSS estimate of take-up rate makes allowance for these and other factors and presents results as ranges within which it can be assumed true take-up lies - 81% to 87% for private tenants in 1992. This estimate also makes an allowance for the interval between application for Housing Benefit and its first receipt. It excludes self-employed tenants from the calculation as survey information on their income is judged to be too poor to allow entitlement to benefit to be calculated accurately.

The advantage of the SEH estimates of take-up rates is that they are based on a sample more than twice the size of the FES and that they can distinguish the types

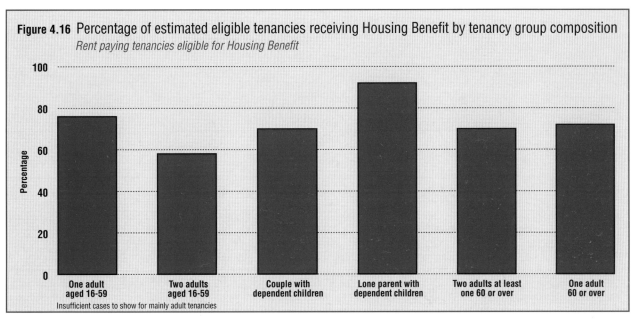

Figure 4.16 Percentage of estimated eligible tenancies receiving Housing Benefit by tenancy group composition

Rent paying tenancies eligible for Housing Benefit

Insufficient cases to show for mainly adult tenancies

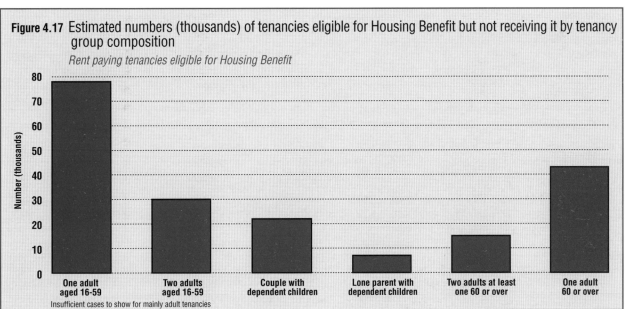

Figure 4.17 Estimated numbers (thousands) of tenancies eligible for Housing Benefit but not receiving it by tenancy group composition

Rent paying tenancies eligible for Housing Benefit

Insufficient cases to show for mainly adult tenancies

of tenancy agreement. Take up of Housing Benefit among eligible groups was highest among lone parents with dependent children, almost all (92%) of those estimated as eligible for benefit were receiving it. This is lower than the DSS estimate of 99% to 100% for 1992. Take up appeared to be lowest among tenancy groups consisting of 2 adults of working age, with just 58% of those eligible receiving the benefit. As the most common tenancy group consists of one person of working age, the largest number of tenancies eligible but not receiving benefit were tenancy groups of this type; there were an estimated 78 thousand of these tenancies estimated to be eligible but who were not receiving Housing Benefit. (Figures 4.16 and 4.17)

As is to be expected, take up of Housing Benefit was highest among eligible tenancy groups in the lower income bands. The vast majority of tenancy groups with incomes under £80 per week who were eligible for Housing Benefit were receiving it and the level of take-up decreased with increasing income. Take up, like eligibility, was not related to the amount of rent charged. (Figures 4.18 and 4.19)

On average tenants receiving Housing Benefit received £49 per week in benefit which brought the average rent actually paid down to £44 per week. The average amount of benefit received ranged from £26 per week for regulated lettings to £66 per week for assured shorthold lettings. (Figure 4.20)

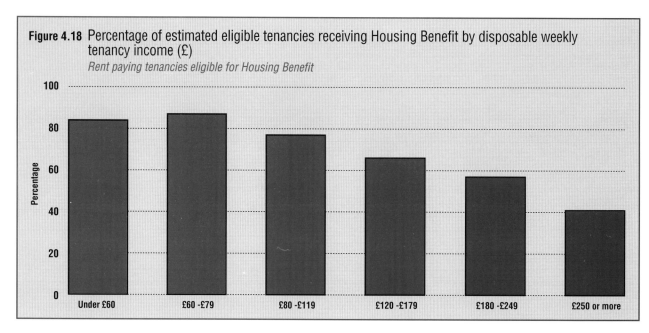

Figure 4.18 Percentage of estimated eligible tenancies receiving Housing Benefit by disposable weekly tenancy income (£)
Rent paying tenancies eligible for Housing Benefit

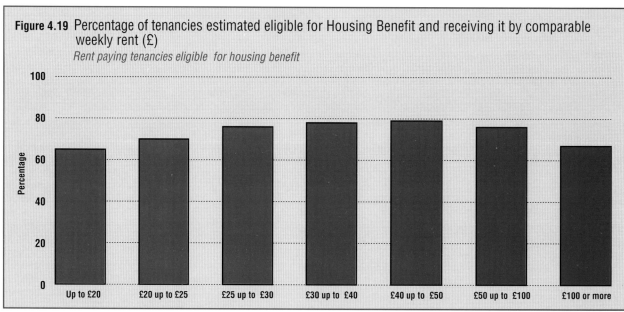

Figure 4.19 Percentage of tenancies estimated eligible for Housing Benefit and receiving it by comparable weekly rent (£)
Rent paying tenancies eligible for housing benefit

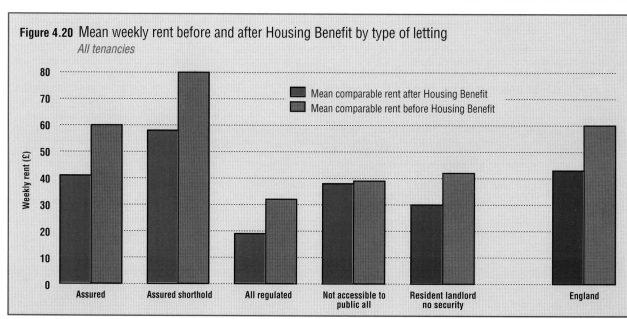

Figure 4.20 Mean weekly rent before and after Housing Benefit by type of letting
All tenancies

Notes and references

1   Hazel Green and Jacqui Hansbro. *Housing in England 1993/94.* HMSO (London 1995).

2   Because type of letting is linked to specific periods in time, different expressions of the length of tenancy have been used in the rent modelling for different letting types. The rent achieved for a property at any given point in time is likely to be affected by other factors operating in the market place such as mortgage interest rates, house prices and the supply of and demand for private rented accommodation, the year in which the tenancy started. The year a tenancy started can be seen to indicate market rents at a particular point in time or as an expression of how long the tenancy group have been renting the accommodation.

3   G Harris. 'The take-up of income-related benefits: inaccuracies in the estimation of take-up rates'. Department of Social Security Analytical Note No. 3. J-Y Duclos 'Understanding the take-up of state benefits using micro data. London School of Economics Welfare State Programme (1992).

4   DSS. *Income related benefits: estimates of take-up in 1992.* Analytical Services Division DSS (1995).

5   A tenancy group was counted as receiving Housing Benefit if any person in the group was receiving the benefit.

5 Income and rent

SUMMARY

- The average tenancy group disposable income in 1993 was £190 per week or approximately £10,000 per annum.

- Tenancy groups in accommodation not accessible to the public had the highest average incomes with a mean disposable income of £240 per week. Tenancy groups with assured shorthold lettings also had a high average disposable income (£220 per week).

- Tenancies with regulated lettings (mostly retired people) and those with resident landlord and no security lettings (mainly young people) had lower average disposable incomes, £140 and £130 per week respectively.

- Although average disposable income varied by letting type there was little difference in the income level defining the lowest tenth of incomes in all letting types.

- Twenty nine per cent of all tenancies were largely dependent on state benefits for their income, that is, they were receiving at least three quarters of their income from benefits.

- On average, tenancies spent 27% of their disposable income on rent. Just over a quarter of tenancies were spending at least a third of their income on rent.

- The proportion of tenancies spending at least a third of their disposable income on rent (after Housing Benefit) was highest (32%) among assured and assured shorthold tenancies. Only one in ten regulated tenants paid a third or more of their disposable income in rent.

5.1 **Calculation of income**

All individuals aged 16 or over in a tenancy group were asked about their income. They were asked about the amounts from each source separately (earnings, state benefits, etc) and about payments of income tax, National Insurance contributions and so on. This was then used to calculate the total weekly income for each tenancy group, as far as possible, and similarly the disposable income excluding income tax and other deductions.[1] Incomes were obtained for 89% of tenancy groups.[2] Disposable income is the measure used in this chapter.

The average disposable income of tenancy groups in 1993 was £190 per week, approximately £10,000 per annum. The Department of the Environment has for some years published estimates of disposable income from the Family Expenditure Survey (FES).[3] Although the FES has a sample less than half the size of the SEH and does not provide a breakdown by type of letting any differences need to be explained. The mean household disposable income of private renters in England from the 1993/94 FES was £11,800 a year, rather higher than the SEH estimate for tenancy groups. One reason for the difference is that grossing reduced the SEH estimate from £10,600 a year based just on the sample to £9,900 based on grossed results. The grossing employed in the SEH compensates for the under-representation of one-person tenancy groups, which tend to have lower incomes. The FES, however, is not grossed. Another reason for the difference is that the FES incomes are for households while the SEH incomes are for tenancy groups. FES households, on average, have slightly more adults than

SEH tenancy groups so must be expected to have a higher total income.

5.2 **Differences in income**

Figure 5.1 shows the estimated numbers of tenancies with different levels of disposable income. The distribution is concentrated around the lower end of the income range with decreasing numbers of tenancies having incomes in the higher ranges. A quarter of all tenancy groups (490 thousand) had disposable income of under £75 per week and a further 20% or 380 thousand tenancies had income between £75 and £125 per week. (Figure 5.1)

Tenancy group income is determined by the number of people in the tenancy group and their economic status. As might be expected there were differences in the disposable income of the tenancy group depending on its composition. People aged 60 or over living alone had the lowest average disposable income at £100 per week, which is just over half the average income for all tenancies. Lone parents with dependent children and younger one-person tenancies had similar mean income levels (£130 per week). Large mainly adult tenancies had the highest mean disposable income at £370 per week. This group and tenancy groups comprising two adults, at least one aged 60 or over included a relatively high proportion of cases for whom income was missing (one fifth). This is likely to have resulted in an underestimation of the mean income of these tenancies.

Mean income values are sensitive to the presence of a few very high or very low incomes. The median, which

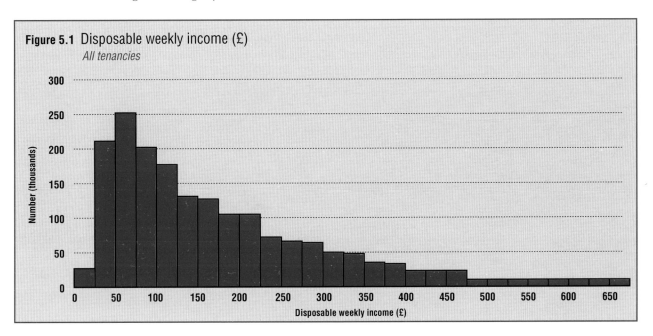

Figure 5.1 Disposable weekly income (£)
All tenancies

divides the distribution in half is less affected by extremes and so provides an alternative and in some ways a better measure of general income level. The median was lower than the mean for all types of tenancy group indicating that some tenancies of each type had a very high income.

As well as showing mean and median disposable income, Figure 5.2 shows the range of income among tenancy groups of different types. The vertical lines represent the range of income between the top and bottom deciles, that is the range of income excluding the 10% of tenancy groups with the highest incomes and the 10% with the lowest income. Couples of working age, couples with dependent children and mainly adult tenancy groups had the widest spread of disposable income and the highest medians; the other types of tenancy group had similar and narrower ranges of income with lower medians. (Figure 5.2)

Figure 5.3 shows the proportion of tenancy groups with disposable income levels under £180 per week. Not surprisingly, very high proportions of tenancy groups consisting of one adult, older couples and lone parents with dependent children had disposable incomes below £180 per week (70% or more) compared with a quarter or less of other groups. Almost half of tenancy groups consisting of one adult of working age and older one-person tenancies had a disposable income of less than £80 per week. (Figure 5.3)

Figure 5.4 shows the close relationship between disposable income and economic status. Over two thirds of tenancies where the tenant was unemployed

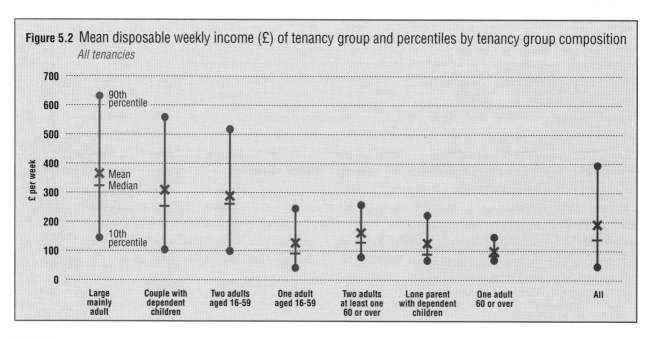

Figure 5.2 Mean disposable weekly income (£) of tenancy group and percentiles by tenancy group composition

All tenancies

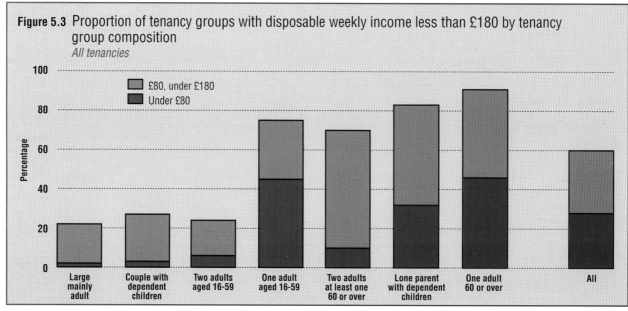

Figure 5.3 Proportion of tenancy groups with disposable weekly income less than £180 by tenancy group composition

All tenancies

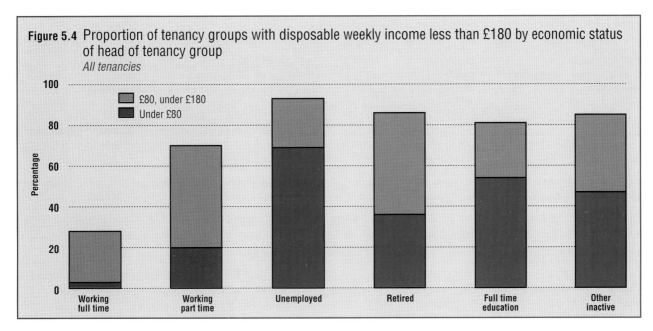

Figure 5.4 Proportion of tenancy groups with disposable weekly income less than £180 by economic status of head of tenancy group
All tenancies

had disposable income less than £80 per week (69%) as did relatively high proportions of tenancies where the head was a student (54%) or economically inactive (47%). Hardly any tenancies headed by a full-time worker had a disposable income under £80 but one fifth of those headed by a part-time worker did. (Figure 5.4)

Tenancy group disposable income also varied according to the type of letting. Tenancy groups in accommodation not accessible to the public had the highest average incomes with a mean disposable income of £240. Most of these tenancies were lettings that went with a job. Tenancy groups with assured shorthold lettings also had a high average weekly disposable income (£220) and had the widest range of income. Tenancies with regulated lettings and those

with other types of lettings had lower mean and median disposable income levels and narrow ranges of income. The mean disposable income of tenancies with regulated lettings was £140, tenants with this type of letting tended to be older retired people. The average disposable income of tenants with resident landlord and no security lettings was lower still at £130, these tenants were predominantly young. Although average incomes varied widely between the different types of letting, the value of the lowest decile was similar for all letting types. (Figure 5.5)

5.3 **Income from state benefits**

Twenty nine per cent of all tenancies were largely dependent on state benefits for their income, that is, they were receiving at least three quarters of their

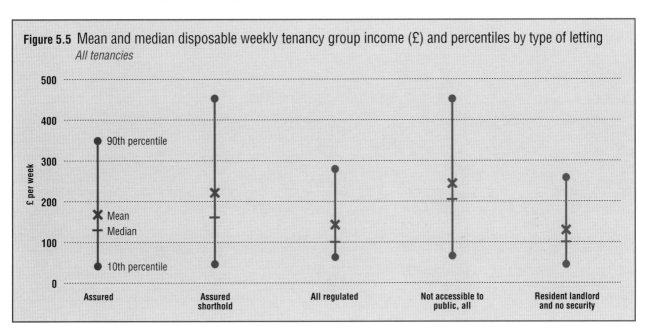

Figure 5.5 Mean and median disposable weekly tenancy group income (£) and percentiles by type of letting
All tenancies

income from benefits. The importance of state benefits as a source of income for lone parents and tenancies comprising one or two older people is clearly shown; almost two thirds of lone parents with dependent children (64%) received at least three quarters of their income in state benefits as did 58% of older one-person tenancies. Large mainly adult tenancy groups and tenancy groups consisting of two adults of working age or couples with dependent children were much less likely to be so dependent; 16% or less received at least three quarters of their income from benefits. These types of tenancy groups tended to have higher than average disposable income (Figure 5.2). (Figure 5.6)

As might be expected from the profiles of different letting types in Chapter 2, tenancy groups in regulated lettings were most likely to be receiving a large part of their income from benefits: almost half received at least three quarters of their income as state benefits (47%). Tenants with this type of letting agreement tended to be older, retired people. Tenancies in lettings not accessible to the public, which had the highest average disposable income, were accordingly least likely to be dependent on income from state benefits with just 11% of tenancies receiving at least three quarters of their income from benefits. (Figure 5.7)

As is to be expected, the proportion of tenancy groups receiving most of their income from state benefits varied with income. Tenancy groups in the lower income bands were most likely to be dependent on state benefits for a large part of their income. Almost three quarters of tenancies with a weekly disposable

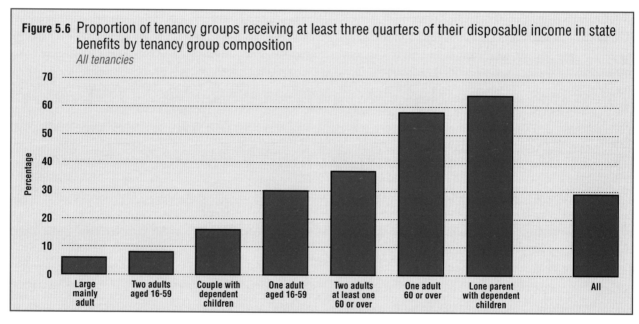

Figure 5.6 Proportion of tenancy groups receiving at least three quarters of their disposable income in state benefits by tenancy group composition
All tenancies

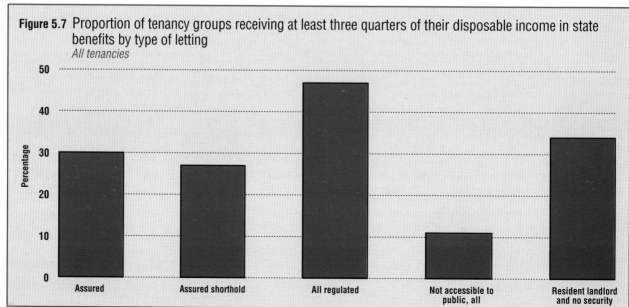

Figure 5.7 Proportion of tenancy groups receiving at least three quarters of their disposable income in state benefits by type of letting
All tenancies

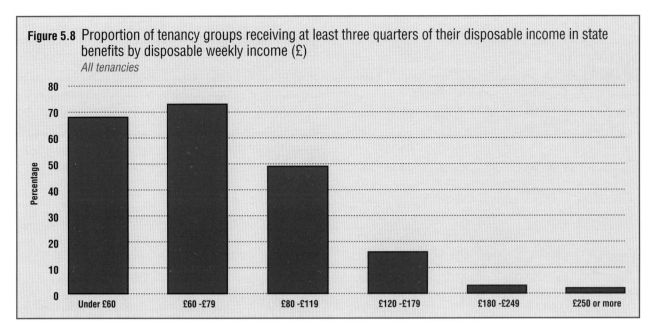

Figure 5.8 Proportion of tenancy groups receiving at least three quarters of their disposable income in state benefits by disposable weekly income (£)
All tenancies

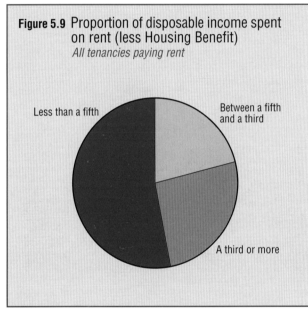

Figure 5.9 Proportion of disposable income spent on rent (less Housing Benefit)
All tenancies paying rent

income of between £60 and £79 (73%) and over two thirds of those with incomes under £60 (68%) received at least three quarters of their income from state benefits. (Figure 5.8)

5.4 **Affordability of rent**

While the analysis of rent (Chapter 4) is of interest in itself, rent and income taken together can provide an indication of the relative affordability of housing. One indicator of affordability is the proportion of disposable income taken up by housing costs - rent in this case - referred to as the rent to income ratio.

Housing Benefit is a subsidy towards rent and can be regarded in one of two ways, either as an element of income or as a deduction from the rent. The way

Housing Benefit is treated has an important impact on the rent to income ratio.[4] For the purposes of reporting on the findings of this survey, Housing Benefit has been deducted from the comparable rent for the tenancy in calculating the rent to income ratio. The income measure is the disposable income of the tenancy group.

On average, tenancies spent 27% of their disposable income on rent. Just over a quarter (26%) were spending a third or more of their income on rent. The mean ratio gives a distorted picture of the proportion of income taken up by rent because of the effect of Housing Benefit and the circumstances of a few tenancies whose rent at the time of interview was very much higher than their disposable income. An alternative measure of general levels of a tenancy's spending on rent is the median proportion of income taken up by rent which divides the distribution at its central point. The median value for all tenancies was 18%. (Figure 5.9)

5.5 **Differences in rent to income ratio**

Figure 5.10 shows, for rent paying tenancies, the proportion spending at least a third of their disposable income on rent after deduction of Housing Benefit analysed by letting type. This proportion was highest (32%) among assured and assured shorthold tenancies. These types of lettings had the highest average rents before Housing Benefit (£60 and £80 respectively) as well as high average income and a wide range of incomes (Figure 5.4). In contrast, only one in ten regulated tenants paid a third or more of their disposable income in rent. These tenancy groups had the lowest average rents as well as low average income. Less than a fifth of tenants in lettings not accessible to the public paid a third or more of their disposable income as rent; these tenancies had the highest average disposable income (£240) and relatively low rents before the deduction of Housing Benefit. (Figure 5.10)

The proportion of tenancies spending at least a third of their disposable income on rent varied with rent level. Almost half of tenancies with comparable weekly rents of £100 or more per week (before Housing Benefit) were paying a third or more of their income as rent (48%). Among tenancies paying the lowest rents (before Housing Benefit), rent accounted for a third or more of disposable income for only a very small proportion of tenancies, 2% of those paying less

than £15 per week and 5% of those with rents of £15, up to £19. (Figure 5.11)

The effect of Housing Benefit on rent to income ratios is shown in Figure 5.12 which shows the number of tenancy groups at each rent level spending a third or more of their disposable income on rent by whether they receive Housing Benefit. Among both groups, a greater number of tenancies paying higher levels of rent (before Housing Benefit) were paying at least a third of their income in rent than tenancies with lower rents. Among tenancies in receipt of Housing Benefit, the number of tenancies paying a third or more of their income in rent was lower at each rent level than among tenancies not receiving Housing Benefit. (Figure 5.12)

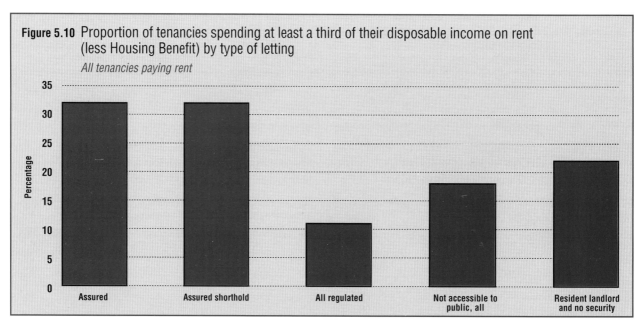

Figure 5.10 Proportion of tenancies spending at least a third of their disposable income on rent (less Housing Benefit) by type of letting

All tenancies paying rent

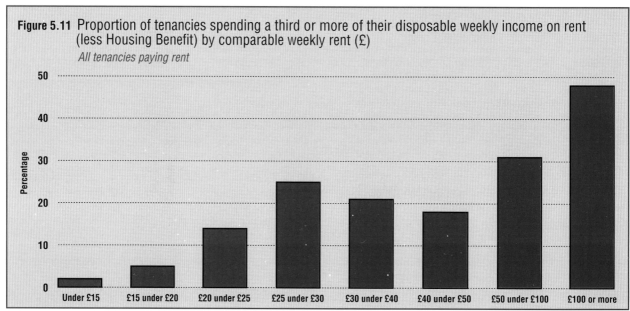

Figure 5.11 Proportion of tenancies spending a third or more of their disposable weekly income on rent (less Housing Benefit) by comparable weekly rent (£)

All tenancies paying rent

Figure 5.13 shows the proportion of tenancies spending at least a third of their disposable income on rent by income level. As is to be expected, the proportion spending a third or more of their disposable income on rent was highest among tenancies with disposable incomes in the lowest band, under £60 per week (37%). Tenancies in the two lowest income bands were most likely to be eligible for Housing Benefit (Figure 4.13) and also had the highest takeup of Housing Benefit (Figure 4.18). The effect of Housing Benefit on the proportion of tenancies that spend at least a third of their disposable income on rent at different income levels is shown in Figure 5.14. Among tenancies which were not receiving Housing Benefit, the proportion spending a third or more of their income on rent was higher for tenancies in the lower income bands. Almost all tenancies (93%) not receiving Housing Benefit with disposable incomes under £60 per week spent at least a third of their income on rent as did 79% of those with incomes of £60 to £79. This means that there were 120 thousand tenancies with disposable incomes of less than £80 per week who were paying at least a third of their disposable income on rent and who were not receiving Housing Benefit. Among tenancies receiving Housing Benefit relatively small proportions in each income band were spending at least a third of their income on rent. (Figures 5.13 and 5.14)

Notes and references

1   Income includes earnings from employment, profit or loss from self-employment, state benefits and pensions, income from investments and other receipts such as maintenance allowances and student grants. Tax, national insurance, pension contributions, union subscriptions and regular maintenance payments have been deducted from earnings to arrive at disposable income.

2   If income from any source was missing for an individual then the total income was not calculated for that person. Likewise, if information was missing for an individual in the tenancy, then the total tenancy group income was not calculated. In order to minimise the number of cases for which tenancy group income could not be calculated, an estimate of the tenancy group income was sought where income for an individual was missing or where the informant felt the tenancy group income was either too high or too low. An estimate was used for 3% of tenancy groups.

3   Department of the Environment. *Housing and Construction Statistics 1983-1993.* HMSO (London 1994).

4   If Housing Benefit is included as income the ratio of rent to income is generally higher for recipients of Housing Benefit than if it is deducted from the rent. This is clearest for people whose rent is entirely covered by Housing Benefit and for whom the ratio is reduced to zero if benefit is deducted from rent but may be very high if it is not. For example, a tenant with an income of £280 per week with rent of £100 per week and Housing Benefit of £70, using the first method would have a rent to income ratio of (100 - 70)/280 =0.11 or 11%. Using the second method, the ratio would be 100 / (280 + 70) = 0.28 or 28%.

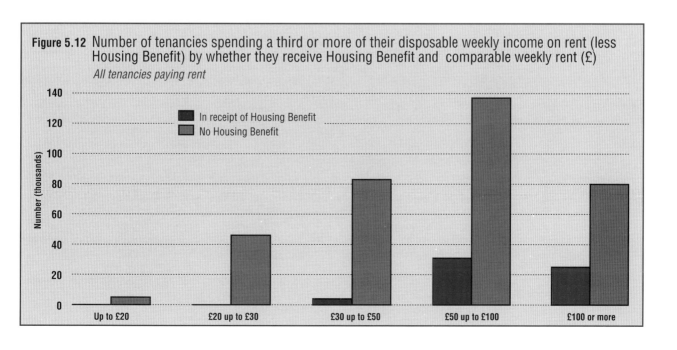

Figure 5.12 Number of tenancies spending a third or more of their disposable weekly income on rent (less Housing Benefit) by whether they receive Housing Benefit and comparable weekly rent (£)

All tenancies paying rent

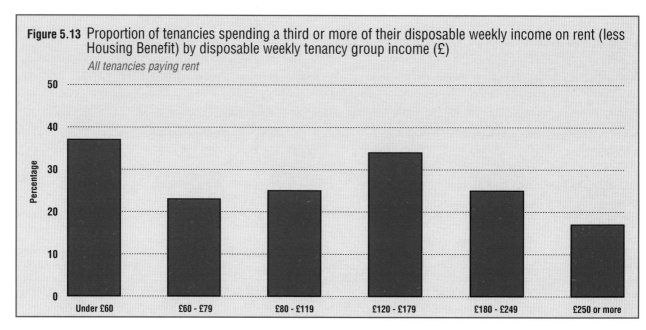

Figure 5.13 Proportion of tenancies spending a third or more of their disposable weekly income on rent (less Housing Benefit) by disposable weekly tenancy group income (£)

All tenancies paying rent

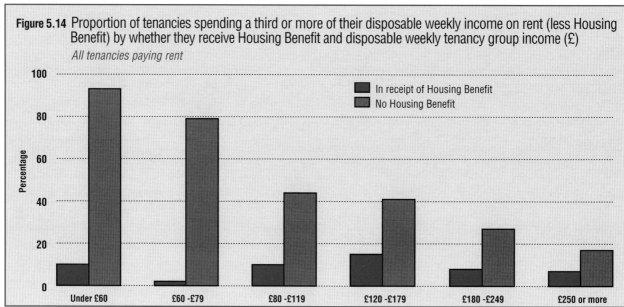

Figure 5.14 Proportion of tenancies spending a third or more of their disposable weekly income on rent (less Housing Benefit) by whether they receive Housing Benefit and disposable weekly tenancy group income (£)

All tenancies paying rent

6 The housing histories and expectations of private tenants

SUMMARY

- Four out of ten tenants (41%) who had been in their accommodation less than five years had found the accommodation through personal contacts such as friends, relatives or people at work.

- Over a third of tenants (38%) had experienced difficulty in finding accommodation. Tenants in assured lettings were twice as likely as other types of tenant to report problems.

- Almost two thirds of tenants (63%) had had to pay a deposit or non-returnable fee in order to secure their accommodation; assured tenants were more than twice as likely as other groups to have had to pay a deposit or fee.

- About a half of regulated tenants and a half of assured tenants said that their accommodation was in need of repair compared with about a third of tenants with other types of letting agreement.

- Almost two thirds of tenants had asked their landlord to carry out repairs and just over four in ten said that it had been difficult to get the work done.

- The majority of tenants (77%) described themselves as being on good terms with their landlord.

- Over three quarters of tenants (1.7 million) had moved in the ten years prior to the interview and 59% (1.3 million) had moved in the previous three years.

- Almost three quarters of tenants expected to move at some time in the future.

- A half of tenants expected to buy a home at some time.

- 290 thousand tenants (13%) were on a waiting list for local authority or housing association accommodation.

This chapter describes features of tenants' past and present accommodation as well as their experiences of looking for and securing privately rented accommodation. It also describes the future housing expectations and aspirations of private tenants.

6.1 **Finding rented accommodation**

Tenants who had been in their present accommodation for five years or less were asked how they had found their present accommodation.[1] Figure 6.1 shows that the main means of finding accommodation was through personal contacts with friends, relatives or people at work - mentioned by 41% overall. This was the most common method for people in each tenancy type but particularly for those

with a resident landlord (62%). Tenants in assured lettings were more likely than other groups to have found their accommodation through an agent (21% compared with 6% or less). The 29% of people in tenancies not accessible to the public who found their accommodation by 'other' methods includes people whose employer arranged the accommodation. (Figure 6.1)

Over one third of tenants (38%) said that it had been difficult to find their accommodation. Tenants in assured lettings were at least twice as likely as those in other groups to report problems. This is related to the way in which the accommodation was found. As Table 6.1 shows, tenants who found their accommodation through an advert or agent were more likely to have difficulty than those using personal contacts. The

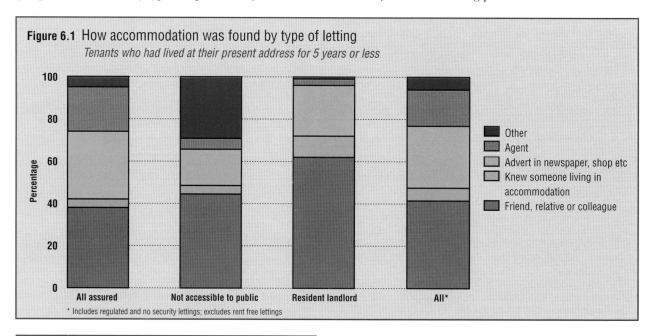

Figure 6.1 How accommodation was found by type of letting
Tenants who had lived at their present address for 5 years or less

Legend:
- Other
- Agent
- Advert in newspaper, shop etc
- Knew someone living in accommodation
- Friend, relative or colleague

* Includes regulated and no security lettings; excludes rent free lettings

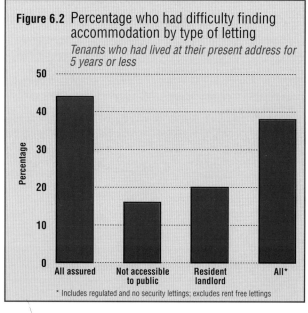

Figure 6.2 Percentage who had difficulty finding accommodation by type of letting
Tenants who had lived at their present address for 5 years or less

* Includes regulated and no security lettings; excludes rent free lettings

Table 6.1 Ease with which accommodation was found by how it was found
*Tenants who had lived at their present address for 5 years or less**   *England*

How accommodation was found	Found with difficulty	Found easily	Total
			thousands
Friend, relative or colleague	212	435	647
Knew someone living in accommodation	13	62	75
Advert in newspaper, shop, etc	206	255	462
Agent	133	135	268
Other	25	94	118
All	589	980	1 569
			percentages
Friend, relative or colleague	33	67	100
Knew someone living in accommodation	17	83	100
Advert in newspaper, shop, etc	45	55	100
Agent	50	50	100
Other	21	79	100
All	38	62	100

* Excluding rent free lettings

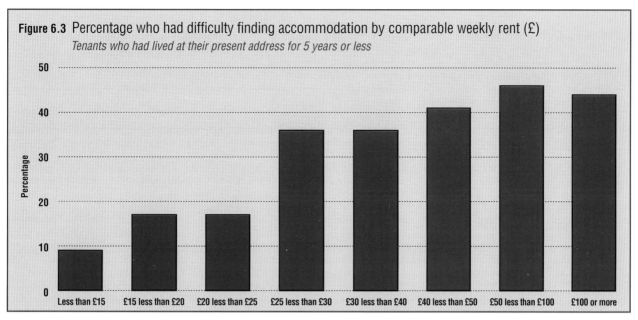

Figure 6.3 Percentage who had difficulty finding accommodation by comparable weekly rent (£)
Tenants who had lived at their present address for 5 years or less

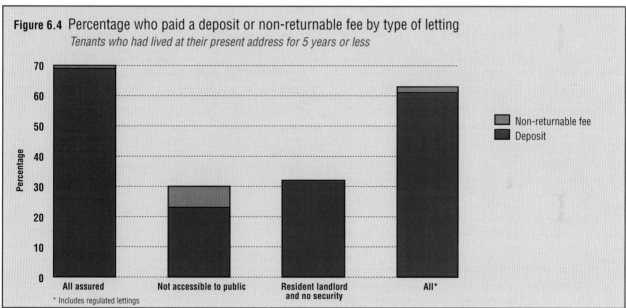

Figure 6.4 Percentage who paid a deposit or non-returnable fee by type of letting
Tenants who had lived at their present address for 5 years or less

former - used more by those with assured tenancies - probably involves more effort and expense than other methods of finding accommodation. (Figure 6.2 and Table 6.1)

Over 70% of tenants reporting problems said that they had had difficulty finding a place they could afford and, as Figure 6.3 illustrates, difficulty finding accommodation was directly related to the amount of rent charged. Those paying £25 per week or more were at least twice as likely to have problems as those paying less. This is related to the type of letting - rents were highest in assured tenancies, particularly assured shortholds and, as shown above, tenants in these lettings were most likely to report problems. Another possibility is that those who had difficulty were forced to pay relatively high rents. (Figure 6.3)

Most tenants (73%) had had to make one rent payment in advance in order to secure their accommodation but 8% had had to make a larger payment. Almost two thirds (63%) had had to pay a deposit or non-returnable fee, usually in addition to the advance rent. Assured tenants were more than twice as likely as other groups to have had to pay a deposit or fee, 70% compared with 30%-32%. As assured tenants were also the group most likely to have had difficulty finding their accommodation, it is likely that such payments contributed to the difficulties. As Figure 6.5 shows, one fifth of assured tenants said that they had had to turn down suitable accommodation because they had not been able to afford the deposit. (Figures 6.4 and 6.5)

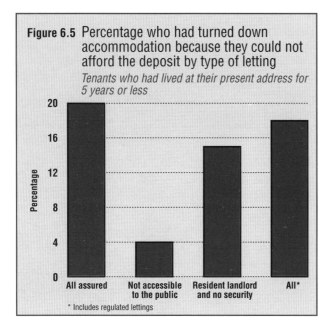

Figure 6.5 Percentage who had turned down accommodation because they could not afford the deposit by type of letting
Tenants who had lived at their present address for 5 years or less

* Includes regulated lettings

6.2 Repairs

At the time of interview, about a half of tenants in regulated lettings and about a half in assured lettings said that their accommodation needed some sort of repair compared with about a third of those in lettings not accessible to the public or with a resident landlord. This variation is probably attributable to differences in the type and age of the property occupied by different groups of tenants. Most of the tenants in lettings not accessible to the public rented their accommodation from their employer. A high proportion of assured tenants lived in converted flats while regulated tenants tended to live in terraced houses - accommodation which tends to be older than other types of property. Figure 6.7 shows that the percentage of tenants saying that repairs were required was highest among occupants of converted flats and terraced houses. Tenants who said that their accommodation was in need of repair were asked what types of repairs were needed. Figure 6.8 shows that the main types of repair needed were external or structural repairs and internal decoration.

Almost all tenants said that the landlord had sole responsibility for at least some types of repair. Figure 6.10 shows the type of repairs for which the landlord was solely responsible. The majority of tenants said that the landlord was responsible for structural or external repairs whereas internal decoration was said to be the sole responsibility of the landlord in only 44% of cases. In regulated lettings only 9% of tenants said that internal decoration was the landlord's responsibility.

Almost two thirds (62%) of tenants had, at some time, asked their landlord to carry out repairs (table not shown) and just over four in ten of these tenants (42%) said that it been difficult to get the work done. Tenants reporting that they had had difficulty in the past in getting repairs done tended to be the same people as those saying that their accommodation was currently in need of repair. Among the latter group, 62% had had difficulty getting work done in the past (table not shown). (Figures 6.6 to 6.11)

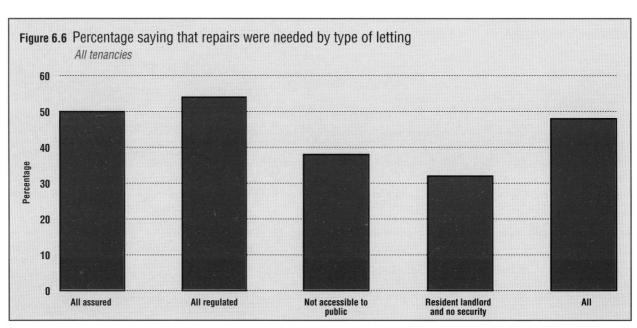

Figure 6.6 Percentage saying that repairs were needed by type of letting
All tenancies

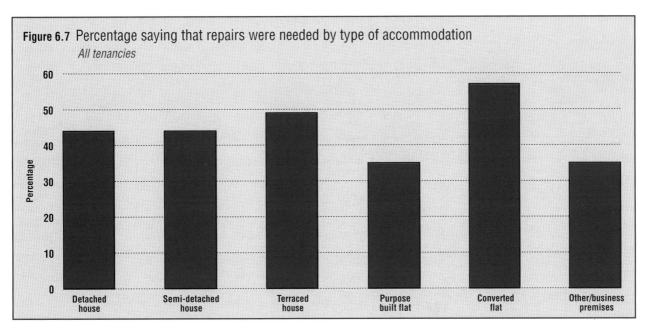

Figure 6.7 Percentage saying that repairs were needed by type of accommodation
All tenancies

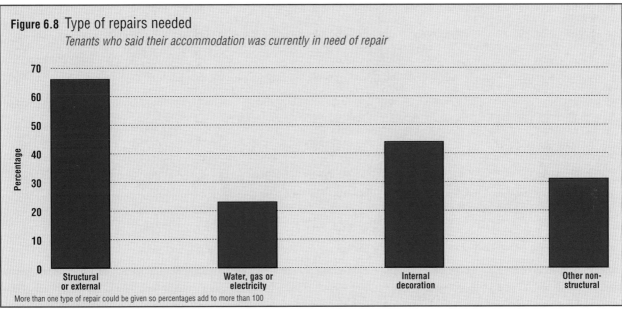

Figure 6.8 Type of repairs needed
Tenants who said their accommodation was currently in need of repair

More than one type of repair could be given so percentages add to more than 100

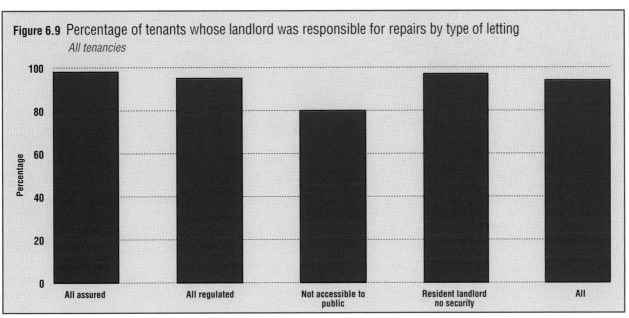

Figure 6.9 Percentage of tenants whose landlord was responsible for repairs by type of letting
All tenancies

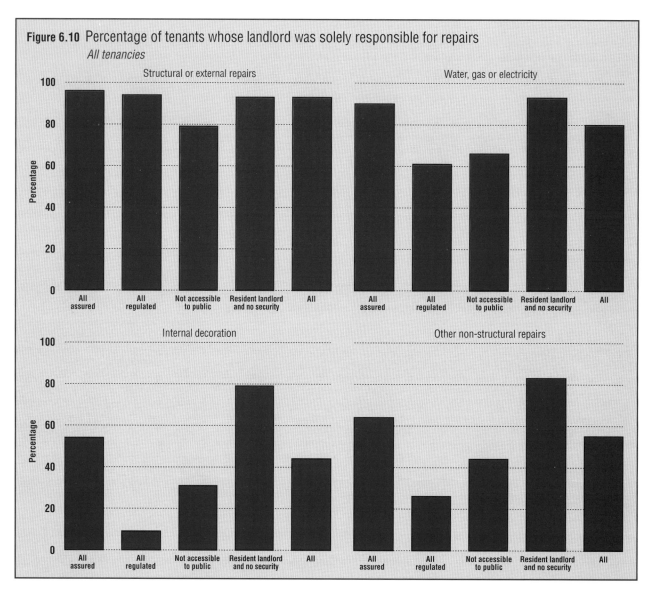

Figure 6.10 Percentage of tenants whose landlord was solely responsible for repairs
All tenancies

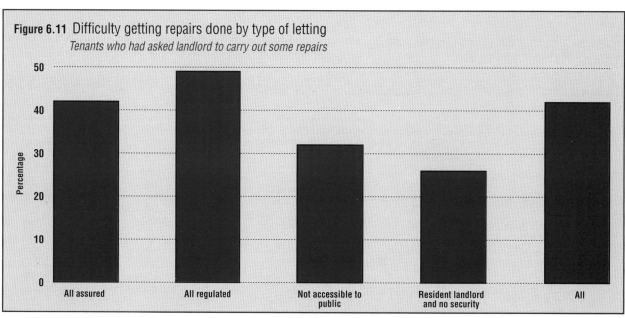

Figure 6.11 Difficulty getting repairs done by type of letting
Tenants who had asked landlord to carry out some repairs

6.3 **Tenant and landlord relationship**

The majority of tenants (77%) described themselves as being on good terms with their landlord while only 5% said they were on poor terms.[2] These proportions compare with 81% and 3% respectively in 1990. Dissatisfaction was greatest among tenants in regulated lettings and those renting from a property company - about one in ten said that they were on poor terms with the landlord. Conversely, only 2% of tenants renting from an employer reported a poor relationship. Repairs were the main cause of contention, mentioned by 58% of those on poor terms. Almost one in ten tenants living in accommodation which was in need of repair said they were on poor terms with their landlord compared to only 1% of those in accommodation not needing

repairs (Table A6.14). Other reasons for a poor relationship were that the tenant thought that the landlord was unpleasant, untrustworthy or difficult (mentioned by 41% of tenants who said that they were on poor terms) or that he or she was difficult to contact (36% of tenants on poor terms). This is, of course, from the tenants' viewpoint. Not all the reasons necessarily imply unreasonable behaviour on the part of the landlord - the financial demands might have arisen because of rent arrears and legal action to evict can only be taken in specified circumstances. All tenants were asked if the landlord had ever tried to get them to leave the accommodation or had done anything to make them feel uncomfortable. Overall, 7% of tenants said that the landlord had done so. The figure includes what may be reasonable actions by the landlord, for example taking legal action to evict

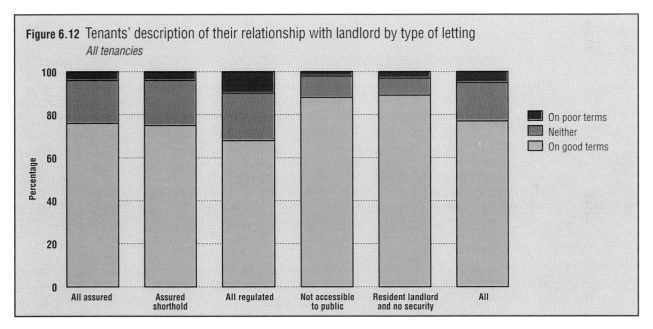

Figure 6.12 Tenants' description of their relationship with landlord by type of letting
All tenancies

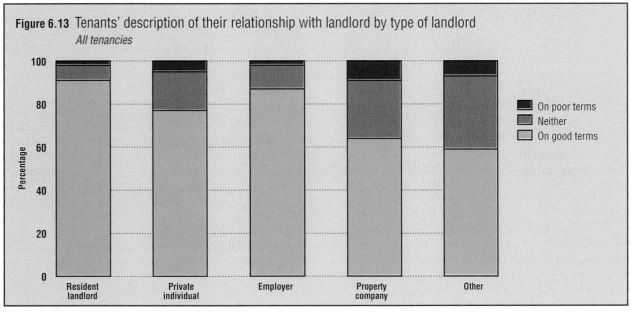

Figure 6.13 Tenants' description of their relationship with landlord by type of landlord
All tenancies

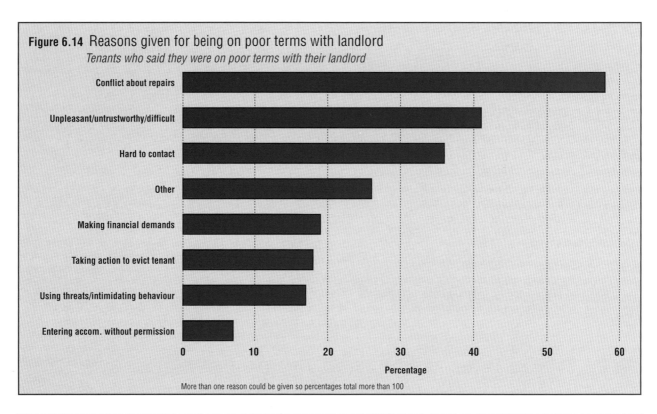

Figure 6.14 Reasons given for being on poor terms with landlord
Tenants who said they were on poor terms with their landlord

More than one reason could be given so percentages total more than 100

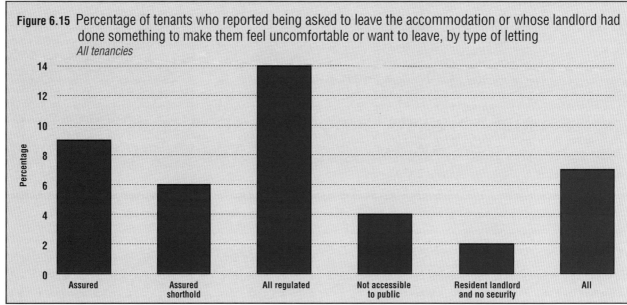

Figure 6.15 Percentage of tenants who reported being asked to leave the accommodation or whose landlord had done something to make them feel uncomfortable or want to leave, by type of letting
All tenancies

tenants who have mistreated the property or failed to pay the rent for more than three months. It also includes actions not necessarily aimed at getting the tenant to leave, such as slow or poor repairs (cited by about a quarter of the 7%). Only 3% reported that the landlord had entered the accommodation without permission or used threats or intimating behaviour. (Figures 6.12 to 6.15)

6.4 **Moving**

Over three quarters of tenants (1.7 million) had moved in the ten years prior to the interview and 59%

(1.3 million) had moved in the previous three years. Both proportions are higher than those recorded by the 1990 survey, 65% and 48%. This trend is at least partly attributable to the greater number of young tenants. As Figure 6.16 shows, 83% of lone parent families and at least 75% of tenancies consisting of one or two people of working age had moved in the last three years. Conversely, only 5% of households consisting of one person aged 60 or over and 12% of elderly couples had moved during this period.

Variation in mobility between people with different types of letting agreement reflect the time period for

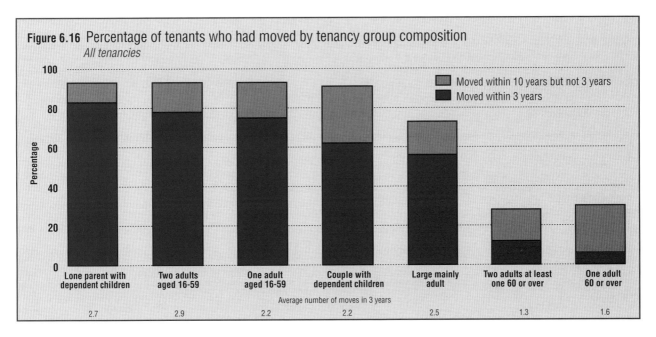

Figure 6.16 Percentage of tenants who had moved by tenancy group composition

All tenancies

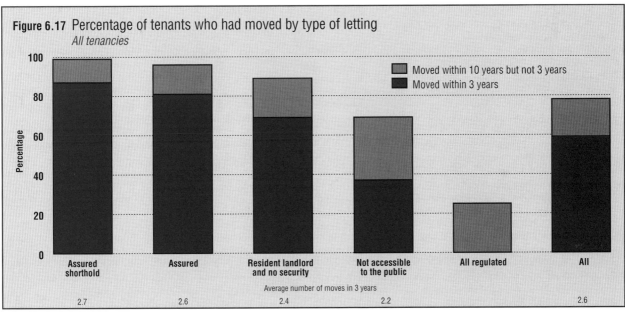

Figure 6.17 Percentage of tenants who had moved by type of letting

All tenancies

which the letting type has been available and the different age profiles of the groups. Thus, assured tenancies were only available for people who had moved since January 1989 and assured tenants were also predominantly young. They were therefore the most mobile group: 81% of those in assured lettings and 87% of those with assured shorthold agreements had moved in the last three years. In contrast, only 25% of tenants in the regulated sector had moved in the last ten years. Such tenants tend to be elderly and would have had to have moved into their accommodation before deregulation in January 1989. (Figures 6.16 and 6.17)

Tenants who had moved in the last three years were asked about their previous accommodation and their reasons for moving. A fifth of tenants had previously been living at home with parents or family and 44%

had moved from other privately rented accommodation. Over one in ten (12%) had owned their previous accommodation, some of whom are probably people renting temporarily before moving back into owner occupation. A fifth of tenants in accommodation not accessible to the public were previously owner occupiers. These may include people who have moved for employment reasons and whose employer was providing rented accommodation: over a half of tenants in accommodation not accessible to the public had moved for reasons connected with their job. A fifth of tenants gave general housing reasons which include wanting larger, smaller or better accommodation.

A third of tenants who had moved in the last three years had moved less than two miles from their last

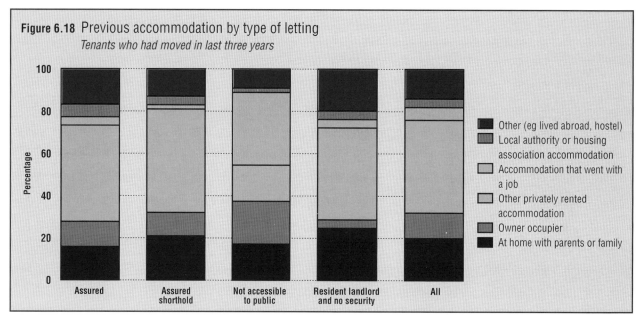

Figure 6.18 Previous accommodation by type of letting
Tenants who had moved in last three years

Legend:
- Other (eg lived abroad, hostel)
- Local authority or housing association accommodation
- Accommodation that went with a job
- Other privately rented accommodation
- Owner occupier
- At home with parents or family

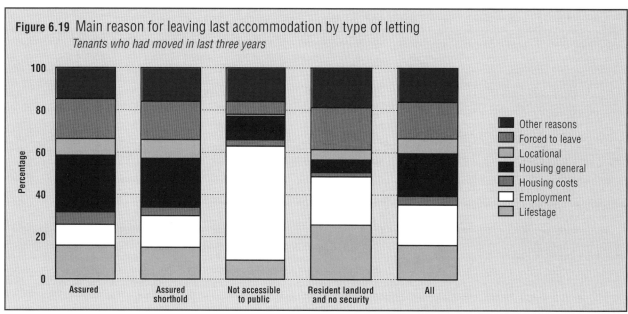

Figure 6.19 Main reason for leaving last accommodation by type of letting
Tenants who had moved in last three years

Legend:
- Other reasons
- Forced to leave
- Locational
- Housing general
- Housing costs
- Employment
- Lifestage

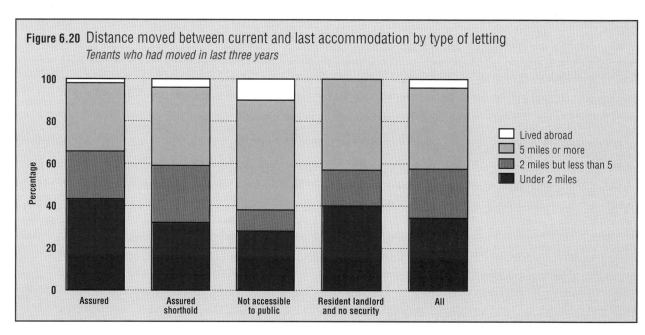

Figure 6.20 Distance moved between current and last accommodation by type of letting
Tenants who had moved in last three years

Legend:
- Lived abroad
- 5 miles or more
- 2 miles but less than 5
- Under 2 miles

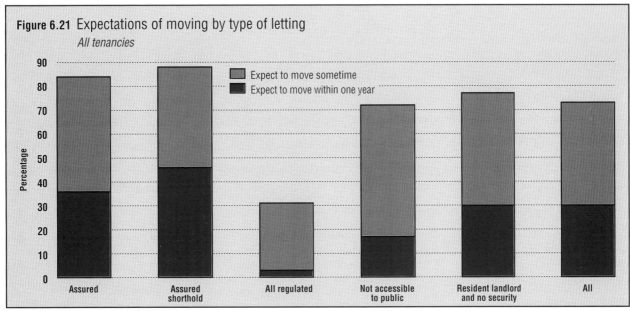

Figure 6.21 Expectations of moving by type of letting
All tenancies

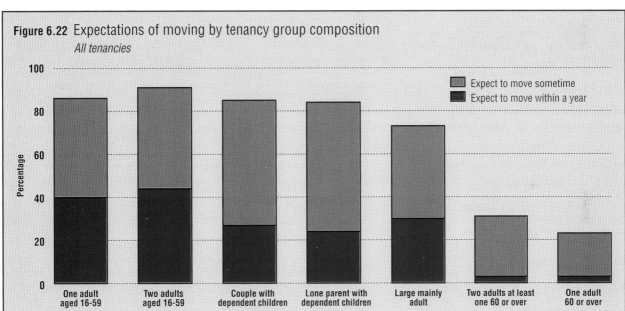

Figure 6.22 Expectations of moving by tenancy group composition
All tenancies

accommodation and just over a half had moved less than five. Tenants in accommodation not accessible to the public tended to have moved a greater distance than other groups: 62% had moved more than five miles, including 10% who had previously lived abroad. (Figures 6.18 to 6.20)

6.5 **Tenants' expectations of moving**

Almost three quarters of tenants (73%) expected to move at some time, a marked increase on the percentage in 1990 (57%). The proportion expecting to move within a year, however, did not change over this period, 30% in 1993 and 29% in 1990. Variations by letting type showed the same pattern as variations in the proportions who had actually moved. Assured tenants were most likely to be expecting to move (84%

of assured and 89% of assured shortholds). Only 31% of tenants in regulated lettings expected to move. As with actual mobility, expectations of moving were related to age. Less than a third of elderly couples and one-person tenancies expected to move compared with at least three quarters of other groups. (Figures 6.21 and 6.22)

Tenants were asked if they thought they had the right to remain in their accommodation as long as they wanted to or if they might have to move at some time. A third of tenants (34%) thought that they might have to move. The proportion was much lower, 8%, among regulated tenants, who have security of tenure, than among those with other types of agreement (37%-44%). The main reasons people gave for possibly having to move were: that the

Table 6.2 Tenants who might have to move and reasons for moving by type of letting
All tenancies   *England*

Type of letting	Reasons for having to move*							Total**
	Tenants who said that they might have to move[1]	If the landlord sold the property	If the landlord needed the accommodation himself/herself	Accommodation goes with job	End of rental contract	Not paying the rent	Other	
								thousands
Assured	135	91	58	2	26	61	10	137
Assured shorthold	338	196	142	2	134	116	17	340
All assured	473	287	200	4	160	177	27	477
All regulated	31	17	7	0	8	12	2	32
Not accessible to public, all	165	31	10	146	7	5	7	165
Other	67	39	37	2	14	26	10	72
All	736	375	254	151	189	220	45	746
								percentages
Assured	37	66	42	1	19	45	7	
Assured shorthold	42	58	42	0	39	34	5	
All assured	40	60	42	1	34	37	6	
All regulated	8	53	22	-	24	36	8	
Not accessible to public, all	44	19	6	88	4	3	4	
Resident landlord and no security	38	55	51	3	19	37	14	
All	34	50	34	20	25	30	6	

1 Based on all tenants
* Based on those who said they might have to move or who were uncertain
**Each tenant could give more than one reason so percentages add to more than 100

landlord might sell the property (50%), the landlord might need the accommodation for him/herself (34%), and the tenant might not be able to pay the rent (30%). As is to be expected, the majority of tenants in lettings which were not accessible to the public said that they might have to leave because the accommodation went with a job. The most common reason cited by tenants in other letting types was that the landlord might sell the property (53%-66%). (Table 6.2)

Tenants were asked if they expected to buy a home at some time. A small proportion of tenants already owned a property elsewhere but these people were still asked if they expected to buy in order to estimate the proportion of current tenants who expected to move out of the private rented sector in the future. A half of tenants (51%) expected to buy a home at some time, a considerably higher proportion than in 1990 when only just over a third (35%) were expecting to buy. The increase between 1990 and 1993 will be partly attributable to a growth in the number of people who are delaying entry to owner occupation but who expect to buy eventually. Another, probably related, explanation is the increase in the number of young tenants: among those of working age, 67% of one-

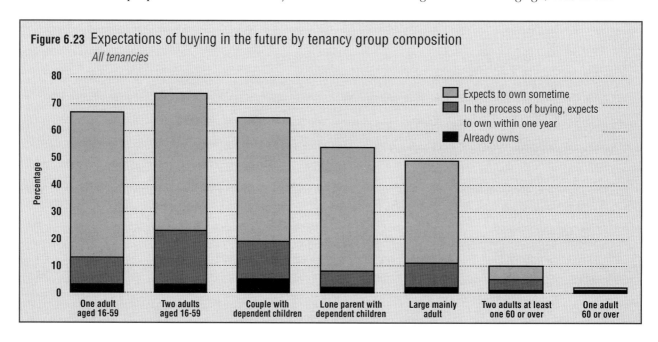

Figure 6.23 Expectations of buying in the future by tenancy group composition

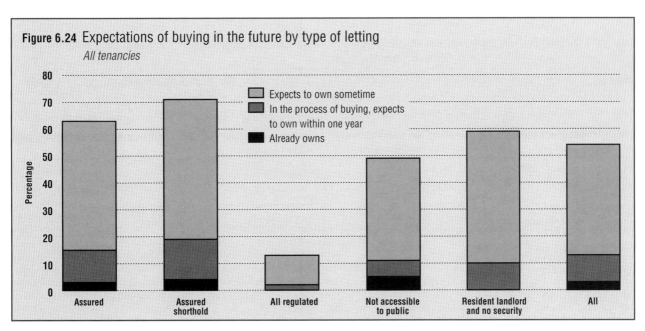

Figure 6.24 Expectations of buying in the future by type of letting

All tenancies

Figure 6.25 Percentage of tenants who would buy their next accommodation by type of letting

Tenants who said they would buy accommodation in the future

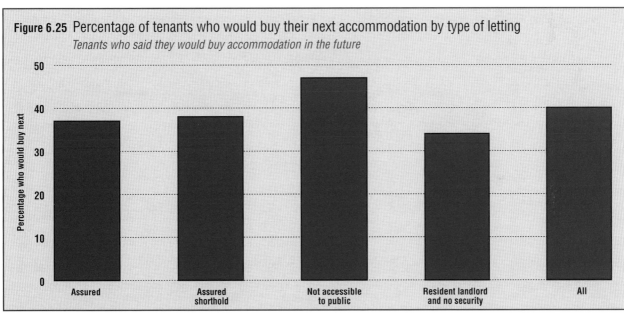

Figure 6.26 Percentage of tenants who would buy their next accommodation by tenancy group composition

Tenants who said they would buy accommodation in the future

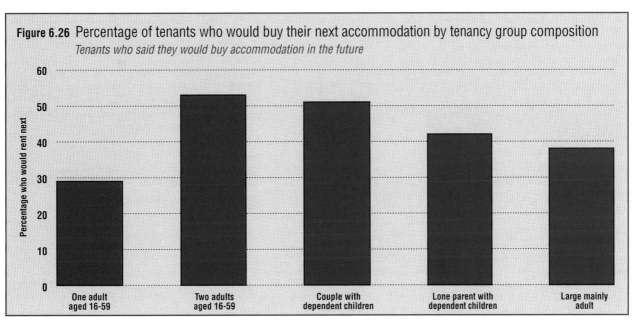

person tenancies and 74% of couples expected to buy compared with 2% and 10% respectively in the older age group. Deregulation may also be a contributory factor: the higher rents in the deregulated sector might make owning cheaper than renting. As Figure 6.24 shows, over 60% of tenants in assured tenancies expected to buy compared with only 13% of tenants in regulated lettings. Less than half of all those expecting to buy thought that they would buy their next accommodation (40%) although the proportion was higher, just over 50%, among couples and families with children. (Figures 6.23 to 6.26)

6.6 **Waiting lists for social rented sector accommodation**

The private rented sector contains a higher proportion of waiting list applicants than any other tenure group.[3] In 1993, 290 thousand tenants, 13% of tenancy groups, were on a waiting list for local authority or housing association accommodation. Figure 6.27 shows that assured tenancies contained the largest number (190 thousand) and highest proportion of tenants on a waiting list (16%) followed by regulated lettings with 60 thousand tenants (14%) on a list. Tenancy groups containing children were more likely than other groups to be on a waiting list. Two fifths of lone parents were on a waiting list as were one fifth of couples with dependent children. Less predictably, almost a fifth (18%) of elderly

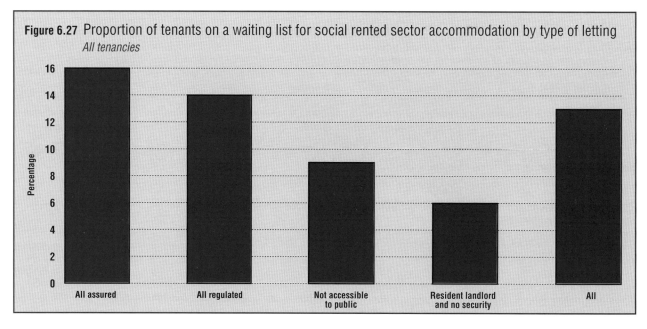

Figure 6.27 Proportion of tenants on a waiting list for social rented sector accommodation by type of letting
All tenancies

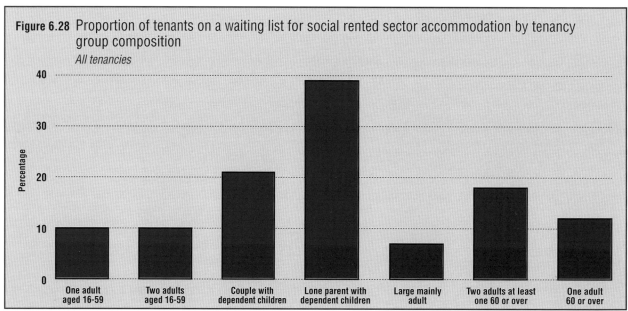

Figure 6.28 Proportion of tenants on a waiting list for social rented sector accommodation by tenancy group composition
All tenancies

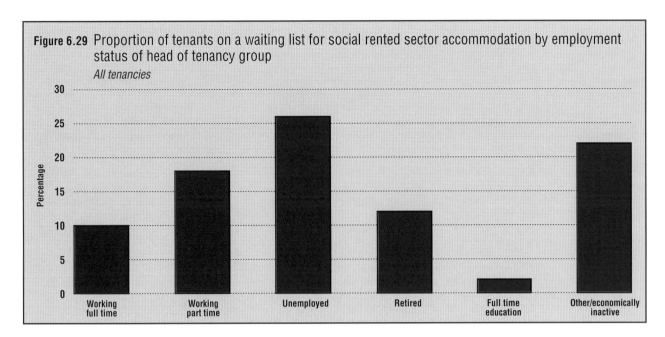

Figure 6.29 Proportion of tenants on a waiting list for social rented sector accommodation by employment status of head of tenancy group

All tenancies

couples were on a list. Regulated tenants tended to live in older accommodation (Figure 2.10) and in houses rather than flats (Figure 2.8) and, on average, were paying low rents (Figure 4.2). Such tenants may have been on a waiting list because their accommodation was in poor condition or was no longer suitable for them and they did not have the means to buy somewhere. Some may have been people wishing to move into sheltered housing. The proportion wanting council housing was also high among unemployed tenants of whom about a quarter were on a waiting list. (Figures 6.27 to 6.29)

Notes and references

1 The questions were restricted to recent movers so as to avoid confounding variations between tenants with changes over time. Rent-free lettings were excluded from the analysis. Data are not shown for tenants in regulated lettings because very few had started their letting in the last five years.

2 The survey gives the tenants' view of their relationship with the landlord. The landlords' views are covered in a separate survey of private landlords. Andrew Thomas and Dawn Snape. *Understanding private landlords.* HMSO (London 1995).

3 Hazel Green and Jacqui Hansbro. *Housing in England 1993/94.* HMSO (London 1995).

Annex tables
Chapter 1

Table A1 Unweighted sample bases for all tenancies
All tenancies = 1958

Characteristic	Base
Letting Type	
Assured	309
Assured shorthold	702
All Assured	**1 011**
Regulated - registered	203
Regulated - not registered	133
All regulated	**336**
Not accessible to public - rent paid	138
Not accessible to public - rent free	209
Not accessible to public	**347**
Resident landlord and no security	**153**
Total	**1 847**
Region	
North	72
North West	203
Yorkshire and Humberside	172
West Midlands	180
East Midlands	180
The North and Midlands	**807**
Rest of South East	385
South West	286
East Anglia	85
Rest of South	**756**
Total	**1 958**

Characteristic	Base
Comparable weekly rent (£)	
Up to £15	81
£15-£20	71
£20-£25	92
£25-£30	120
£30-£40	262
£40-£50	148
£50-£100	536
£100 or more	227
Total	**1 958**
Disposable income of tenancy group (£)	
Under £60	212
£60-£79	180
£80-£119	254
£120-£179	254
£180-£249	225
£250 or more	479
Total	**1 604**
Type of accommodation	
Detached house	242
Semi-detached	392
Terraced	616
Purpose-built flat	231
Converted flat	451
Caravan/boat	9
Other	7
Total	**1 958**

Characteristic	Base
Age and sex of Tenant	
Male	
Under 30	447
30 to 59	626
60 or over	226
Total male	**1 299**
Female	
Under 30	234
30 to 59	171
60 or over	145
Total female	**550**
Total	**1 849**
Tenancy Group composition	
One adult aged 16-59	4 641
Two adults aged 16-59	4 641
Couple with dependent child(ren)	7 943
Lone parent and dependent child(ren)	1 118
Large mainly adult	1 563
Two adults at least one 60 or over	1 925
One adult 60 or over	3 117
Total	**1 849**

Table A1.1 Trends in tenure: 1981 to 1993
All households   *England*

Year	Owner occupied			Social rented			Private rented			All tenures
	Owned outright	Buying with a mortgage	All	council	housing association	All	unfurnished	furnished	All	
										thousands
1981	4 310	5 550	9 860	5 100	360	5 460	1 490	420	1 910	17 230
1984	4 590	6 400	10 990	4 660	370	5 030	1 410	510	1 920	17 940
1988	4 834	7 414	12 248	4 246	460	4 706	1 218	484	1 702	18 656
1991	4 795	8 255	13 050	3 872	564	4 436	1 236	588	1 824	19 309
1993	4 991	8 462	13 453	3 708	732	4 440	1 307	620	1 927	19 819
										percentages
1981	25	32	57	30	2	32	8.6	2.4	11.1	100
1984	26	36	61	26	2	28	7.9	2.8	10.7	100
1988	26	40	66	23	2	25	6.5	2.6	9.1	100
1991	25	43	68	20	3	23	6.4	3	9.4	100
1993	25	43	68	19	4	23	6.6	3.1	9.7	100

Table A1.2 Type of letting: 1988 to 1993
All tenancies   *England*

Type of letting	1988	1990	1993	
			Excluding non-privately rented households	Including non-privately rented households
				thousands
Assured	0	360	375	378
Assured shorthold	0	140	825	826
All assured	**0**	**500**	**1 199**	**1 204**
Regulated, rent registered	470	320	245	245
Regulated, rent not registered	600	270	162	162
All regulated	**1 070**	**590**	**407**	**407**
Not accessible to public, rent paid	240	230	146	146
Not accessible to public, rent free	270	250	230	230
Not accessible to public, all	**510**	**480**	**375**	**375**
Resident landlord	110	90	73	158
No security	60	90	22	22
Protected shorthold and pre-89 assured	60	40	0	0
Other	**230**	**220**	**95**	**180**
All	**1 810**	**1 790**	**2 077**	**2 166**
				percentages
Assured	-	20	18	17
Assured shorthold	-	8	40	38
All assured	**-**	**28**	**58**	**56**
Regulated, rent registered	26	18	12	11
Regulated, rent not registered	33	15	8	8
All regulated	**59**	**33**	**20**	**19**
Not accessible to public, rent paid	13	13	7	7
Not accessible to public, rent free	15	14	11	11
Not accessible to public, all	**28**	**27**	**18**	**17**
Resident landlord	6	4	4	7
No security	4	5	1	1
Protected shorthold and pre-89 assured	4	2	-	-
Other	**14**	**11**	**5**	**8**
All	**100**	**100**	**100**	**100**

Table A1.3 Type of landlord: 1988 to 1993
All tenancies   *England*

Type of landlord	1988	1990	1993	
			Excluding non-privately rented households	Including non-privately rented households
				thousands
Resident landlord	..	53	77	166
Private individual	..	1 022	1 445	1 445
Employer	..	351	280	280
Property company	..	146	170	170
Other	..	128	104	104
All	**..**	**1 698**	**2 077**	**2 166**
				percentages
Resident landlord	5	3	4	8
Private individual	53	60	70	67
Employer	25	21	13	13
Property company	9	9	8	8
Other	8	7	5	5
All	**100**	**100**	**100**	**100**

Table A1.4 Type of accommodation: 1988 to 1993
All tenancies *England*

Type of accommodation	1988	1990	1993	
			Excluding non-privately rented households	Including non-privately rented households
				thousands
Detached house	218	214	208	213
Semi-detached	350	342	368	390
Terraced house	517	502	605	646
Purpose-built flat	197	186	249	260
Converted flat	299	283	554	561
Other/Business premises	110	163	93	97
All	**1 692**	**1 698**	**2 077**	**2 166**
				percentages
Detached house	13	13	10	10
Semi-detached	20	20	18	18
Terraced house	30	30	29	30
Purpose-built flat	11	11	12	12
Converted flat	17	17	27	26
Other/Business premises	9	10	4	5
All	**100**	**100**	**100**	**100**

Accommodation occupied by household. In most cases this is the same as the tenancy group but some households contain more than one tenancy group.

Table A1.5 Tenancy group composition: 1988 to 1993
All tenancies *England*

Tenancy group composition	1988	1990	1993	
			Excluding non-privately rented households	Including non-privately rented households
				thousands
One adult aged 16-59	436	476	729	809
Two adults aged 16-59	268	288	370	374
Couple with dependent child(ren)	241	263	274	274
Lone parent with dependent child(ren)	37	66	112	113
Large mainly adult	184	142	170	170
Two adults at least one 60 or over	233	199	130	130
One adult 60 or over	332	261	292	297
All	**1 741**	**1 698**	**2 077**	**2 166**
				percentages
One adult aged 16-59	25	28	35	37
Two adults aged 16-59	15	17	18	17
Couple with dependent child(ren)	14	16	13	13
Lone parent with dependent child(ren)	2	4	5	5
Large mainly adult	11	8	8	8
Two adults at least one 60 or over	13	12	6	6
One adult 60 or over	20	15	14	14
All	**100**	**100**	**100**	**100**

Table A1.6 Proportion of households who rent privately by region: 1990 and 1993

All households   *England*

Region	1990	1993	1990	1993
		thousands	*Percentages*	
North	65	78	5	6
North West	166	210	7	8
Yorkshire and Humberside	149	163	8	8
West Midlands	125	168	6	8
East Midlands	119	161	7	10
The North and Midlands	**624**	**780**	**7**	**8**
Greater London	**348**	**405**	**13**	**14**
Rest of South East	346	372	8	8
South West	188	283	10	14
East Anglia	95	88	12	10
The South	**978**	**1 147**	**10**	**11**
All	**1 602**	**1 927**	**8**	**10**

Table A1.7 Type of letting by region

All tenancies   *England*

Region	Assured	Assured shorthold	All assured	Regulated With registered rent	Regulated Without registered rent	All regulated	No access to public Rented	No access to public Rent free	No access to public Not accessible to public, all	Resident landlord	No security	Resident landlord and no security, all	Total
													thousands
North	16	25	41	8	11	19	12	9	21	3	0	3	63
North West	50	83	133	35	18	52	12	22	34	11	0	11	196
Yorkshire and Humberside	47	48	95	23	16	40	21	24	45	7	3	10	145
West Midlands	30	70	100	31	19	50	9	19	28	19	2	21	171
East Midlands	32	72	104	22	18	40	16	17	34	9	8	17	161
The North and Midlands	**175**	**298**	**473**	**119**	**82**	**201**	**71**	**91**	**162**	**49**	**13**	**62**	**899**
Greater London	**88**	**189**	**277**	**59**	**26**	**85**	**17**	**27**	**44**	**38**	**4**	**42**	**448**
Rest of South East	63	169	231	35	23	58	34	52	86	27	1	28	317
South West	38	147	184	19	20	39	22	39	61	34	4	38	261
East Anglia	15	23	38	13	11	24	2	20	22	10	0	10	72
The South	**115**	**339**	**454**	**67**	**54**	**121**	**58**	**112**	**169**	**71**	**5**	**76**	**820**
All	**378**	**826**	**1 204**	**245**	**162**	**407**	**146**	**230**	**375**	**158**	**22**	**180**	**2 166**
													percentages
North	20	29	49	10	13	22	14	11	25	4	-	4	100
North West	22	36	58	15	8	23	5	10	15	5	-	5	100
Yorkshire and Humberside	25	25	50	12	9	21	11	13	24	4	2	5	100
West Midlands	15	35	50	16	10	25	5	10	14	9	1	10	100
East Midlands	16	37	53	11	9	21	8	9	17	5	4	9	100
The North and Midlands	**20**	**33**	**53**	**13**	**9**	**22**	**8**	**10**	**18**	**5**	**2**	**7**	**100**
Greater London	**20**	**42**	**62**	**13**	**6**	**19**	**4**	**6**	**10**	**8**	**1**	**9**	**100**
Rest of South East	16	42	57	9	6	14	8	13	21	7	0	7	100
South West	12	46	57	6	6	12	7	12	19	10	1	12	100
East Anglia	16	25	40	14	12	25	2	22	23	11	-	11	100
The South	**14**	**41**	**55**	**8**	**7**	**15**	**7**	**14**	**21**	**9**	**1**	**9**	**100**
All	**17**	**38**	**56**	**11**	**8**	**19**	**7**	**11**	**17**	**7**	**1**	**8**	**100**

Table A1.8 Type of landlord by region

All tenancies   *England*

Region	Type of landlord					
	Resident landlord	Private individual	Employer	Property company	Other	Total
						thousands
North	3	55	18	2	6	84
North West	14	164	18	28	7	231
Yorkshire and Humberside	7	131	28	12	11	189
West Midlands	19	140	22	10	9	199
East Midlands	9	145	24	6	12	196
The North and Midlands	**52**	**635**	**110**	**58**	**45**	**899**
Greater London	**46**	**293**	**31**	**61**	**17**	**448**
Rest of South East	26	240	73	28	37	404
South West	32	217	48	19	4	321
East Anglia	10	60	18	5	1	94
The South	**69**	**517**	**139**	**52**	**42**	**820**
All	**166**	**1 445**	**280**	**170**	**104**	**2 166**
						percentages
North	4	65	21	3	7	100
North West	6	71	8	12	3	100
Yorkshire and Humberside	4	69	15	6	6	100
West Midlands	9	70	11	5	5	100
East Midlands	5	74	12	3	6	100
The North and Midlands	**6**	**71**	**12**	**6**	**5**	**100**
Greater London	**10**	**66**	**7**	**14**	**4**	**100**
Rest of South East	6	59	18	7	9	100
South West	10	68	15	6	1	100
East Anglia	11	64	19	5	1	100
The South	**8**	**63**	**17**	**6**	**5**	**100**
All	**8**	**67**	**13**	**8**	**5**	**100**

Table A1.9 Type of accommodation by region
All tenancies *England*

Region	Type of accommodation							
	Detached house	Semi-detached house	Terraced house	Purpose-built flat	Converted flat	With Business premises	Other	Total
								thousands
North	12	16	24	12	13	7	0	84
North West	14	34	85	27	62	8	1	231
Yorkshire and Humberside	14	45	79	8	29	12	1	189
West Midlands	20	47	66	19	42	6	0	199
East Midlands	25	48	76	6	35	3	2	196
The North and Midlands	**84**	**191**	**331**	**72**	**181**	**35**	**4**	**899**
Greater London	**8**	**40**	**101**	**112**	**175**	**10**	**1**	**448**
Rest of South East	49	91	104	59	81	14	7	404
South West	47	50	85	15	101	16	7	321
East Anglia	25	18	24	2	23	2	0	94
The South	**120**	**159**	**214**	**76**	**205**	**32**	**14**	**820**
All	**213**	**390**	**646**	**260**	**561**	**77**	**19**	**2 166**
								Percentages
North	14	20	28	14	16	8	-	100
North West	6	15	37	12	27	3	0	100
Yorkshire and Humberside	8	24	42	4	15	6	1	100
West Midlands	10	24	33	10	21	3	-	100
East Midlands	13	25	39	3	18	2	1	100
The North and Midlands	**9**	**21**	**37**	**8**	**20**	**4**	**0**	**100**
Greater London	**2**	**9**	**23**	**25**	**39**	**2**	**0**	**100**
Rest of South East	12	22	26	14	20	4	2	100
South West	14	16	27	5	32	5	2	100
East Anglia	27	19	26	2	24	2	-	100
The South	**15**	**19**	**26**	**9**	**25**	**4**	**2**	**100**
All	**10**	**18**	**30**	**12**	**26**	**4**	**1**	**100**

Accommodation occupied by household. In most cases this is the same as the tenancy group but some households contain more than one tenancy group.

Table A1.10 Year tenancy started by region
All tenancies   *England*

Region	Year tenancy started						
	Before 1968	1968-1978	1979-1988	1989-1990	1991-1992	1993-1994	Total
							thousands
North	7	10	15	8	14	30	84
North West	22	18	29	22	70	69	231
Yorkshire and Humberside	23	6	27	15	53	64	189
West Midlands	24	13	26	20	62	54	199
East Midlands	23	14	22	17	63	57	196
The North and Midlands	**100**	**61**	**119**	**83**	**262**	**275**	**899**
Greater London	**45**	**19**	**63**	**32**	**128**	**159**	**446**
Rest of South East	30	27	45	41	125	133	402
South West	22	19	43	31	93	114	321
East Anglia	15	6	17	4	19	33	94
The South	**67**	**52**	**105**	**76**	**237**	**280**	**817**
All	**212**	**132**	**286**	**191**	**628**	**714**	**2 162**
							percentages
North	9	12	18	9	17	36	100
North West	9	8	13	10	30	30	100
Yorkshire and Humberside	12	3	14	8	28	34	100
West Midlands	12	6	13	10	31	27	100
East Midlands	12	7	11	9	32	29	100
The North and Midlands	**11**	**7**	**13**	**9**	**29**	**31**	**100**
Greater London	**10**	**4**	**14**	**7**	**29**	**36**	**100**
Rest of South East	8	7	11	10	31	33	100
South West	7	6	13	10	29	35	100
East Anglia	16	6	18	4	20	35	100
The South	**8**	**6**	**13**	**9**	**29**	**34**	**100**
All	**10**	**6**	**13**	**9**	**29**	**33**	**100**

Table A1.11 Tenancy group composition by region
All tenancies   *England*

Region	One adult aged 16-59	Two adults aged 16-59	Couple with dependent child(ren)	Lone parent with dependent child(ren)	Large mainly adult	Two adults at least one 60 or over	One adult 60 or over	Total
								thousands
North	36	8	14	5	7	6	8	84
North West	84	36	21	18	12	16	43	231
Yorkshire and Humberside	68	32	20	12	14	10	33	189
West Midlands	78	28	26	6	24	18	20	199
East Midlands	85	24	23	11	6	15	32	196
The North and Midlands	**351**	**128**	**104**	**53**	**63**	**64**	**135**	**899**
Greater London	**163**	**106**	**42**	**23**	**44**	**13**	**58**	**448**
Rest of South East	136	71	65	21	30	27	55	404
South West	126	57	45	15	27	15	35	321
East Anglia	32	13	17	1	6	11	14	94
The South	**294**	**140**	**127**	**37**	**63**	**53**	**104**	**820**
All	**809**	**374**	**274**	**113**	**170**	**130**	**297**	**2 166**
								percentages
North	43	10	17	6	9	7	9	100
North West	37	16	9	8	5	7	19	100
Yorkshire and Humberside	36	17	10	6	7	5	17	100
West Midlands	39	14	13	3	12	9	10	100
East Midlands	44	12	12	6	3	8	16	100
The North and Midlands	**39**	**14**	**12**	**6**	**7**	**7**	**15**	**100**
Greater London	**36**	**24**	**10**	**5**	**10**	**3**	**13**	**100**
Rest of South East	34	17	16	5	7	7	14	100
South West	39	18	14	5	8	5	11	100
East Anglia	34	14	18	1	6	12	15	100
The South	**36**	**17**	**16**	**4**	**8**	**6**	**13**	**100**
All	**37**	**17**	**13**	**5**	**8**	**6**	**14**	**100**

Table A1.12 Type of letting by type of area

All tenancies   *England*

Type of area	Assured	Assured shorthold	**All assured**	Regulated			No access to public		**Not accessible to public, all**	Resident landlord	No security	**Resident landlord and no security, all**	Total
				With registered rent	Without registered rent	**All regulated**	Rented	Rent free					
													thousands
More rural	77	196	272	49	62	112	63	94	157	49	1	50	591
More urban	301	630	931	195	100	295	82	136	218	109	21	130	1 575
All	**378**	**826**	**1 204**	**245**	**162**	**407**	**146**	**230**	**376**	**158**	**22**	**180**	**2 166**
													percentages
More rural	13	33	46	8	11	19	11	16	27	8	0	8	100
More urban	19	40	59	12	6	19	5	9	14	7	1	8	100
All	**17**	**38**	**56**	**11**	**7**	**19**	**7**	**11**	**17**	**7**	**1**	**8**	**100**

Table A1.13 Whether accommodation goes with someone's job by type of letting and type of area

Tenancies: not accessible to public   *England*

Type of area	Not accessible to the public - rent paid			Not accessible to the public - rent free		
	Accommodation with job	Accommodation not with job	**Total**	Accommodation with job	Accommodation not with job	**Total**
						thousands
More rural	62	1	63	61	33	94
More urban	66	16	82	68	68	136
All	**128**	**17**	**146**	**129**	**101**	**230**
						percentages
More rural	10	0	11	10	6	16
More urban	4	1	5	4	4	9
All	**6**	**1**	**7**	**6**	**5**	**11**

Annex tables
Chapter 2

Table A2.1   Number of tenancies in household and size of tenancy group by type of letting
All lettings   *England*

Type of letting	Number of tenancies in household			Number of people in tenancy					
	One	More than one	Total	One	Two	Three	Four or more	Total	Mean
			thousands					*thousands*	*number*
Assured	316	62	378	216	94	35	33	378	1.7
Assured shorthold	756	69	826	349	255	117	105	826	2.0
All assured	**1 072**	**131**	**1 204**	**565**	**349**	**152**	**139**	**1 204**	**1.9**
Regulated, rent registered	245	0	245	143	64	19	18	245	1.7
Regulated, rent not registered	161	1	162	100	34	17	11	162	1.7
All regulated	**406**	**1**	**407**	**243**	**98**	**36**	**30**	**407**	**1.7**
Not accessible to public, rent paid	128	17	146	47	32	21	46	146	2.5
Not accessible to public, rent free	226	4	230	94	62	27	47	230	2.2
Not accessible to public, all	**354**	**22**	**375**	**141**	**94**	**48**	**93**	**375**	**2.3**
Resident landlord	119	40	158	141	13	3	1	158	1.1
No security	[12]	[10]	[22]	[16]	[1]	[2]	[3]	[22]	*
Resident landlord and no security, all	**130**	**50**	**180**	**157**	**14**	**5**	**4**	**180**	**1.2**
All	**1 962**	**204**	**2 166**	**1 105**	**555**	**241**	**265**	**2 166**	**1.9**
			percentages					*percentages*	
Assured	84	16	100	57	25	9	9	100	
Assured shorthold	92	8	100	42	31	14	13	100	
All assured	**89**	**11**	**100**	**47**	**29**	**13**	**12**	**100**	
Regulated, rent registered	100	-	100	58	26	8	8	100	
Regulated, rent not registered	99	1	100	61	21	11	7	100	
All regulated	**100**	**-**	**100**	**60**	**24**	**9**	**7**	**100**	
Not accessible to public, rent paid	88	12	100	32	22	14	31	100	
Not accessible to public, rent free	98	2	100	41	27	12	20	100	
Not accessible to public, all	**94**	**6**	**100**	**38**	**25**	**13**	**25**	**100**	
Resident landlord	75	25	100	89	8	2	1	100	
No security	*	*	*	*	*	*	*	*	
Resident landlord and no security, all	**72**	**28**	**100**	**87**	**8**	**3**	**2**	**100**	
All	**91**	**9**	**100**	**51**	**26**	**11**	**12**	**100**	

Table A2.2 Age group and sex of head of tenancy group by type of letting

All tenancies *England*

Type of letting	Age group and sex of head of tenancy group						
	Under 30		30-59		60 or over		
	Male	Female	Male	Female	Male	Female	Total
							thousands
Assured	133	79	109	33	16	8	378
Assured shorthold	300	149	250	90	24	12	826
All assured	**433**	**229**	**359**	**123**	**40**	**20**	**1 204**
Regulated, rent registered	2	1	51	19	88	83	245
Regulated, rent not registered	6	3	37	4	57	55	162
All regulated	**8**	**4**	**89**	**24**	**145**	**138**	**407**
Not accessible to public, rent paid	27	16	84	8	10	0	146
Not accessible to public, rent free	31	5	92	17	48	37	230
Not accessible to public, all	**58**	**21**	**176**	**25**	**58**	**37**	**375**
Resident landlord	61	20	51	11	6	10	158
No security	[5]	[12]	[3]	[0]	[1]	[1]	[22]
Resident landlord and no security, all	**66**	**32**	**54**	**11**	**7**	**11**	**180**
All	**565**	**286**	**677**	**182**	**249**	**207**	**2 166**
							percentages
Assured	35	21	29	9	4	2	100
Assured shorthold	36	18	30	11	3	2	100
All assured	**36**	**19**	**30**	**10**	**3**	**2**	**100**
Regulated, rent registered	1	0	21	8	36	34	100
Regulated, rent not registered	4	2	23	3	35	34	100
All regulated	**2**	**1**	**22**	**6**	**36**	**34**	**100**
Not accessible to public, rent paid	19	11	58	6	7	-	100
Not accessible to public, rent free	13	2	40	7	21	16	100
Not accessible to public, all	**16**	**6**	**47**	**7**	**15**	**10**	**100**
Resident landlord	38	13	32	7	4	7	100
No security	*	*	*	*	*	*	*
Resident landlord and no security, all	**37**	**18**	**30**	**6**	**4**	**6**	**100**
All	**26**	**13**	**31**	**8**	**12**	**10**	**100**

Table A2.3 Economic status of head of tenancy group by type of letting
All tenancies *England*

Type of letting	Economic status of head of tenancy						
	Working full time	Working part time	Unemployed	Retired	Full-time education	Other	Total
							thousands
Assured	182	20	67	18	46	44	378
Assured shorthold	420	42	155	22	106	80	825
All assured	**602**	**62**	**221**	**40**	**153**	**124**	**1 203**
Regulated, rent registered	43	9	14	157	0	21	244
Regulated, rent not registered	40	6	11	88	1	17	162
All regulated	**83**	**15**	**25**	**245**	**1**	**38**	**406**
Not accessible to public, rent paid	124	3	2	1	16	0	146
Not accessible to public, rent free	126	15	8	61	6	14	230
Not accessible to public, all	**250**	**19**	**10**	**61**	**21**	**14**	**375**
Resident landlord	72	6	44	15	10	11	158
No security	[7]	[2]	[2]	[3]	[8]	[0]	[22]
Resident landlord and no security, all	**79**	**8**	**46**	**18**	**18**	**11**	**180**
All	**1 014**	**104**	**302**	**364**	**194**	**187**	**2 164**
							percentages
Assured	48	5	18	5	12	12	100
Assured shorthold	51	5	19	3	13	10	100
All assured	**50**	**5**	**18**	**3**	**13**	**10**	**100**
Regulated, rent registered	18	4	6	64	-	9	100
Regulated, rent not registered	25	4	7	54	1	10	100
All regulated	**20**	**4**	**6**	**60**	**0**	**9**	**100**
Not accessible to public, rent paid	85	2	1	1	11	-	100
Not accessible to public, rent free	55	7	4	26	2	6	100
Not accessible to public, all	**66**	**5**	**3**	**16**	**6**	**4**	**100**
Resident landlord	45	4	28	9	6	7	100
No security	*	*	*	*	*	*	*
Resident landlord and no security, all	**44**	**5**	**25**	**10**	**10**	**6**	**100**
All	**47**	**5**	**14**	**17**	**9**	**9**	**100**

Table A2.4 Socio-economic group of head of tenancy group by type of letting
All tenancies *England*

Type of letting	Socio-economic group of head of tenancy				
	Professional and managerial	Other non-manual	Skilled manual	Semi- and unskilled manual	Total
					thousands
Assured	69	80	70	90	309
Assured shorthold	181	207	160	134	682
All assured	**250**	**287**	**229**	**224**	**991**
Regulated, rent registered	27	47	74	74	223
Regulated, rent not registered	29	21	32	58	140
All regulated	**56**	**68**	**106**	**132**	**363**
Not accessible to public, rent paid	46	15	26	18	103
Not accessible to public, rent free	71	37	38	65	212
Not accessible to public, all	**117**	**52**	**64**	**82**	**315**
Resident landlord	20	42	38	34	135
No security	[1]	[3]	[0]	[10]	[14]
Resident landlord and no security, all	**22**	**45**	**38**	**43**	**149**
All	**445**	**452**	**438**	**482**	**1 817**
					percentages
Assured	22	26	23	29	100
Assured shorthold	26	30	23	20	100
All assured	**25**	**29**	**23**	**23**	**100**
Regulated, rent registered	12	21	33	33	100
Regulated, rent not registered	21	15	23	42	100
All regulated	**16**	**19**	**29**	**36**	**100**
Not accessible to public, rent paid	44	14	25	17	100
Not accessible to public, rent free	34	18	18	31	100
Not accessible to public, all	**37**	**16**	**20**	**26**	**100**
Resident landlord	15	31	29	25	100
No security	*	*	*	*	*
Resident landlord and no security, all	**14**	**30**	**26**	**29**	**100**
All	**24**	**25**	**24**	**26**	**100**

Table A2.5 Ethnic group of head of tenancy by type of letting
All tenancies   *England*

Type of letting	Ethnic group		
	White	Other	Total
			thousands
Assured	325	53	378
Assured shorthold	750	75	826
All assured	**1 075**	**129**	**1 204**
Regulated, rent registered	243	1	245
Regulated, rent not registered	158	5	162
All regulated	**401**	**6**	**407**
Not accessible to public, rent paid	142	4	146
Not accessible to public, rent free	221	9	230
Not accessible to public, all	**362**	**13**	**375**
Resident landlord	137	21	158
No security	[20]	[2]	[22]
Resident landlord and no security, all	**157**	**23**	**180**
All	**1 995**	**171**	**2 166**
			percentages
Assured	86	14	100
Assured shorthold	91	9	100
All assured	**89**	**11**	**100**
Regulated, rent registered	99	1	100
Regulated, rent not registered	97	3	100
All regulated	**98**	**2**	**100**
Not accessible to public, rent paid	97	3	100
Not accessible to public, rent free	96	4	100
Not accessible to public, all	**96**	**4**	**100**
Resident landlord	87	13	100
No security	*	*	*
Resident landlord and no security, all	**87**	**13**	**100**
All	**92**	**8**	**100**

Table A2.6 Year tenancy started by type of letting
All tenancies   *England*

Type of tenancy	Year tenancy started						
	Before 1968	1968-1978	1979-1988	1989-1990	1991-1992	1993-1994	Total
							thousands
Assured	0	0	0	55	152	171	378
Assured shorthold	0	0	31	64	322	408	824
All assured	**0**	**0**	**31**	**119**	**473**	**579**	**1 202**
Regulated, rent registered	120	52	73	0	0	0	245
Regulated, rent not registered	59	31	72	0	0	0	162
All regulated	**179**	**83**	**145**	**0**	**0**	**0**	**407**
Not accessible to public, rent paid	7	13	26	24	42	33	146
Not accessible to public, rent free	18	35	64	34	49	28	227
Not accessible to public, all	**25**	**48**	**90**	**58**	**91**	**61**	**373**
Resident landlord	7	1	19	12	61	57	158
No security	[0]	[0]	[2]	[2]	[2]	[16]	[22]
Resident landlord and no security, all	**7**	**1**	**20**	**15**	**64**	**73**	**180**
All	**212**	**132**	**286**	**191**	**628**	**714**	**2 162**
							percentages
Assured	-	-	-	15	40	45	100
Assured shorthold	-	-	4	8	39	50	100
All assured	**-**	**-**	**3**	**10**	**39**	**48**	**100**
Regulated, rent registered	49	21	30	..	..	..	100
Regulated, rent not registered	36	19	44	..	..	..	100
All regulated	**44**	**20**	**36**	**..**	**..**	**..**	**100**
Not accessible to public, rent paid	5	9	18	17	29	23	100
Not accessible to public, rent free	8	15	28	15	21	12	100
Not accessible to public, all	**7**	**13**	**24**	**16**	**24**	**16**	**100**
Resident landlord	4	1	12	8	39	36	100
No security	-	-	*	*	*	*	*
Resident landlord and no security, all	**4**	**1**	**11**	**8**	**35**	**41**	**100**
All	**10**	**6**	**13**	**9**	**29**	**33**	**100**

Table A2.7 Type of property by type of letting
All tenancies   *England*

Type of letting	Type of property						
	Detached house	Semi-detached house	Terraced house	Purpose-built flat	Converted flat	Other	Total
							thousands
Assured	12	65	124	42	123	13	378
Assured shorthold	81	104	244	128	258	11	826
All assured	**94**	**169**	**367**	**169**	**381**	**24**	**1 204**
Regulated, rent registered	10	55	110	34	35	2	245
Regulated, rent not registered	21	51	36	5	39	10	162
All regulated	**31**	**105**	**146**	**39**	**74**	**11**	**407**
Not accessible to public, rent paid	26	31	35	19	9	25	146
Not accessible to public, rent free	56	61	39	15	27	31	230
Not accessible to public, all	**83**	**92**	**74**	**34**	**37**	**56**	**375**
Resident landlord	4	21	42	16	68	6	158
No security	[1]	[2]	[17]	[1]	[2]	[0]	[22]
Resident landlord and no security, all	**5**	**23**	**59**	**17**	**70**	**6**	**180**
All	**213**	**390**	**646**	**260**	**561**	**96**	**2 166**
							percentages
Assured	3	17	33	11	33	3	100
Assured shorthold	10	13	30	16	31	1	100
All assured	**8**	**14**	**30**	**14**	**32**	**2**	**100**
Regulated, rent registered	4	22	45	14	14	1	100
Regulated, rent not registered	13	31	22	3	24	6	100
All regulated	**8**	**26**	**36**	**10**	**18**	**3**	**100**
Not accessible to public, rent paid	18	21	24	13	6	17	100
Not accessible to public, rent free	24	27	17	6	12	14	100
Not accessible to public, all	**22**	**25**	**20**	**9**	**10**	**15**	**100**
Resident landlord	3	13	27	10	43	4	100
No security	*	*	*	*	*	*	*
Resident landlord and no security, all	**3**	**13**	**33**	**10**	**39**	**3**	**100**
All	**10**	**18**	**30**	**12**	**26**	**4**	**100**

Table A2.8 Whether accommodation rented furnished or unfurnished by type of letting
All tenancies   *England*

Type of letting	Whether furnished or unfurnished		
	Furnished	Unfurnished*	Total
			thousands
Assured	182	196	378
Assured shorthold	411	414	825
All assured	**592**	**610**	**1 203**
Regulated, rent registered	4	240	245
Regulated, rent not registered	16	146	162
All regulated	**21**	**386**	**407**
Not accessible to public, rent paid	29	116	146
Not accessible to public, rent free	38	192	230
Not accessible to public, all	**67**	**309**	**375**
Resident landlord	117	41	158
No security	[16]	[6]	[22]
Resident landlord and no security, all	**134**	**46**	**180**
All	**814**	**1 352**	**2 165**
			percentages
Assured	48	52	100
Assured shorthold	50	50	100
All assured	**49**	**51**	**100**
Regulated, rent registered	2	98	100
Regulated, rent not registered	10	90	100
All regulated	**5**	**95**	**100**
Not accessible to public, rent paid	20	80	100
Not accessible to public, rent free	16	84	100
Not accessible to public, all	**18**	**82**	**100**
Resident landlord	74	26	100
No security	*	*	*
Resident landlord and no security, all	**74**	**26**	**100**
All	**38**	**62**	**100**

* Includes partly furnished

Table A2.9 Age of building by type of letting
All tenancies   *England*

Type of letting	Age of building					
	Pre-1919	1919-1944	1945-1964	1965-1984	1985 or later	Total
						thousands
Assured	166	88	41	32	24	351
Assured shorthold	341	181	74	120	62	778
All assured	**507**	**269**	**115**	**152**	**86**	**1 129**
Regulated, rent registered	137	83	17	4	0	241
Regulated, rent not registered	96	52	7	4	0	160
All regulated	**233**	**135**	**25**	**8**	**0**	**401**
Not accessible to public, rent paid	51	26	32	30	1	140
Not accessible to public, rent free	101	44	44	31	11	230
Not accessible to public, all	**152**	**69**	**76**	**62**	**11**	**370**
Resident landlord	73	34	16	21	5	149
No security	[13]	[5]	[0]	[1]	[1]	[20]
Resident landlord and no security, all	**86**	**39**	**16**	**22**	**6**	**169**
All	**977**	**513**	**231**	**243**	**104**	**2 068**
						percentages
Assured	47	25	12	9	7	100
Assured shorthold	44	23	10	15	8	100
All assured	**45**	**24**	**10**	**13**	**8**	**100**
Regulated, rent registered	57	34	7	2	-	100
Regulated, rent not registered	60	33	5	3	-	100
All regulated	**58**	**34**	**6**	**2**	**-**	**100**
Not accessible to public, rent paid	36	18	23	22	1	100
Not accessible to public, rent free	44	19	19	14	5	100
Not accessible to public, all	**41**	**19**	**20**	**17**	**3**	**100**
Resident landlord	49	23	11	14	3	100
No security	*	*	*	*	*	*
Resident landlord and no security, all	**51**	**23**	**10**	**13**	**3**	**100**
All	**47**	**25**	**11**	**12**	**5**	**100**

Table A2.10 Difference from the bedroom standard and rooms per person by type of letting

All tenancies   *England*

Type of letting	Difference from bedroom standard				Rooms per person					Mean
	Below	Equal	Above	Total	Less than one	1-1.5	1.5-2	2 or more	Total	
									thousands	*number*
Assured	21	210	148	378	7	86	156	129	378	2.1
Assured shorthold	32	432	361	826	18	205	326	276	826	2.0
All assured	**53**	**642**	**509**	**1 204**	**25**	**291**	**483**	**405**	**1 204**	**2.0**
Regulated, rent registered	5	60	179	245	2	27	48	168	245	2.5
Regulated, rent not registered	1	56	105	162	1	21	28	112	162	2.4
All regulated	**6**	**117**	**284**	**407**	**3**	**48**	**76**	**280**	**407**	**2.5**
Not accessible to public, rent paid	4	31	110	146	2	30	62	51	146	2.1
Not accessible to public, rent free	7	55	167	230	5	30	74	122	230	2.3
Not accessible to public, all	**11**	**86**	**278**	**375**	**7**	**60**	**136**	**172**	**375**	**2.2**
Resident landlord	16	95	47	158	1	43	61	53	158	2.0
No security	[1]	[12]	[9]	[22]	[0]	[5]	[16]	[2]	[22]	*
Resident landlord and no security, all	**17**	**107**	**57**	**180**	**1**	**48**	**77**	**55**	**180**	**2.0**
All	**87**	**952**	**1 128**	**2 166**	**35**	**448**	**771**	**912**	**2 166**	**2.0**
									percentages	
Assured	5	55	39	100	2	23	41	34	100	
Assured shorthold	4	52	44	100	2	25	40	33	100	
All assured	**4**	**53**	**42**	**100**	**2**	**24**	**40**	**34**	**100**	
Regulated, rent registered	2	25	73	100	1	11	19	69	100	
Regulated, rent not registered	1	35	65	100	0	13	17	69	100	
All regulated	**2**	**29**	**70**	**100**	**1**	**12**	**19**	**69**	**100**	
Not accessible to public, rent paid	3	21	76	100	1	21	43	35	100	
Not accessible to public, rent free	3	24	73	100	2	13	32	53	100	
Not accessible to public, all	**3**	**23**	**74**	**100**	**2**	**16**	**36**	**46**	**100**	
Resident landlord	10	60	30	100	1	27	39	34	100	
No security	*	*	*	*	*	*	*	*	*	
Resident landlord and no security, all	**9**	**59**	**32**	**100**	**0**	**27**	**43**	**30**	**100**	
All	**4**	**44**	**52**	**100**	**2**	**21**	**36**	**42**	**100**	

Table A2.11 Sharing amenities and circulation space by type of letting
All tenancies   *England*

Type of letting	Shared amenities (kitchen, bath/toilet and WC)				
	None shared	At least one shared	Lacking at least one	**Total**	Sharing circulation space
					thousands
Assured	313	42	23	378	77
Assured shorthold	738	52	36	826	91
All assured	**1 052**	**93**	**59**	**1 204**	**169**
Regulated, rent registered	209	2	33	245	10
Regulated, rent not registered	143	3	16	162	10
All regulated	**353**	**5**	**49**	**407**	**19**
Not accessible to public, rent paid	140	0	5	146	3
Not accessible to public, rent free	217	5	8	230	17
Not accessible to public, all	**357**	**5**	**13**	**375**	**19**
Resident landlord	125	21	13	158	34
No security	[20]	[2]	[0]	[22]	[3]
Resident landlord and no security, all	**145**	**22**	**13**	**180**	**37**
All	**1 907**	**126**	**134**	**2 166**	**244**
					percentages
Assured	83	11	6	100	20
Assured shorthold	89	6	4	100	11
All assured	**87**	**8**	**5**	**100**	**14**
Regulated, rent registered	86	1	14	100	4
Regulated, rent not registered	88	2	10	100	6
All regulated	**87**	**1**	**12**	**100**	**5**
Not accessible to public, rent paid	96	-	4	100	2
Not accessible to public, rent free	94	2	3	100	7
Not accessible to public, all	**95**	**1**	**3**	**100**	**5**
Resident landlord	79	13	8	100	21
No security	*	*	*	*	*
Resident landlord and no security, all	**80**	**12**	**7**	**100**	**20**
All	**76**	**5**	**18**	**100**	**11**

Table A2.12 Council tax band by type of letting
All tenancies   *England*

Type of letting	Council tax band						
	A Up to £40,000	**B** £40,000 - £52,000	**C** £52,000 - £68,000	**D** £68,000 - £88,000	**E** £88,000 - £120,000	**F - H** £120,000 or more	**Total**
							thousands
Assured	90	36	29	28	10	4	196
Assured shorthold	154	111	108	69	45	25	512
All assured	**244**	**147**	**136**	**97**	**55**	**29**	**708**
Regulated, rent registered	78	37	32	31	7	13	198
Regulated, rent not registered	34	26	24	18	12	10	124
All regulated	**113**	**63**	**55**	**49**	**19**	**23**	**321**
Not accessible to public, rent paid	22	19	12	13	14	20	99
Not accessible to public, rent free	35	26	27	29	20	26	163
Not accessible to public, all	**57**	**44**	**39**	**41**	**34**	**46**	**262**
Resident landlord	37	26	21	12	7	4	106
No security	[0]	[2]	[2]	[1]	[0]	[0]	[5]
Resident landlord and no security	**37**	**28**	**23**	**12**	**7**	**4**	**111**
All	**451**	**282**	**254**	**199**	**115**	**101**	**1 402**
							percentages
Assured	46	18	14	14	5	2	100
Assured shorthold	30	22	21	13	9	5	100
All assured	**34**	**21**	**19**	**14**	**8**	**4**	**100**
Regulated, rent registered	40	19	16	16	4	7	100
Regulated, rent not registered	28	21	19	15	9	8	100
All regulated	**35**	**20**	**17**	**15**	**6**	**7**	**100**
Not accessible to public, rent paid	22	19	12	13	14	20	100
Not accessible to public, rent free	22	16	16	18	12	16	100
Not accessible to public, all	**22**	**17**	**15**	**16**	**13**	**17**	**100**
Resident landlord	34	24	20	11	6	4	100
No security	*	*	*	*	*	*	*
Resident landlord and no security	**33**	**25**	**21**	**11**	**6**	**4**	**100**
All	**32**	**20**	**18**	**14**	**8**	**7**	**100**

Table A2.13 Type of landlord by type of letting

All tenancies   *England*

Type of letting	Type of landlord					
	Resident landlord	Private individual	Employer	Property company	Other - not known	Total
						thousands
Assured	0	341	6	16	15	378
Assured shorthold	0	699	4	88	35	826
All assured	0	1 040	10	104	50	1 204
Regulated, rent registered	0	156	4	56	29	245
Regulated, rent not registered	0	134	6	11	13	162
All regulated	0	289	10	67	41	407
Not accessible to public, rent paid	0	8	127	0	11	146
Not accessible to public, rent free	7	93	128	0	3	230
Not accessible to public, all	7	100	255	0	14	375
Resident landlord	152	4	2	0	0	158
No security	[0]	[18]	[4]	[0]	[0]	[22]
Resident landlord and no security, all	152	22	5	0	0	180
All	159	1 445	280	170	104	2 166
						percentages
Assured	-	90	2	4	4	100
Assured shorthold	-	85	0	11	4	100
All assured	-	86	1	9	4	100
Regulated, rent registered	-	64	2	23	12	100
Regulated, rent not registered	-	82	4	6	8	100
All regulated	-	71	2	16	10	100
Not accessible to public, rent paid	-	5	87	-	7	100
Not accessible to public, rent free	3	40	56	-	1	100
Not accessible to public, all	2	27	68	-	4	100
Resident landlord	96	2	1	-	-	100
No security	*	*	*	*	*	*
Resident landlord and no security, all	85	12	3	-	-	100
All	7	67	13	8	5	100

Table A2.14 Characteristics of tenants in non-privately renting households compared with tenants in privately renting households

All tenancies   *England*

Characteristics of tenant or tenancy group	Tenants in non-privately renting households	Tenants in privately renting households
		percentages
Type of letting		
Resident landlord	100	4
Assured	0	18
Assured shorthold	0	40
Other	0	39
Number of persons in tenancy group		
One	94	49
More than one	6	51
Age		
Under 30	58	38
30 to 59	36	40
60 or over	5	22
Sex		
Male	82	68
Female	18	32
Marital status		
Married or cohabiting	7	36
Single	71	38
Widowed	2	11
Divorced or separated	20	16
Economic activity status		
Working full time	40	47
Working part time	6	5
Unemployed	30	13
Retired	6	17
Full-time student	9	9
Other economically inactive	10	9
Type of property		
Detached house	5	10
Semi-detached house	24	18
Terraced house	46	29
Purpose-built flat	13	12
Converted flat	8	27
Other	4	4
Age of property		
Before 1919	39	48
1919-1944	23	25
1945-1964	9	11
1965-1984	23	11
1985 or later	5	5
Duration of tenancy		
1990 or earlier	20	39
1991-1992	44	28
1993-1994	36	33
Characteristics of household head		
Age		
Under 30	42	38
30 or over	58	62
Marital status		
Married or cohabiting	14	36
Single	54	37
Widowed	5	11
Divorced or separated	26	16
Economic activity status		
Working full time	70	48
Working part time	3	5
Unemployed	8	14
Retired	4	17
Full-time student	4	8
Other economically inactive	11	8
Tenure		
Own outright	8	-
Buying with a mortgage	83	-
Renting from council	8	-
Renting from housing association	1	-
Renting privately	-	100

Annex tables
Chapter 3

Table A3.1 Age and sex of head of tenancy group: 1988 to 1993

All tenancies   *England*

Age and sex of tenant		1988	1990	1993	
				Excluding non-privately renting households	Including non-privately renting households
					thousands
Under 30	Male	358	404	521	565
	Female	149	185	278	286
	All	**507**	**589**	**799**	**942**
30-59	Male	552	521	651	677
	Female	98	112	176	182
	All	**650**	**633**	**827**	**859**
60 or over	Male	321	276	246	249
	Female	263	197	205	207
	All	**584**	**473**	**451**	**456**
All	Male	1 231	1 201	1 418	1 491
	Female	510	494	659	675
	All	**1 741**	**1 695**	**2 077**	**2 166**
					percentages
Under 30	Male	20	24	25	26
	Female	9	11	13	13
	All	**29**	**35**	**38**	**39**
30-59	Male	32	31	31	31
	Female	6	7	8	8
	All	**38**	**38**	**40**	**40**
60 or over	Male	18	16	12	12
	Female	15	12	10	10
	All	**33**	**28**	**22**	**21**
All	Male	70	71	68	69
	Female	30	30	32	31
	All	**100**	**100**	**100**	**100**

Table A3.2 Economic status of head of tenancy group: 1988 to 1993

All tenancies   *England*

Age and sex of tenant	1988	1990	1993	
			Excluding non-privately renting households	Including non-privately renting households
				thousands
Working full time	924	985	978	1 014
Working part time	86	70	99	104
Unemployed	115	89	275	302
Retired	434	351	359	364
Full-time education	56	65	186	194
Other inactive	126	97	178	187
All	**1 741**	**1 698**	**2 075**	**2 164**
				percentages
Working full time	53	59	47	47
Working part ime	5	4	5	5
Unemployed	7	5	13	14
Retired	25	21	17	17
Full-time education	3	4	9	9
Other inactive	7	7	9	9
All	**100**	**100**	**100**	**100**

Table A3.3 Economic status of head of tenancy group by tenancy group composition

All tenancies   *England*

Tenancy group composition	Economic status of head of tenancy						
	Working full time	Working part time	Unemployed	Retired	Full-time education	Other	Total
							thousands
One adult aged 16-59	391	38	185	6	128	60	809
Two adults aged 16-59	281	13	38	3	26	14	374
Couple with dependent child(ren)	205	10	40	1	4	13	273
Lone parent with dependent child(ren)	18	16	19	0	4	54	112
Large mainly adult	85	11	13	14	33	14	170
Two adults at least one 60 or over	19	6	4	96	0	6	130
One adult 60 or over	14	11	3	244	0	25	297
All	1 014	104	302	364	194	187	2 164
							percentages
One adult aged 16-59	48	5	23	1	16	7	100
Two adults aged 16-59	75	3	10	1	7	4	100
Couple with dependent child(ren)	75	4	15	0	1	5	100
Lone parent with dependent child(ren)	16	14	17	-	3	49	100
Large mainly adult	50	6	8	8	19	8	100
Two adults at least one 60 or over	15	5	3	74	-	4	100
One adult 60 or over	5	4	1	82	-	8	100
All	47	5	14	17	9	9	100

Table A3.4 Socio-economic group* of tenant by tenancy group composition

All tenancies   *England*

Tenancy group composition	Socio-economic group of head of tenancy				
	Professional and managerial	Other non-manual	Skilled manual	Semi- and unskilled manual	Total known
					thousands
One adult aged 16-59	135	208	142	159	643
Two adults aged 16-59	109	73	75	72	329
Couple with dependent child(ren)	91	38	73	46	247
Lone parent with dependent child(ren)	9	41	12	32	94
Large mainly adult	39	21	33	38	132
Two adults at least one 60 or over	17	13	48	41	119
One adult 60 or over	44	59	55	94	253
All	445	452	438	482	1 817
					percentages
One adult aged 16-59	21	32	22	25	100
Two adults aged 16-59	33	22	23	22	100
Couple with dependent child(ren)	37	15	30	18	100
Lone parent with dependent child(ren)	10	43	13	34	100
Large mainly adult	30	16	25	29	100
Two adults at least one 60 or over	14	11	40	34	100
One adult 60 or over	18	23	22	37	100
All	24	25	24	26	100

* Based on present occupation for those currently working and last occupation for others.
  Social class could not be determined for all tenancy groups

Table A3.5   Age of building by type of accommodation
All tenancies   *England*

Type of accommodation	Age of building					
	Pre - 1919	1919-1944	1945-1964	1965-1984	1985 or later	Total known*
						thousands
Detached house	89	41	30	43	8	212
Semi-detached house	114	113	85	43	26	381
Terraced house	346	160	39	65	19	630
Purpose-built flat	22	57	51	74	45	249
Converted flat	349	128	20	6	2	506
Other/business premises	57	13	5	12	4	90
All	**977**	**513**	**231**	**243**	**104**	**2 068**
						percentages
Detached house	42	19	14	20	4	100
Semi-detached house	30	30	22	11	7	100
Terraced house	55	25	6	10	3	100
Purpose-built flat	9	23	20	30	18	100
Converted flat	69	25	4	1	0	100
Other/business premises	63	14	6	13	4	100
All	**47**	**25**	**11**	**12**	**5**	**100**

* Year the property was built was not known for all tenancies

Table A3.6   Whether accommodation rented furnished or unfurnished by type of accommodation
All tenancies   *England*

Type of accommodation	Whether furnished or unfurnished		
	Furnished	Unfurnished *	Total
			thousands
Detached house	44	168	213
Semi-detached house	102	287	390
Terraced house	259	387	646
Purpose-built flat	119	140	259
Converted flat	267	294	561
Other/business premises	22	75	97
All	**814**	**1 352**	**2 165**
			percentages
Detached house	21	79	100
Semi-detached house	26	74	100
Terraced house	40	60	100
Purpose-built flat	46	54	100
Converted flat	48	52	100
Other/business premises	23	77	100
All	**38**	**62**	**100**

* Includes partly furnished

Table A3.7   Type of landlord by type of accommodation
All tenancies   *England*

Type of accommodation*	Type of landlord					
	Resident landlord	Private individual	Employer	Property company	Other - not known	Total
						thousands
Detached house	4	129	66	2	12	213
Semi-detached house	23	247	70	30	20	390
Terraced house	43	468	49	52	33	646
Purpose-built flat	17	170	22	34	17	260
Converted flat	75	400	20	49	18	561
Other/business premises	4	31	54	3	5	97
All	**166**	**1 445**	**280**	**170**	**104**	**2 166**
						percentages
Detached house	2	60	31	1	6	100
Semi-detached house	6	63	18	8	5	100
Terraced house	7	72	8	8	5	100
Purpose-built flat	7	66	8	13	6	100
Converted flat	13	71	4	9	3	100
Other/business premises	4	33	56	3	5	100
All	**8**	**67**	**13**	**8**	**5**	**100**

* Accommodation occupied by the household. In most cases this is the same as the tenancy group but some households contain more than one tenancy group.

Table A3.8 Council tax band by type of accommodation
All tenancies   *England*

Type of accommodation	Council tax band								
	A up to £40,000	B £40,000 - £52,000	C £52,000 - £68,000	D £68,000 - £88,000	E £88,000 - £120,000	F £120,000 - £160,000	G £160,000- £320,000	H £320,000 or more	Total known*
									thousands
Detached house	5	16	25	38	40	19	16	5	163
Semi-detached house	42	65	74	60	31	14	5	0	291
Terraced house	189	101	77	43	20	3	6	0	438
Purpose-built flat	54	39	43	30	7	3	0	0	176
Converted flat	142	56	28	21	11	7	8	0	272
Other/business premises	19	6	8	7	6	6	4	4	62
All	451	282	254	199	115	53	39	8	1 402
									percentages
Detached house	3	10	15	23	25	12	10	3	100
Semi-detached house	15	22	25	21	10	5	2	-	100
Terraced house	43	23	18	10	4	1	1	-	100
Purpose-built flat	31	22	24	17	4	2	-	-	100
Converted flat	52	20	10	8	4	2	3	-	100
Other/business premises	31	10	13	12	10	10	6	6	100
All	32	20	18	14	8	4	3	1	100

* Council tax band was not available for all tenancies

Table A3.9 Sharing amenities and whether accommodation self-contained by type of accommodation
All tenancies   *England*

Type of accommodation†	Shared amenities (kitchen, bath or shower and inside WC)				Non self-contained accommodation*
	None shared	At least one shared	Missing at least one	Total	
	thousands				
Detached house	206	3	5	213	6
Semi-detached house	383	0	7	390	0
Terraced house	613	5	28	646	10
Purpose-built flat	243	2	15	260	18
Converted flat	374	116	70	561	201
Other/business premises	88	0	9	97	9
All	1 907	126	134	2 166	245
	percentages				
Detached house	97	1	2	100	2
Semi-detached house	98	-	2	100	-
Terraced house	95	1	4	100	2
Purpose-built flat	94	1	6	101	7
Converted flat	67	21	13	100	36
Other/business premises	91	-	9	100	10
All	88	6	6	100	11

*Although some households said they shared the building with another household such as a granny flat, they still considered their accommodation to be fully self-contained.
† Accommodation occupied by household. In most cases this is the same as the tenancy group but some households contained more than one tenancy group

Table A3.10 Type of accommodation by tenancy group composition

All tenancies *England*

Tenancy group composition	Type of accommodation*						Total
	Detached house	Semi-detached house	Terraced house	Purpose-built flat	Converted flat	Other/business premises	
							thousands
One adult aged 16-59	34	97	224	94	330	29	809
Two adults aged 16-59	37	58	81	76	104	17	374
Couple with dependent child(ren)	60	70	81	17	23	23	274
Lone parent with dependent child(ren)	8	25	45	10	21	5	113
Large mainly adult	26	37	70	11	16	10	170
Two adults at least one 60 or over	23	33	45	13	10	8	130
One adult 60 or over	25	71	100	39	58	5	297
All	**213**	**390**	**646**	**260**	**561**	**97**	**2 166**
							percentages
One adult aged 16-59	4	12	28	12	41	4	100
Two adults aged 16-59	10	16	22	20	28	5	100
Couple with dependent child(ren)	22	25	30	6	8	8	100
Lone parent with dependent child(ren)	7	22	40	9	18	4	100
Large mainly adult	15	22	41	6	9	6	100
Two adults at least one 60 or over	17	25	34	10	7	6	100
One adult 60 or over	8	24	34	13	19	2	100
All	**10**	**18**	**30**	**12**	**26**	**4**	**100**

* Accommodation occupied by the household. In most cases this is the same as the tenancy group but some households contained more than one tenancy group.

Table A3.11 Whether accommodation rented furnished or unfurnished by tenancy group composition

All tenancies *England*

Tenancy group composition	Whether furnished or unfurnished		Total
	Furnished	Unfurnished *	
			thousands
One adult aged 16-59	468	341	809
Two adults aged 16-59	154	219	373
Couple with dependent child(ren)	58	217	274
Lone parent with dependent child(ren)	38	75	113
Large mainly adult	73	97	170
Two adults at least one 60 or over	2	128	130
One adult 60 or over	21	276	297
All	**814**	**1 352**	**2 165**
			percentages
One adult aged 16-59	58	42	100
Two adults aged 16-59	41	59	100
Couple with dependent child(ren)	21	79	100
Lone parent with dependent child(ren)	33	67	100
Large mainly adult	43	57	100
Two adults at least one 60 or over	2	98	100
One adult 60 or over	7	93	100
All	**38**	**62**	**100**

* Includes partly furnished

Table A3.12 Sharing amenities and whether accommodation self-contained by tenancy group composition
All tenancies *England*

| Tenancy group composition | Shared amenities (kitchen, bath or shower and inside WC) | | | | Non self-contained accommodation* |
	None shared	At least one shared	Missing at least one	Total	
					thousands
One adult aged 16-59	633	100	76	809	178
Two adults aged 16-59	353	13	8	374	30
Couple with dependent child(ren)	267	2	5	274	9
Lone parent with dependent child(ren)	105	5	3	113	9
Large mainly adult	169	1	0	170	4
Two adults at least one 60 or over	123	1	7	130	1
One adult 60 or over	257	4	35	297	13
All	1 907	126	134	2 166	244
					percentages
One adult aged 16-59	78	12	9	100	22
Two adults aged 16-59	94	4	2	100	8
Couple with dependent child(ren)	97	1	2	100	3
Lone parent with dependent child(ren)	93	4	2	100	8
Large mainly adult	99	1	0	100	2
Two adults at least one 60 or over	94	0	5	100	1
One adult 60 or over	87	2	12	100	4
All	88	6	6	100	11

*Although some households said they shared the building with another household such as a granny flat, they still considered their accommodation to be fully self-contained.

Table A3.13 Difference from the bedroom standard and rooms per person by tenancy group composition
All tenancies *England*

| Tenancy group composition | Difference from bedroom standard* | | | | Rooms per person | | | | | Mean |
	Below	Equal	Above	Total	Less than one	1-1.5	1.5-2	2 or more	Total	
									thousands	*number*
One adult aged 16-59	25	455	328	809	8	179	228	393	809	2.3
Two adults aged 16-59	10	162	202	374	8	48	197	121	374	2.0
Couple with dependent child(ren)	18	108	148	274	15	128	113	18	274	1.5
Lone parent with dependent child(ren)	18	58	37	113	3	23	65	22	113	1.8
Large mainly adult	14	79	77	170	1	53	105	11	170	1.7
Two adults at least one 60 or over	1	19	111	130	0	2	50	79	130	2.4
One adult 60 or over	0	71	225	297	0	14	14	268	297	3.2
All types	87	952	1 128	2 166	35	448	771	912	2 166	2.1
									percentages	
One adult aged 16-59	3	56	40	100	1	22	28	49	100	
Two adults aged 16-59	3	43	54	100	2	13	53	32	100	
Couple with dependent child(ren)	7	39	54	100	6	47	41	6	100	
Lone parent with dependent child(ren)	16	51	33	100	2	20	57	20	100	
Large mainly adult	8	46	46	100	1	32	62	6	100	
Two adults at least one 60 or over	1	14	85	100	-	1	38	60	100	
One adult 60 or over	-	24	76	100	-	5	5	90	100	
All types	4	44	52	100	2	21	36	42	100	

* Bedroom standard for the household rather than the tenancy group. One person tenancy groups can be below the bedroom standard where there is more than one tenancy group in the household and the accommodation for the household is below the standard.

Table A3.14 Satisfaction with accommodation by difference from the bedroom standard and whether accommodation self-contained

All tenancies   *England*

Difference from the bedroom standard and whether self-contained	Satisfaction with accommodation					
	Very satisfied	Fairly satisfied	Neither satisfied nor dissatisfied	Slightly dissatisfied	Very dissatisfied	Total known*
						thousands
Above standard	20	39	8	7	12	87
Equal to standard	336	362	70	104	75	947
Below standard	506	425	62	82	50	1 125
All	**863**	**826**	**140**	**193**	**137**	**2 159**
Self-contained accommodation	804	732	115	163	101	1 914
Not self-contained	59	95	25	30	36	245
All	**863**	**826**	**140**	**193**	**137**	**2 159**
						percentages
Below standard	24	45	9	8	14	100
Equal to standard	36	38	7	11	8	100
Above standard	45	38	6	7	4	100
All	**40**	**38**	**6**	**9**	**6**	**100**
Self-contained accommodation	42	38	6	8	5	100
Not self-contained	24	39	10	12	15	100
All	**40**	**38**	**6**	**9**	**6**	**100**

* A small number of tenants did not answer the question on satisfaction

Table A3.15 Satisfaction with accommodation by year property built

All tenancies   *England*

Year property built	Satisfaction with accommodation					
	Very satisfied	Fairly satisfied	Neither satisfied nor dissatisfied	Slightly dissatisfied	Very dissatisfied	Total known*
						thousands
Before 1919	387	347	67	99	75	975
1919-1944	197	200	37	37	40	511
1945-1964	94	95	11	17	11	229
1965-1984	111	96	12	14	10	243
1985 or later	44	48	5	6	0	103
All	**833**	**786**	**133**	**173**	**136**	**2 061**
						percentages
Before 1919	40	36	7	10	8	100
1919-1944	39	39	7	7	8	100
1945-1964	41	42	5	7	5	100
1965-1984	46	39	5	6	4	100
1985 or later	42	47	5	6	-	100
All	**40**	**38**	**6**	**8**	**7**	**100**

* A small number of tenants did not answer the question on satisfaction

Table A3.16 Satisfaction with accommodation by type of accommodation
All tenancies   *England*

Type of accommodation*	Satisfaction with accommodation					
	Very satisfied	Fairly satisfied	Neither satisfied nor dissatisfied	Slightly dissatisfied	Very dissatisfied	Total known*
						thousands
Detached house	113	76	8	9	7	213
Semi-detached	182	150	16	27	11	386
Terraced	273	221	48	62	40	644
Purpose built flat	104	108	22	17	8	259
Converted flat	149	235	43	67	68	561
Business premises/Other	41	37	5	10	4	97
All	**863**	**826**	**140**	**193**	**137**	**2 159**
						percentages
Detached house	53	36	4	4	3	100
Semi-detached	47	39	4	7	3	100
Terraced	42	34	7	10	6	100
Purpose built flat	40	42	8	7	3	100
Converted flat	26	42	8	12	12	100
Business premises/Other	42	38	5	10	5	100
All	**40**	**38**	**6**	**9**	**6**	**100**

* Accommodation occupied by the household. In most cases this is the same as the tenancy group but some households contained more than one tenancy group.

Annex tables
Chapter 4

Table A4.1 Comparable weekly rent by type of letting
Tenancies paying rent
England

Type of letting	Comparable weekly rent										
	Up to £15	£15, up to £20	£20, up to £25	£25, up to £30	£30, up to £40	£40, up to £50	£50, up to £100	£100 or more	Total	Mean rent	Median rent
									thousands		£ per week
Assured	11	4	22	35	53	47	142	41	354	60	50
Assured shorthold	16	6	9	30	83	67	410	194	816	80	70
All assured	28	10	31	65	136	113	552	235	1 170	73	65
Regulated, rent registered	12	33	28	40	84	30	14	0	240	31	30
Regulated, rent not registered	25	15	13	12	38	10	13	3	129	32	29
All regulated	37	48	41	52	122	41	27	3	369	31	30
Not accessible to public, rent paid	19	14	23	13	17	5	19	8	119	39	26
All not accessible to public	19	14	23	13	17	5	19	8	119	39	26
Resident landlord	9	12	10	14	40	26	31	2	142	41	35
No security	[0]	[1]	[4]	[2]	[8]	[0]	[2]	[2]	[18]	*	*
Resident landlord and no security	9	13	13	16	48	26	32	4	161	42	35
All	92	84	108	146	322	186	630	251	1 819	60	48
									percentages		
Assured	3	1	6	10	15	13	40	12	100		
Assured shorthold	2	1	1	4	10	8	50	24	100		
All assured	2	1	3	6	12	10	47	20	100		
Regulated, rent registered	5	14	12	16	35	13	6	-	100		
Regulated, rent not registered	20	12	10	9	29	8	10	3	100		
All regulated	10	13	11	14	33	11	7	1	100		
Not accessible to public, rent paid	16	12	20	11	14	4	16	7	100		
All not accessible to public	16	12	20	11	14	4	16	7	100		
Resident landlord	6	8	7	10	28	18	22	1	100		
No security	*	*	*	*	*	*-	*	*	*		
Resident landlord and no security	5	8	8	10	30	16	20	3	100		
All	5	5	6	8	18	10	34	14	100		

Table A4.2 Comparable weekly rent by region
Tenancies paying rent
England

Region	Comparable weekly rent										
	Up to £15	£15, up to £20	£20, up to £25	£25, up to £30	£30, up to £40	£40, up to £50	£50, up to £100	£100 or more	Total	Mean rent	Median rent
									thousands		£ per week
North	6	5	8	6	11	7	20	2	66	41	35
North West	9	18	20	19	35	19	55	21	196	50	39
Yorkshire and Humberside	11	10	16	25	29	11	45	5	152	43	35
West Midlands	7	10	13	19	42	16	61	7	174	47	38
East Midlands	19	11	15	30	35	15	41	4	170	39	32
The North and midlands	53	55	71	99	152	69	222	39	759	45	36
Greater London	10	10	11	11	55	42	108	148	395	89	75
Rest of South East	10	6	14	14	59	30	150	48	333	66	60
South West	15	6	10	14	50	33	124	14	267	55	53
East Anglia	4	7	3	7	6	12	25	2	66	47	46
Rest of South	30	20	26	35	115	75	300	64	665	60	55
All	92	84	108	146	322	186	630	251	1 819	60	48
									percentages		
North	10	8	12	10	17	11	31	3	100		
North West	4	9	10	10	18	10	28	11	100		
Yorkshire and Humberside	8	7	10	17	19	8	30	3	100		
West Midlands	4	6	7	11	24	9	35	4	100		
East Midlands	11	6	9	17	21	9	24	3	100		
The North	7	7	9	13	20	9	29	5	100		
Greater London	2	3	3	3	14	10	27	37	100		
Rest of South East	3	2	4	4	18	9	45	14	100		
South West	6	2	4	5	19	12	47	5	100		
East Anglia	6	11	4	11	9	18	39	3	100		
Rest of South	4	3	4	5	17	11	45	10	100		
All	5	5	6	8	18	10	35	14	100		

Table A4.3 Comparable weekly rent by year tenancy started

Tenancies paying rent   *England*

Year tenancy started	Comparable weekly rent										
	Up to £15	£15, up to £20	£20, up to £25	£25, up to £30	£30, up to £40	£40, up to £50	£50, up to £100	£100 or more	Total	Mean rent	Median rent
									thousands		*£ per week*
Before 1968	19	24	21	27	53	16	12	1	173	30	28
1968-1978	17	14	12	11	22	5	6	1	88	27	25
1979-1988	17	22	10	20	64	26	31	2	192	36	33
1989-1990	4	2	21	11	22	21	48	14	142	53	45
1991-1992	18	13	29	39	74	59	237	86	555	67	58
1993-1994	18	9	14	38	89	58	297	146	669	74	65
All	**92**	**84**	**108**	**146**	**322**	**186**	**630**	**250**	**1 818**	**60**	**48**
									percentages		
Before 1968	11	14	12	16	30	9	7	1	100		
1968-1978	19	16	14	12	24	6	6	2	100		
1979-1988	9	12	5	10	33	14	16	1	100		
1989-1990	2	1	15	8	16	15	34	10	100		
1991-1992	3	2	5	7	13	11	43	16	100		
1993-1994	3	1	2	6	13	9	44	22	100		
All	**5**	**5**	**6**	**8**	**18**	**10**	**35**	**14**	**100**		

Table A4.4 Opinion about rent level by type of letting

Tenancies paying rent   *England*

Type of letting	Opinion of rent level					
	Very high	Slightly high	About right	Slightly low	Very low	Total
						thousands
Assured	36	74	192	42	18	362
Assured shorthold	98	251	390	52	28	819
All assured	**134**	**325**	**582**	**93**	**46**	**1 180**
Regulated, rent registered	31	45	145	13	8	243
Regulated, rent not registered	10	19	71	11	26	137
All regulated	**41**	**64**	**216**	**24**	**34**	**380**
Not accessible to public, rent paid	12	25	73	9	25	144
All not accessible to public	**12**	**25**	**73**	**9**	**25**	**144**
Resident landlord	5	20	94	15	17	151
No security	[2]	[5]	[9]	[2]	[0]	[18]
Resident landlord and no security	**6**	**26**	**103**	**17**	**17**	**170**
All	**194**	**440**	**975**	**143**	**122**	**1 874**
						percentages
Assured	10	20	53	12	5	100
Assured shorthold	12	31	48	6	3	100
All assured	**11**	**28**	**49**	**8**	**4**	**100**
Regulated, rent registered	13	19	60	5	3	100
Regulated, rent not registered	7	14	52	8	19	100
All regulated	**11**	**17**	**57**	**6**	**9**	**100**
Not accessible to public, rent paid	8	18	51	6	17	100
All not accessible to public	**8**	**18**	**51**	**6**	**17**	**100**
Resident landlord	3	14	62	10	11	100
No security	*	*	*	*	*	*
Resident landlord and no security	**4**	**15**	**61**	**10**	**10**	**100**
All	**10**	**24**	**52**	**8**	**6**	**100**

Table A4.5   Opinion of rent level by comparable weekly rent level
Tenancies paying rent   *England*

Comparable weekly rent	Opinion of rent level					
	Very high	Slightly high	About right	Slightly low	Very low	**Total**
						thousands
Up to £15	3	7	40	6	34	89
£15, up to £20	8	5	53	8	10	84
£20, up to £25	0	13	63	15	16	108
£25, up to £30	8	22	89	12	12	142
£30, up to £40	26	71	173	27	20	317
£40, up to £50	25	26	110	16	8	184
£50, up to £100	99	193	285	41	14	630
£100 or more	21	93	120	13	1	249
All	**189**	**430**	**933**	**138**	**114**	**1 805**
						percentages
Up to £15	3	8	45	6	38	100
£15, up to £20	9	6	63	9	12	100
£20, up to £25	-	12	59	14	15	100
£25, up to £30	5	16	63	8	8	100
£30, up to £40	8	22	54	9	6	100
£40, up to £50	14	14	60	9	4	100
£50, up to £100	16	31	45	6	2	100
£100 or more	9	37	48	5	0	100
All	**10**	**24**	**52**	**8**	**6**	**100**

Table A4.6   Estimated eligibility for Housing Benefit by tenancy group composition
Tenancies paying rent   *England*

Tenancy group composition	Eligibility for Housing Benefit				Tenancies in receipt of Housing Benefit	Eligible tenancies who receive Housing Benefit
	Eligible for : all rent	part of rent	Not eligible	Total		
						thousands
One adult aged 16-59	244	87	389	721	260	254
Two adults aged 16-59	45	25	206	276	51	40
Couple with dependent child(ren)	55	18	119	191	55	51
Lone parent with dependent child(ren)	79	12	12	103	84	84
Large mainly adult	20	7	82	109	25	[19]
Two adults at least one 60 or over	37	14	38	89	41	36
One adult 60 or over	98	55	47	199	116	109
All	**579**	**217**	**892**	**1 687**	**632**	**592**
						percentages
One adult aged 16-59	34	12	54	100	36	76
Two adults aged 16-59	16	9	75	100	17	58
Couple with dependent child(ren)	29	9	62	100	27	70
Lone parent with dependent child(ren)	77	11	12	100	80	92
Large mainly adult	18	6	76	100	23	*
Two adults at least one 60 or over	42	15	42	100	44	70
One adult 60 or over	49	27	24	100	55	72
All	**34**	**13**	**53**	**100**	**36**	**74**

Table A4.7   Estimated eligibility for Housing Benefit by disposable weekly tenancy group income
Tenancies paying rent   *England*

Tenancy group disposable weekly income	Eligibility for Housing Benefit				Tenancies in receipt of Housing Benefit	Eligible tenancies who receive Housing Benefit
	Eligible for: all rent	part of rent	Not eligible	Total		
						thousands
Under £60	206	25	59	290	195	194
£60-£79	148	24	29	201	151	150
£80-£119	104	80	69	254	151	142
£120-£179	44	52	164	260	71	63
£180-£249	22	17	178	217	33	22
£250 or more	22	13	363	398	20	14
All	**546**	**212**	**862**	**1 620**	**620**	**586**
						percentages
Under £60	71	9	20	100	67	84
£60-£79	74	12	14	100	75	87
£80-£119	41	32	27	100	59	77
£120-£179	17	20	63	100	27	66
£180-£249	10	8	82	100	14	57
£250 or more	6	3	91	100	5	41
All	**34**	**13**	**53**	**100**	**36**	**77**

Table A4.8   Estimated eligibility for Housing Benefit by type of letting
Tenancies paying rent   *England*

Type of letting	Eligibility for Housing Benefit				Tenancies in receipt of Housing Benefit	Eligible tenancies who receive Housing Benefit
	Eligible for: all rent	part of rent	Not eligible	Total		
						thousands
Assured	113	38	169	320	122	114
Assured shorthold	251	92	411	754	283	266
All assured	**364**	**130**	**580**	**1 074**	**405**	**380**
Regulated, rent registered	102	38	78	219	118	110
Regulated, rent not registered	48	20	50	118	51	49
All regulated	**150**	**58**	**128**	**337**	**168**	**159**
Not accessible to public, rent paid	8	10	107	125	5	[4]
Not accessible to public, all	**8**	**10**	**107**	**125**	**5**	**4**
Resident landlord	52	15	68	135	51	46
No security	[4]	[3]	[9]	[16]	[3]	[3]
Resident landlord and no security, all	**56**	**18**	**78**	**151**	**54**	**49**
All	**579**	**217**	**892**	**1 687**	**632**	**592**
						percentages
Assured	35	12	53	100	36	75
Assured shorthold	33	12	54	100	37	78
All assured	**34**	**12**	**54**	**100**	**36**	**77**
Regulated, rent registered	47	18	36	100	52	78
Regulated, rent not registered	41	17	42	100	41	72
All regulated	**45**	**17**	**38**	**100**	**48**	**76**
Not accessible to public, rent paid	7	8	85	100	4	*
Not accessible to public, all	**7**	**8**	**85**	**100**	**4**	**21**
Resident landlord	38	11	51	100	36	69
No security	*	*	*	*	*	*
Resident landlord and no security, all	**37**	**12**	**51**	**100**	**34**	**66**
All	**34**	**13**	**53**	**100**	**36**	**74**

Table A4.9 Estimated eligibility for Housing Benefit by comparable weekly rent

Tenancies paying rent *England*

Comparable weekly rent	Eligibility for Housing Benefit				Tenancies in receipt of Housing Benefit	Eligible tenancies who receive Housing Benefit
	Eligible for : all rent	part of rent	Not eligible	Total		
						thousands
Up to £15	24	7	49	80	23	[18]
£15, up to £20	25	8	38	72	24	[24]
£20, up to £25	35	7	55	97	31	30
£25, up to £30	38	17	87	142	45	42
£30, up to £40	99	32	162	293	109	103
£40, up to £50	78	20	74	172	82	77
£50, up to £100	205	100	270	575	243	232
£100 or more	64	25	123	212	62	59
All	**568**	**217**	**858**	**1 642**	**619**	**584**
						percentages
Up to £15	30	9	61	100	28	} 65
£15, up to £20	35	12	53	100	32	
£20, up to £25	36	8	57	100	31	70
£25, up to £30	27	12	61	100	33	76
£30, up to £40	34	11	55	100	35	78
£40, up to £50	45	11	43	100	46	79
£50, up to £100	36	17	47	100	41	76
£100 or more	30	12	58	100	28	67
All	**35**	**13**	**52**	**100**	**36**	**75**

Table A4.10 Comparable weekly rent less Housing Benefit by type of letting

Tenancies paying rent *England*

Type of letting	Comparable weekly rent less Housing Benefit							Mean Rent	Median Rent
	Up to £20	£20, up to £40	£40, up to £60	£60, up to £80	£80, up to £100	£100 or more	Total		
							thousands		*£ per week*
Assured	90	99	60	32	15	20	316	41	33
Assured shorthold	215	109	88	109	76	132	728	58	48
All assured	305	208	147	141	92	152	1 044	53	40
Regulated, rent registered	117	79	24	1	0	0	221	18	18
Regulated, rent not registered	68	24	13	4	1	1	111	20	12
All regulated	185	103	37	5	1	1	332	19	16
Not accessible to public, rent paid	25	52	10	8	3	8	106	38	26
All not accessible to public	25	52	10	8	3	8	106	38	26
Resident landlord	52	44	19	6	1	2	125	28	27
No security	[3]	[11]	[0]	[0]	[0]	[2]	[16]	*	*
Resident landlord and no security	55	55	19	6	1	4	141	30	29
All	**569**	**419**	**214**	**160**	**97**	**165**	**1 624**	**43**	**31**
							percentages		
Assured	28	31	19	10	5	6	100		
Assured shorthold	30	15	12	15	10	18	100		
All assured	29	20	14	14	9	15	100		
Regulated, rent registered	53	38	11	-	-	-	100		
Regulated, rent not registered	61	22	12	4	1	1	100		
All regulated	56	31	11	1	0	0	100		
Not accessible to public, rent paid	24	49	9	8	3	8	100		
All not accessible to public	24	49	9	8	3	8	100		
Resident landlord	42	35	16	5	1	2	100		
No security	*	*	*	*	*	*	*		
Resident landlord and no security	39	39	14	5	1	3	100		
All	**35**	**26**	**13**	**10**	**6**	**10**	**100**		

Table A4.11 Housing Benefit by type of letting

Tenancies paying rent — *England*

Type of letting	Housing Benefit (weekly)														
	No Housing Benefit	Up to £10	£10, up to £20	£20, up to £30	£30, up to £40	£40, up to £50	£50, up to £60	£60, up to £70	£70, up to £80	£80, up to £90	£90, up to £100	£100 or more	Total	Mean	Median
													thousands		*£ per week*
Assured	215	0	10	15	18	18	16	13	6	2	7	4	323	49	46
Assured shorthold	490	5	4	17	26	28	43	33	24	18	10	33	732	66	58
All assured	705	5	13	32	44	46	59	46	30	20	17	37	1 055	61	55
Regulated, rent registered	110	11	20	40	26	4	9	1	0	0	0	0	222	27	25
Regulated, rent not registered	73	6	6	20	12	4	0	0	0	0	0	0	120	26	27
All regulated	184	17	26	60	37	8	9	1	0	0	0	0	342	26	26
Not accessible to public, rent paid	127	0	0	1	3	0	0	0	0	0	0	1	132	47	39
All not accessible to public	127	0	0	1	3	0	0	0	0	0	0	1	132	47	39
Resident landlord	91	1	1	5	13	9	9	1	1	1	0	0	132	41	40
No security	[13]	[0]	[0]	[1]	[0]	[0]	[0]	[0]	[0]	[2]	[0]	[0]	[16]	*	*
Resident landlord and no security	105	1	1	7	13	9	9	1	1	3	0	0	149	42	40
All	1 120	23	40	100	98	63	77	48	31	23	17	38	1 677	49	42
													percentages		
Assured	67	-	3	5	6	6	5	4	2	1	2	1	100		
Assured shorthold	67	1	1	2	4	4	6	4	3	2	1	5	100		
All assured	67	0	1	3	4	4	6	4	3	2	2	4	100		
Regulated, rent registered	50	5	9	18	12	2	4	1	-	-	-	-	100		
Regulated, rent not registered	61	5	5	16	10	3	-	-	-	-	-	-	100		
All regulated	54	5	8	18	11	2	3	0	-	-	-	-	100		
Not accessible to public, rent paid	96	-	-	1	2	-	-	-	-	-	-	-	100		
All not accessible to public	96	-	-	1	2	-	-	-	-	-	-	1	100		
Resident landlord	69	1	1	4	10	7	7	1	1	1	-	-	100		
No security	*	-	-	*	-	-	-	-	-	*	-	-	*		
Resident landlord and no security	70	1	1	5	9	6	6	1	1	2	-	-	100		
All	67	1	2	6	6	4	5	3	2	1	1	2	100		

Table A4.12 Comparable weekly rent by council tax band

Tenancies paying rent — *England*

Council tax band	Comparable weekly rent										
	Up to £15	£15, up to £20	£20, up to £25	£25, up to £30	£30, up to £40	£40, up to £50	£50, up to £100	£100 or more	Total	Mean	Median
									thousands		*£ per week*
Up to £40,000	24	32	31	36	77	53	149	1	403	42	40
£40,000, up to £52,000	10	10	17	24	34	24	106	20	243	55	52
£52,000, up to £68,000	8	5	7	17	43	12	87	28	207	62	58
£68,000, up to £88,000	6	3	13	7	35	12	39	41	156	67	50
£88,000, up to £120,000	4	2	2	1	10	9	27	32	89	85	70
£120,000 or more	3	4	3	2	4	7	10	25	59	111	65
All	55	55	73	88	202	117	419	147	1 158	59	48
									Percentages		
Up to £40,000	6	8	8	9	19	13	37	0	100		
£40,000, up to £52,000	4	4	7	10	14	10	43	8	100		
£52,000, up to £68,000	4	2	3	8	21	6	42	14	100		
£68,000, up to £88,000	4	2	8	5	22	8	25	26	100		
£88,000, up to £120,000	5	2	3	1	11	11	31	36	100		
£120,000 or more	6	7	6	4	6	12	17	42	100		
All	5	5	6	8	18	10	36	13	100		

Annex tables
Chapter 5

Table A5.1 Disposable weekly tenancy group income by tenancy group composition
All tenancies   *England*

Tenancy group composition	Disposable weekly income of tenancy group								
	Under £60	£60-£79	£80-£119	£120-£179	£180-£249	£250 or more	**Total**	*Mean*	*Median*
							thousands		*£ per week*
One adult aged 16-59	269	63	85	139	107	76	739	127	92
Two adults aged 16-59	6	14	19	40	60	187	326	288	263
Couple with dependent child(ren)	1	5	28	26	40	123	224	309	254
Lone parent with dependent child(ren)	4	31	37	18	7	11	108	125	89
Large mainly adult	2	1	5	22	17	87	134	366	325
Two adults at least one 60 or over	3	7	30	31	18	13	102	163	129
One adult 60 or over	19	103	96	22	9	14	263	99	82
All	**303**	**224**	**300**	**297**	**258**	**512**	**1 894**	**191**	**138**
							percentages		
One adult aged 16-59	36	8	12	19	14	10	100		
Two adults aged 16-59	2	4	6	12	18	57	100		
Couple with dependent child(ren)	0	2	13	12	18	55	100		
Lone parent with dependent child(ren)	3	29	34	17	7	10	100		
Large mainly adult	2	1	4	16	12	65	100		
Two adults at least one 60 or over	3	7	29	30	18	13	100		
One adult 60 or over	7	39	37	8	4	5	100		
All	**16**	**12**	**16**	**16**	**14**	**27**	**100**		

Table A5.2 Disposable weekly tenancy group income by economic status of head of tenancy group
All tenancies   *England*

Economic status of tenant	Disposable weekly income of tenancy group								
	Under £60	£60-£79	£80-£119	£120-£179	£180-£249	£250 or more	**Total**	*Mean*	*Median*
							thousands		*£ per week*
Working full time	15	8	44	168	195	419	848	288	236
Working part time	7	12	24	24	12	17	96	161	126
Unemployed	163	37	47	23	11	11	291	82	45
Retired	15	96	113	44	20	25	314	117	94
Full-time education	67	28	26	21	12	21	175	121	70
Other inactive	35	44	47	17	9	18	170	122	81
All	**303**	**224**	**300**	**297**	**258**	**512**	**1 894**	**191**	**138**
							percentages		
Working full time	2	1	5	20	23	49	100		
Working part time	8	12	25	25	13	18	100		
Unemployed	56	13	16	8	4	4	100		
Retired	5	31	36	14	6	8	100		
Full-time education	38	16	15	12	7	12	100		
Other inactive	21	26	28	10	5	11	100		
All	**16**	**12**	**16**	**16**	**14**	**27**	**100**		

Table A5.3 Disposable weekly tenancy group income by type of letting
All tenancies   *England*

Type of letting	Disposable weekly income of tenancy group								
	Under £60	£60-£79	£80-£119	£120-£179	£180-£249	£250 or more	Total	Mean	Median
							thousands		*£ per week*
Assured	71	35	44	55	62	61	328	167	130
Assured shorthold	139	54	96	119	99	244	750	219	162
All assured	210	89	140	174	161	305	1 079	203	150
Regulated, rent registered	14	64	58	32	20	32	219	137	97
Regulated, rent not registered	14	30	37	21	15	22	139	146	104
All regulated	27	94	95	53	35	54	359	141	100
Not accessible to public, rent paid	9	4	11	10	14	69	118	290	262
Not accessible to public, rent free	9	16	32	27	27	65	176	211	179
Not accessible to public, all	18	20	43	37	41	135	293	243	206
Resident landlord	42	19	18	30	21	15	144	125	104
No security	[7]	[2]	[4]	[3]	[1]	[3]	[20]	*	*
Resident landlord and no security, all	48	21	22	33	22	18	164	128	100
All	303	224	300	297	258	512	1 894	191	138
							percentages		
Assured	22	11	14	17	19	19	100		
Assured shorthold	18	7	13	16	13	32	100		
All assured	19	8	13	16	15	28	100		
Regulated, rent registered	6	29	26	14	9	15	100		
Regulated, rent not registered	10	22	27	15	11	16	100		
All regulated	8	26	26	15	10	15	100		
Not accessible to public, rent paid	8	3	9	9	12	59	100		
Not accessible to public, rent free	5	9	18	15	15	37	100		
Not accessible to public, all	6	7	15	13	14	46	100		
Resident landlord	29	13	12	21	14	10	100		
No security	*	*	*	*	*	*	*		
Resident landlord and no security, all	30	13	13	20	13	11	100		
All	16	12	16	16	14	27	100		

Table A5.4 Income from state benefits as a proportion of tenancy group disposable income by tenancy group composition
All tenancies   *England*

Tenancy group composition	Income from state benefits as a proportion of disposable weekly income					
	No income from benefits	Less than 25%	25%, less than 50%	50%, less than 75%	75% or more	Total *
						thousands
One adult aged 16-59	506	12	9	10	234	770
Two adults aged 16-59	257	36	9	5	27	334
Couple with dependent child(ren)	15	170	16	7	40	247
Lone couple with dependent child(ren)	3	16	11	9	69	108
Large mainly adult	81	29	11	6	8	135
Two adults at least one 60 or over	9	22	17	25	43	117
One adult 60 or over	20	17	16	61	157	271
All	891	302	88	123	579	1 982
						percentages
One adult aged 16-59	68	2	1	1	30	100
Two adults aged 16-59	77	11	3	2	8	100
Couple with dependent child(ren)	6	69	7	3	16	100
Lone couple with dependent child(ren)	3	15	10	8	64	100
Large mainly adult	60	22	8	4	6	100
Two adults at least one 60 or over	8	19	15	22	37	100
One adult 60 or over	8	6	6	22	58	100
All	45	15	4	6	29	100

* Includes tenancy groups who did not receive any income from benefits but whose disposable weekly income was not known.

Table A5.5 Income from state benefits as a proportion of tenancy group disposable weekly income by type of letting
All tenancies   *England*

Type of letting	Income from state benefits as a proportion of disposable weekly income					
	No income from benefits	Less than 25%	25%, less than 50%	50%, less than 75%	75% or more	Total*
						thousands
Assured	188	37	9	5	102	341
Assured shorthold	413	101	27	19	211	771
All assured	**601**	**138**	**37**	**23**	**313**	**1 112**
Regulated, rent registered	33	34	10	37	113	228
Regulated, rent not registered	25	15	18	26	61	145
All regulated	**59**	**50**	**28**	**62**	**174**	**373**
Not accessible to public, rent paid	65	53	7	4	2	131
Not accessible to public, rent free	78	53	13	23	33	199
Not accessible to public, all	**143**	**106**	**20**	**27**	**35**	**330**
Resident landlord	73	8	4	11	51	147
No security	[14]	[1]	[0]	[0]	[5]	[20]
Resident landlord and no security, all	**87**	**8**	**4**	**11**	**56**	**167**
All	**891**	**302**	**88**	**123**	**579**	**1 982**
						percentages
Assured	55	11	3	1	30	100
Assured shorthold	54	13	4	2	27	100
All assured	**54**	**12**	**3**	**2**	**28**	**100**
Regulated, rent registered	15	15	4	16	50	100
Regulated, rent not registered	17	11	12	18	42	100
All regulated	**16**	**13**	**7**	**17**	**47**	**100**
Not accessible to public, rent paid	50	40	6	3	2	100
Not accessible to public, rent free	39	26	6	12	16	99
Not accessible to public, all	**43**	**32**	**6**	**8**	**11**	**100**
Resident landlord	50	5	3	7	35	100
No security	*	*	*	*	*	*
Resident landlord and no security, all	**52**	**5**	**2**	**6**	**34**	**100**
All	**45**	**15**	**4**	**6**	**29**	**100**

* Includes tenancy groups who did not receive any income from benefits but whose disposable weekly income was not known.

Table A5.6 Income from state benefits as a proportion of tenancy group disposable weekly income by disposable income
All tenancies   *England*

Disposable weekly income of tenancy group	Income from state benefits as a proportion of disposable weekly tenancy group income					
	No income from benefits	Less than 25%	25%, less than 50%	50%, less than 75%	75% or more	Total
						thousands
Under £60	80	8	4	4	204	300
£60-£79	34	3	5	18	164	223
£80-£119	78	3	9	61	146	297
£120-£179	171	24	25	25	47	291
£180-£249	163	48	27	11	8	256
£250 or more	301	162	19	4	10	496
All	**827**	**247**	**88**	**123**	**579**	**1 864**
						percentages
Under £60	27	3	1	1	68	100
£60-£79	15	1	2	8	73	100
£80-£119	26	1	3	21	49	100
£120-£179	59	8	8	8	16	100
£180-£249	64	19	11	4	3	100
£250 or more	61	33	4	1	2	100
All	**44**	**13**	**5**	**7**	**31**	**100**

Table A5.7 Proportion of disposable income spent on rent (after Housing Benefit) by type of letting
All tenancies paying rent *England*

Type of letting	Proportion of disposable income spent on rent (less Housing Benefit)			
	Less than 20%	20%, less than 33%	33% or more	Total*
				thousands
Assured	142	56	94	292
Assured shorthold	300	171	220	691
All assured	442	228	313	983
Regulated, rent registered	153	33	25	211
Regulated, rent not registered	78	17	10	106
All regulated	231	50	36	316
Not accessible to public, rent paid	64	14	18	95
Not accessible to public, all	64	14	18	95
Resident landlord	65	32	22	119
No security	[5]	[2]	[8]	[15]
Resident landlord and no security, all	70	34	30	135
All	807	325	397	1 529
				Percentages
Assured	49	19	32	100
Assured shorthold	44	25	32	100
All assured	45	23	32	100
Regulated, rent registered	72	16	12	100
Regulated, rent not registered	74	16	10	100
All regulated	73	16	11	100
Not accessible to public, rent paid	67	14	18	100
Not accessible to public, all	67	14	18	100
Resident landlord	55	27	18	100
No security	*	*	*	*
Resident landlord and no security, all	52	26	22	100
All	53	21	26	100

* Total number of cases is lower as information was missing on one of the variables for some tenancy groups

Table A5.8 Proportion of disposable income spent on rent (after Housing Benefit) by comparable weekly rent
All tenancies paying rent *England*

Comparable weekly rent	Proportion of disposable income spent on rent (less Housing Benefit)			
	Less than 20%	20%, less than 33%	33% or more	Total*
				thousands
Up to £15	70	3	2	74
£15, up to £20	55	10	3	68
£20, up to £25	63	14	13	91
£25, up to £30	79	19	33	131
£30, up to £40	161	59	58	278
£40, up to £50	105	32	29	166
£50, up to £100	226	139	167	532
£100 or more	47	50	92	189
All	807	325	397	1 529
				percentages
Up to £15	94	4	2	100
£15, up to £20	81	14	5	100
£20, up to £25	70	16	14	100
£25, up to £30	60	14	25	100
£30, up to £40	58	21	21	100
£40, up to £50	63	19	18	100
£50, up to £100	42	26	31	100
£100 or more	25	26	48	100
All	53	21	26	100

* Total number of cases is lower as information was missing on one of the variables for some tenancy groups

Table A5.9 Proportion of disposable income spent on rent (after Housing Benefit) by comparable weekly rent (before Housing Benefit) and whether receives Housing Benefit

All tenancies paying rent   *England*

Comparable weekly rent (before Housing Benefit)	Tenancies not receiving Housing Benefit				Tenancies receiving Housing Benefit			
	Proportion of disposable income spent on rent (less Housing Benefit)							
	Less than 20%	20%, less than 33%	33% or more	Total*	Less than 20%	20%, less than 33%	33% or more	Total*
								thousands
Up to £20	84	13	5	102	41	0	0	41
£20, up to £30	75	30	46	151	68	3	0	71
£30, up to £50	102	85	83	270	164	6	4	174
£50, up to £100	70	116	137	323	156	23	31	210
£100 or more	20	43	80	142	28	7	11	46
All	**351**	**286**	**351**	**987**	**457**	**39**	**46**	**542**
								percentages
Up to £20	83	13	5	100	100	-	-	100
£20, up to £30	50	20	31	100	96	4	-	100
£30, up to £50	38	31	31	100	94	4	2	100
£50, up to £100	22	36	42	100	74	11	15	100
£100 or more	14	30	56	100	60	16	24	100
All	**36**	**29**	**36**	**100**	**84**	**7**	**8**	**100**

* Total number of cases is lower as information was missing on one of the variables for some tenancy groups

Table A5.10 Proportion of disposable income spent on rent (after Housing Benefit) by disposable weekly income of tenancy group

All tenancies paying rent   *England*

Disposable weekly income of tenancy group	Proportion of disposable income spent on rent (after housing benefit)			
	Less than 20%	20%, less than 33%	33% or more	Total*
				thousands
Under £60	145	16	93	254
£60-£79	133	9	43	186
£80-£119	122	48	57	228
£120-£179	93	73	85	251
£180-£249	98	59	52	208
£250 or more	216	120	67	403
All	**807**	**325**	**397**	**1 529**
				percentages
Under £60	57	6	37	100
£60-£79	72	5	23	100
£80-£119	54	21	25	100
£120-£179	37	29	34	100
£180-£249	47	28	25	100
£250 or more	54	30	17	100
All	**53**	**21**	**26**	**100**

* Total number of cases is lower as information was missing on one of the variables for some tenancy groups

Table A5.11 Proportion of disposable income spent on rent (after Housing Benefit) by disposable weekly income of tenancy group and whether receives Housing Benefit

All tenancies paying rent

England

Disposable weekly income of tenancy group	Tenancies not receiving Housing Benefit				Tenancies receiving Housing Benefit			
	Proportion of disposable income spent on rent (less Housing Benefit)							
	Less than 20%	20%, less than 33%	33% or more	Total*	Less than 20%	20%, less than 33%	33% or more	Total*
								thousands
Under £60	1	5	76	82	143	12	17	171
£60-£79	6	4	40	50	127	5	3	136
£80-£119	18	37	44	99	104	11	14	129
£120-£179	44	66	75	185	49	6	10	65
£180-£249	81	53	50	184	17	5	2	24
£250 or more	201	120	66	387	15	0	1	17
All	**351**	**286**	**351**	**987**	**457**	**39**	**46**	**542**
								percentages
Under £60	2	6	93	100	84	7	10	100
£60-£79	13	8	79	100	94	4	2	100
£80-£119	18	38	44	100	81	9	10	100
£120-£179	24	36	41	100	76	10	15	100
£180-£249	44	29	27	100	70	22	8	100
£250 or more	52	31	17	100	93	-	7	100
All	**36**	**29**	**36**	**100**	**84**	**7**	**8**	**100**

* Total number of cases is lower as information was missing on one of the variables for some tenancy groups

Annex tables
Chapter 6

Table A6.1 How accommodation was found by type of letting
Tenants who had lived at their present address for 5 years or less *England*

Type of letting	How tenant first heard of accommodation					
	Friend, relative or colleague	Knew someone living in accommodation	Advert in newspaper, shop, etc	Agent	Other	Total
						thousands
All assured	447	48	379	250	54	1 179
Regulated	[10]	[2]	[2]	[1]	[2]	[21]
Not accessible to the public, all	101	10	37	14	65	226
Resident landlord	84	13	32	4	2	135
No security	[11]	[1]	[9]	[0]	[0]	[21]
All	652	75	463	269	123	1 582
						percentages
All assured	38	4	32	21	5	100
Regulated	*	*	*	*	*	*
Not accessible to the public, all	44	4	17	6	29	100
Resident landlord	62	10	25	3	1	100
No security	*	*	*	*	*	*
All	41	5	29	17	8	100

*Excludes rent free lettings

Table A6.2 Ease with which accommodation was found by type of letting
*Tenants who had lived at their present address for 5 years or less** *England*

Type of letting	Found with difficulty	Found easily	Total
			thousands
All assured	515	661	1 176
Regulated	[5]	[16]	[21]
Not accessible to the public, all	36	183	219
Resident landlord	27	107	134
No security	5	15	20
All	589	982	1 570
			percentages
All assured	44	56	100
Regulated	*	*	*
Not accessible to the public, all	16	84	100
Resident landlord	20	80	100
No security	26	74	100
All	38	62	100

*Excludes rent free lettings

Table A6.3 Ease with which accommodation was found by comparable weekly rent
Tenants who had lived at their present address for 5 years or less *England*

Comparable weekly rent	Found with difficulty	Found easily	Total
			thousands
Less than £15	4	41	45
£15 less than £20	5	24	29
£20 less than £25	11	54	65
£25 less than £30	32	57	88
£30 less than £40	70	124	194
£40 less than £50	57	81	137
£50 less than £100	275	317	592
£100 or more	107	139	246
All	560	836	1 397
			percentages
Less than £15	9	91	100
£15 less than £20	17	83	100
£20 less than £25	17	83	100
£25 less than £30	36	64	100
£30 less than £40	36	64	100
£40 less than £50	41	59	100
£50 less than £100	46	54	100
£100 or more	44	56	100
All	40	60	100

Table A6.4 Whether a non-returnable fee or deposit was paid by type of letting
Tenants who had lived at their present address for 5 years or less *England*

Type of letting	Deposit	Non-return-able fee	Did not have to pay deposit or fee	Total
				thousands
All assured	805	13	349	1 167
Regulated	[8]	[0]	[11]	[18]
Not accessible to the public, all	26	7	77	110
Resident landlord and no security	48	0	101	150
All	887	21	538	1 445
				percentages
All assured	69	1	30	100
Regulated	*	*	*	*
Not accessible to the public, all	23	7	70	100
Resident landlord and no security	32	-	68	100
All	61	1	37	100

Table A6.5 Whether suitable accommodation had ever been turned down because the deposit was too high by type of letting
Tenants who had lived at their present address for 5 years or less *England*

Type of letting	Had turned down	Had not turned down	Total
			thousands
All assured	231	937	1 169
Regulated	[3]	[16]	[18]
Not accessible to the public	4	106	110
Resident landlord and no security	23	127	150
All	261	1 186	1 447
			percentages
All assured	20	80	100
Regulated	*	*	*
Not accessible to the public, all	4	96	100
Resident landlord and no security	15	85	100
All	18	82	100

Table A6.6 Need for repairs by type of letting
All tenancies *England*

Type of letting	Needs repairs	Does not need repairs	Total
			thousands
All assured	606	595	1 201
All regulated	220	186	406
Not accessible to public, all	143	232	375
Resident landlord and no security	58	122	180
All	1 027	1 135	2 162
			percentages
All assured	50	50	100
All regulated	54	46	100
Not accessible to public, all	38	62	100
Resident landlord and no security	32	68	100
All	48	52	100

Table A6.7 Need for repairs by type of accommodation
All tenancies *England*

Type of accommodation	Needs repairs	Does not need repairs	Total
			thousands
Detached house	94	119	213
Semi-detached house	170	218	388
Terraced house	318	327	645
Purpose-built flat	90	170	260
Converted flat	322	239	560
Other/business premises	34	63	97
All	1 027	1 136	2 162
			percentages
Detached house	44	56	100
Semi-detached house	44	56	100
Terraced house	49	51	100
Purpose-built flat	35	65	100
Converted flat	57	43	100
Other/business premises	35	65	100
All	48	52	100

Table A6.8 Landlord's responsibility for repairs by type of letting
All tenancies *England*

Type of letting	Responsibility for repairs		Total
	Landlord is responsible for some repairs	Landlord is not responsible for any repairs	
			thousands
All assured	1 114	27	1 141
All regulated	359	20	380
Not accessible to public	298	76	375
Resident landlord and no security	173	5	177
All	1 944	129	2 073
			percentages
All assured	98	2	100
All regulated	95	5	100
Not accessible to public	80	20	100
Resident landlord and no security	97	3	100
All	94	6	100

Table A6.9   Responsibility for different types of repairs
All tenancies   *England*

Type of letting and type of repair	Responsibility for repairs				
	Landlord	Tenant	Both landlord and tenant	Other	Total
					thousands
Structural or external					
All assured	1 147	30	5	7	1 188
All regulated	383	14	9	0	406
Not accessible to public, all	295	52	20	9	375
Resident landlord and no security	167	1	3	10	180
All	**1 992**	**96**	**36**	**25**	**2 149**
Water, gas or electricity					
All assured	1 061	101	16	6	1 184
All regulated	243	123	27	4	397
Not accessible to public, all	249	94	22	10	375
Resident landlord and no security	168	3	1	8	180
All	**1 722**	**321**	**66**	**29**	**2 138**
Internal decoration					
All assured	643	475	54	8	1 179
All regulated	38	366	1	1	406
Not accessible to public, all	117	228	26	4	375
Resident landlord and no security	140	27	9	2	179
All	**938**	**1 096**	**90**	**15**	**2 139**
Other non-structural repairs					
All assured	743	361	63	3	1 169
All regulated	103	270	15	1	389
Not accessible to public, all	164	180	26	5	375
Resident landlord and no security	148	18	9	4	179
All	**1 157**	**829**	**113**	**13**	**2 112**
					percentages
Structural or external					
All assured	97	2	0	0	100
All regulated	94	3	2	-	100
Not accessible to public, all	79	14	5	2	100
Resident landlord and no security	93	1	1	5	100
All	**93**	**4**	**2**	**1**	**100**
Water, gas or electricity					
All assured	90	8	1	0	100
All regulated	61	31	7	1	100
Not accessible to public, all	66	25	6	3	100
Resident landlord and no security	93	2	0	5	100
All	**80**	**15**	**3**	**1**	**100**
Internal decoration					
All assured	54	40	5	1	100
All regulated	9	90	0	0	100
Not accessible to public, all	31	61	7	1	100
Resident landlord and no security	79	15	5	1	100
All	**44**	**51**	**4**	**1**	**100**
Other non-structural repairs					
All assured	64	31	5	0	100
All regulated	26	69	4	0	100
Not accessible to public, all	44	48	7	1	100
Resident landlord and no security	83	10	5	2	100
All	**55**	**39**	**5**	**1**	**100**

Table A6.10 Difficulty getting repairs done by type of letting
All tenants who had asked landlord to carry out some repairs *England*

Type of letting	Had difficulty	Did not have difficulty	Total
			thousands
All assured	319	432	751
All regulated	161	168	329
Not accessible to public, all	66	139	205
Resident landlord and no security	16	46	62
All	**563**	**785**	**1 347**
			percentages
All assured	42	58	100
All regulated	49	51	100
Not accessible to public, all	32	68	100
Resident landlord and no security	26	74	100
All	**42**	**58**	**100**

Table A6.11 Tenants' description of their relationship with landlord by type of letting
All tenancies *England*

Type of letting	Relationship with landlord			
	On good terms	On poor terms	Neither	Total
				thousands
Assured	286	13	76	376
Assured shorthold	616	36	173	825
All regulated	274	41	89	405
Not accessible to public, all	331	6	39	375
Resident landlord and no security	159	5	16	179
All	**1 666**	**101**	**393**	**2 160**
				percentage
Assured	76	4	20	100
Assured shorthold	75	4	21	100
All regulated	68	10	22	100
Not accessible to public, all	88	2	10	100
Resident landlord and no security	89	3	9	100
All	**77**	**5**	**18**	**100**

Table A6.12 Tenants' description of their relationship with landlord by type of landlord
All tenancies *England*

Type of landlord	Relationship with landlord			
	On good terms	On poor terms	Neither	Total
				thousands
Resident landlord	150	3	12	165
Private individual	1 101	70	268	1 439
Employer	243	5	32	280
Property company	110	15	46	170
Other	62	7	35	104
All	**1 666**	**101**	**393**	**2 160**
				percentages
Resident landlord	91	2	7	100
Private individual	76	5	19	100
Employer	87	2	12	100
Property company	64	9	27	100
Other	59	7	34	100
All	**77**	**5**	**18**	**100**

Table A6.13 Reasons given for being on poor terms with their landlord
Tenants who said they were on poor terms with their landlord *England*

Reason	*thousands*	*percentage**
Conflict about repairs	46	58
Landlord unpleasant/untrustworthy/difficult	33	41
Landlord hard to contact	29	36
Other	21	26
Landlord making financial demands	15	19
Landlord taking action to evict tenant	14	18
Landlord using threats/intimidating behaviour	13	17
Landlord entering premises without permission	6	7
Total	**176**	

*Each tenancy group could give more than one reason for being on poor terms with the landlord so the percentages add to more than 100

Table A6.14 Tenants' description of their relationship with landlord by the need for repairs in the accommodation
All tenancies *England*

Need for repairs	Relationship with landlord			
	On good terms	On poor terms	Neither	Total
				thousands
Accommodation needs some kind of repairs	662	88	275	1 025
Accommodation does not need repairs	1 002	13	119	1 134
Total	**1 664**	**101**	**393**	**2 158**
				percentages
Accommodation needs some kind of repairs	65	9	27	100
Accommodation does not need repairs	88	1	10	100
Total	**77**	**5**	**18**	**100**

Table A6.15 Tenants who reported being asked to leave the accommodation or whose landlord had done something to make them uncomfortable or want to leave, by type of letting
All tenancies *England*

Type of letting	Tenant has:		Total
	reported being asked to leave/made uncomfortable	not reported such problems	
			thousands
Assured	34	342	376
Assured shorthold	49	775	825
All regulated	56	351	407
Not accessible to public	15	361	375
Resident landlord and no security	5	175	179
All	**159**	**2 003**	**2 162**
			percentages
Assured	9	91	100
Assured shorthold	6	94	100
All regulated	14	86	100
Not accessible to public	4	96	100
Resident landlord and no security	2	98	100
All	**7**	**93**	**100**

Table A6.16 Number of moves by type of letting
All tenancies   *England*

Type of letting	Number of moves							
	No moves in previous 10 years	Moved within 10 years but not 3 years	**Number of moves in last three years**			Total who have moved in last 3 years	Total	*Mean number of moves in last three years**
			One move	Two moves	Three or more moves			
							thousands	
Assured	14	56	97	77	124	298	372	2.6
Assured shorthold	6	101	222	153	339	714	821	2.7
All assured	20	156	319	230	467	1 016	1 193	2.7
All regulated	306	100	0	0	0	0	406	-
Not accessible to public, all	118	118	72	30	37	139	375	2.2
Resident landlord and no security	19	36	39	43	41	123	178	2.4
All	**463**	**410**	**430**	**304**	**545**	**1 279**	**2 153**	**2.6**
							percentages	
Assured	4	15	26	21	34	81	100	
Assured shorthold	1	12	27	19	41	87	100	
All assured	2	13	27	19	39	85	100	
All regulated	75	25	-	-	-	-	100	
Not accessible to public, all	31	32	19	8	10	37	100	
Resident landlord and no security	11	20	22	24	23	69	100	
All	**22**	**19**	**20**	**14**	**25**	**59**	**100**	

* The mean is based on number of tenants who had moved in the last three years

Table A6.17 Number of moves by tenancy group composition
All tenancies   *England*

Tenancy group composition	Number of moves							
	No moves in previous 10 years	Moved within 10 years but not 3 years	**Number of moves in last three years**			Total who have moved in last 3 years	Total	*Mean number of moves in last three years**
			One move	Two moves	Three or more moves			
							thousands	
One adult aged 16-59	57	144	191	145	265	601	803	2.7
Two adults aged 16-59	27	56	77	65	147	289	372	2.9
Couple with dependent child(ren)	25	78	75	38	55	168	272	2.2
Lone parent with dependent child(ren)	7	11	38	23	33	94	112	2.2
Large mainly adult	45	29	27	26	41	94	168	2.5
Two adults at least one 60 or over	94	21	13	1	2	16	130	1.3
One adult 60 or over	209	72	9	5	2	16	297	1.6
All types	**463**	**410**	**430**	**304**	**545**	**1 279**	**2 153**	**2.6**
							percentages	
One adult aged 16-59	7	18	24	18	33	75	100	
Two adults aged 16-59	7	15	21	18	40	78	100	
Couple with dependent child(ren)	9	29	28	14	20	62	100	
Lone parent with dependent child(ren)	6	10	34	21	29	83	100	
Large mainly adult	27	17	16	16	24	56	100	
Two adults at least one 60 or over	72	16	10	1	1	12	100	
One adult 60 or over	70	24	3	2	1	5	100	
All types	**22**	**19**	**20**	**14**	**25**	**59**	**100**	

* The mean is based on the number of tenants who had moved in the last three years

Table A6.18 Previous accommodation by type of letting

Tenants who had moved in last three years   *England*

Type of letting	Last accommodation							
	At home with parents or family	Owner occupier	Other privately rented accommodation	Accommodation that went with a job	Local authority or housing association	Lived abroad	Other (e.g. hostel, student accommodation)	Total
								thousands
Assured	47	35	140	11	17	7	45	302
Assured shorthold	153	82	350	15	25	17	74	716
All assured	200	116	490	26	42	24	119	1 018
Not accessible to public, all	23	28	24	48	3	5	8	139
Resident landlord and no security	31	5	53	5	5	1	23	123
All	**254**	**150**	**568**	**79**	**50**	**30**	**150**	**1 280**
								percentages
Assured	16	12	46	4	6	2	15	100
Assured shorthold	21	11	49	2	4	2	10	100
All assured	20	11	48	3	4	2	12	100
Not accessible to public, all	17	20	17	34	2	4	6	100
Resident landlord and no security	25	4	44	4	4	1	19	100
All	**20**	**12**	**44**	**6**	**4**	**2**	**12**	**100**

Table A6.19 Main reason for leaving last accommodation by type of letting

Tenants who had moved in last three years   *England*

Type of letting	Reason for leaving last accommodation							
	Lifestage	Employment	Housing costs	Housing general	Locational	Forced to leave	Other reasons	Total
								thousands
Assured	36	21	12	59	18	41	32	220
Assured shorthold	71	71	21	111	43	89	78	483
All assured	107	92	33	170	61	130	111	703
Not accessible to public, all	9	53	3	11	1	6	16	99
Resident landlord and no security	28	25	2	6	5	22	20	109
All	**145**	**171**	**39**	**187**	**67**	**157**	**146**	**911***
								percentages
Assured	16	10	6	27	8	19	15	100
Assured shorthold	15	15	4	23	9	18	16	100
All assured	15	13	5	24	9	18	16	100
Not accessible to public, all	9	54	3	11	1	6	16	100
Resident landlord and no security	26	23	2	6	5	20	18	100
All	**16**	**19**	**4**	**20**	**7**	**17**	**16**	**100**

*Cases for which information was available

Table A6.20 Distance moved between current and last accommodation by type of letting

Tenants who had moved in last three years   *England*

Type of letting	Distance moved							
	Less than 1 mile	1 mile but less than 2	2 miles but less than 5	5 miles but less than 10	10 miles but less than 50	50 miles or further	Lived abroad	Total
								thousands
Assured	53	30	43	16	21	25	3	190
Assured shorthold	79	66	124	46	60	65	19	458
All assured	132	96	167	62	80	90	22	648
Not accessible to public, all	20	9	10	12	12	29	11	102
Resident landlord and no security	8	4	5	2	3	8	0	30
All	**159**	**110**	**182**	**75**	**95**	**126**	**33**	**779***
								percentages
Assured	28	16	23	8	11	13	2	100
Assured shorthold	17	14	27	10	13	14	4	100
All assured	20	15	26	10	12	14	3	100
Not accessible to public, all	19	9	10	11	12	28	11	100
Resident landlord and no security	26	14	17	7	10	26	-	100
All	**20**	**14**	**23**	**10**	**12**	**16**	**4**	**100**

*Cases for which information was available

Table A6.21 Expectations of moving by type of letting

All tenancies* *England*

Type of letting	Expectations of moving					
	Expect to move within one year	Expect to move sometime	**All expecting to move**	Do not expect to move	Uncertain	**Total**
						thousands
Assured	131	172	303	42	17	362
Assured shorthold	364	335	699	65	24	788
All assured	495	507	1 002	107	41	1 151
All regulated	13	113	126	257	20	403
Not accessible to public, all	63	204	267	94	8	369
Resident landlord and no security	51	79	130	25	13	168
All	**621**	**904**	**1 525**	**483**	**82**	**2 090**
						percentages
Assured	36	48	84	12	5	100
Assured shorthold	46	42	89	8	3	100
All assured	43	44	87	9	4	100
All regulated	3	28	31	64	5	100
Not accessible to public, all	17	55	72	25	2	100
Resident landlord and no security	30	47	77	15	8	100
All	**30**	**43**	**73**	**23**	**4**	**100**

*Questions on future intentions were only asked if the informant was the head of tenancy group or his partner

Table A6.22 Expectations of moving by tenancy group composition

All tenancies• *England*

Tenancy group composition	Expectations of moving					
	Expect to move within one year	Expect to move sometime	**All expecting to move**	Do not expect to move	Uncertain	**Total**
						thousands
One adult aged 16-59	312	359	671	75	41	787
Two adults aged 16-59	156	166	322	25	9	357
Couple with dependent child(ren)	72	156	228	34	8	270
Lone parent with dependent child(ren)	27	68	95	13	5	112
Large mainly adult	43	62	105	36	2	143
Two adults at least one 60 or over	4	35	39	86	2	127
One adult 60 or over	8	58	66	213	16	294
All	**621**	**904**	**1 525**	**483**	**82**	**2 090**
						percentages
One adult aged 16-59	40	46	85	10	5	100
Two adults aged 16-59	44	47	90	7	3	100
Couple with dependent child(ren)	27	58	84	13	3	100
Lone parent with dependent child(ren)	24	60	85	12	4	100
Large mainly adult	30	43	73	25	1	100
Two adults at least one 60 or over	3	28	31	68	2	100
One adult 60 or over	3	20	22	72	5	100
All	**30**	**43**	**73**	**23**	**4**	**100**

*Questions on future intentions were only asked if the informant was the head of tenancy group or his partner

Table A6.23 Expectations of buying in the future by type of letting
All tenancies   *England*

| Type of letting | Expectations of buying | | | | | |
	Already owns	In the process of buying, expects to own within one year	Expects to own sometime	Does not expect to own	Uncertain	Total
						thousands
Assured	9	44	176	124	10	363
Assured shorthold	31	116	408	212	21	788
All assured	40	160	584	336	31	1 151
All regulated	0	7	44	352	0	403
Not accessible to public, all	18	29	139	181	2	370
Resident landlord and no security	0	16	82	67	3	168
All	**59**	**212**	**849**	**936**	**36**	**2 092**
						percentages
Assured	3	12	48	34	3	100
Assured shorthold	4	15	52	27	3	100
All assured	4	14	51	29	3	100
All regulated	-	2	11	88	-	100
Not accessible to public, all	5	8	38	49	0	100
Resident landlord and no security	-	10	49	40	2	100
All	**3**	**10**	**41**	**45**	**2**	**100**

Table A6.24 Expectations of buying in the future by tenancy group composition
All tenancies   *England*

| Tenancy group composition | Expectations of buying | | | | | |
	Already owns	In the process of buying, expects to own within one year	Expects to own sometime	Does not expect to own	Uncertain	Total
						thousands
One adult aged 16-59	27	77	421	240	22	787
Two adults aged 16-59	10	72	184	88	3	358
Couple with dependent child(ren)	13	39	126	90	4	271
Lone parent with dependent child(ren)	2	7	53	46	4	112
Large mainly adult	3	13	55	71	1	143
Two adults at least one 60 or over	2	5	7	112	2	127
One adult 60 or over	3	0	4	288	0	294
All	**59**	**212**	**849**	**936**	**36**	**2 092**
						percentages
One adult aged 16-59	3	10	54	30	3	100
Two adults aged 16-59	3	20	51	25	1	100
Couple with dependent child(ren)	5	14	46	33	1	100
Lone parent with dependent child(ren)	2	6	47	42	3	100
Large mainly adult	2	9	38	50	1	100
Two adults at least one 60 or over	1	4	5	88	1	100
One adult 60 or over	1	-	1	98	-	100
All	**3**	**10**	**41**	**45**	**2**	**100**

Table A6.25 Whether tenants expected to buy their next accommodation by type of letting

Tenants who said they would buy accommodation in the future　　　　　　　　　*England*

Type of letting	Next move			
	Rent again	Buy	Don't know	Total
				thousands
Assured	117	77	16	210
Assured shorthold	299	195	14	508
All assured	417	273	31	721
All regulated	7	24	3	34
Not accessible to public, all	80	75	4	159
Resident landlord and no security	63	33	2	98
All	**567**	**405**	**40**	**1 011**
				percentages
Assured	56	37	8	100
Assured shorthold	59	38	3	100
All assured	58	38	4	100
All regulated	21	71	9	100
Not accessible to public, all	50	47	2	100
Resident landlord and no security	64	34	2	100
All	**56**	**40**	**4**	**100**

Table A6.26 Whether tenants expected to buy their next accommodation by tenancy group composition

Tenants who said they would buy accommodation in the future　　　　　　　　　*England*

Tenancy group composition	Next move			
	Rent again	Buy	Don't know	Total
				thousands
One adult aged 16-59	316	144	29	489
Two adults aged 16-59	112	129	4	245
Couple with dependent child(ren)	70	78	4	152
Lone parent with dependent child(ren)	27	21	2	50
Large mainly adult	37	24	1	62
Two adults at least one 60 or over	[3]	[5]	[0]	[8]
One adult 60 or over	[1]	[4]	[0]	[5]
All	**567**	**405**	**40**	**1 011**
				percentages
One adult aged 16-59	65	29	6	100
Two adults aged 16-59	46	53	2	100
Couple with dependent child(ren)	46	51	3	100
Lone parent with dependent child(ren)	54	42	4	100
Large mainly adult	59	38	2	100
Two adults at least one 60 or over	*	*	*	*
One adult 60 or over	*	*	*	*
All	**56**	**40**	**4**	**100**

Table A6.27 Whether tenant is on a waiting list for social rented sector accommodation by type of letting

All tenancies　　　　　　　　　*England*

Type of letting	Whether on waiting list		
	On list	Not on list	Total
			thousands
All assured	187	1 017	1 204
All regulated	59	349	407
Not accessible to public, all	34	341	375
Resident landlord and no security	11	169	180
All	**291**	**1 875**	**2 166**
			percentages
All assured	16	84	100
All regulated	14	86	100
Not accessible to public, all	9	91	100
Resident landlord and no security	6	94	100
All	**13**	**87**	**100**

Table A6.28 Whether tenant is on a waiting list for social rented sector accommodation by tenancy group composition

All tenancies　　　　　　　　　*England*

Tenancy group composition	Whether on waiting list		
	On list	Not on list	Total
			thousands
One adult aged 16-59	81	728	809
Two adults aged 16-59	37	337	374
Couple with dependent child(ren)	57	217	274
Lone parent with dependent child(ren)	44	69	113
Large mainly adult	12	158	170
Two adults at least one 60 or over	24	106	130
One adult 60 or over	37	260	297
All	**291**	**1 875**	**2 166**
			percentages
One adult aged 16-59	10	90	100
Two adults aged 16-59	10	90	100
Couple with dependent child(ren)	21	79	100
Lone parent with dependent child(ren)	39	61	100
Large mainly adult	7	93	100
Two adults at least one 60 or over	18	82	100
One adult 60 or over	12	88	100
All	**13**	**87**	**100**

Table A6.29 Whether tenant is on a waiting list for social rented sector accommodation by employment status of head of tenancy group

All tenancies　　　　　　　　　*England*

Employment status	Whether on waiting list		
	On list	Not on list	Total
			thousands
Working full time	102	912	1014
Working part time	19	86	104
Unemployed	80	222	302
Retired	45	319	364
Full-time education	5	189	194
Other/economically inactive	41	146	187
All	**291**	**1 873**	**2 164**
			percentages
Working full time	10	90	100
Working part time	18	82	100
Unemployed	26	74	100
Retired	12	88	100
Full-time education	2	98	100
Other/economically inactive	22	78	100
All	**13**	**87**	**100**

Appendix A
Definitions and terms

Arrears

Rent arrears was defined as being at least two weeks behind with the rent.

Bedroom standard

This concept is used as an indicator of occupation density. A standard number of bedrooms is allocated to each household in accordance with its age/sex/marital status composition and the relationship of the members to one another. A separate bedroom is allocated to each married couple, any other person aged 21 or over, each pair of adolescents aged 10 - 20 of the same sex, and each pair of children under 10. Any unpaired person aged 10 - 20 is paired, if possible with a child under 10 of the same sex, or, if that is not possible, he or she is given a separate bedroom, as is any unpaired child under 10. This standard is then compared with the actual number of bedrooms (including bedsitters) available for the sole use of the household, and differences are tabulated. Bedrooms converted to other uses are not counted as available unless they have been denoted as bedrooms by the informants; bedrooms not actually in use are counted unless uninhabitable.

Dependent children

Dependent children are persons aged under 16, or single persons aged 16 to 18 and in full-time education.

Economic activity

Working: employees and self-employed persons, people on Government Training Schemes.

Unemployed: people without a job who were available to start work in the two weeks after interview and had either looked for work in the four weeks before the interview or were waiting to start a new job they had already obtained; this is the ILO definition of unemployed.

Economically inactive: all others who were not working; they include people who were permanently sick or disabled, retired, in full-time education or looking after the family or home.

Economically active persons are those who were working or unemployed in the week before interview. Full-time students are classified according to their reports of what they were doing in the reference week (for example, if they had a full-time job in their vacation, they would be classified as working full time. The exception is people working part time because they are at school or college who are classified as full-time students.

Persons on Government Training Schemes are classified as working full time.

Family

A family unit is defined as one of:

a   a married or cohabiting couple with no children
b   a married or cohabiting couple/lone parent and their never-married child(ren), provided these children have no children of their own
c   one person

Two people of the same sex who described themselves as 'partners' were classified as a cohabiting couple.

In general families cannot span more than two generations, ie grandparents and grandchildren cannot belong to the same family. The exception to this is where there is no parent in the household and it is established that a grandparent is acting in place of a parent.

Adopted and step-children belong to the same family as their adoptive/step-parents. Foster children, however, are not part of the foster-parents' family.

Household

A household is defined as one person living alone or group of people who have the address as their only or main residence and who either share one meal a day or share a living room.

Head of household

The head of the household is a member of the household and (in order of precedence) either the husband of the person, or the person, who:

a   owns the household accommodation
b   is legally responsible for the rent or
c   has the accommodation by virtue of some relationship to the owner in cases where the owner or tenant is not a household member

When two members of a different sex have equal claim, the male is taken as the household head. When two members of the same sex have equal claim, the elder is taken as the household head.

Household membership

People are regarded as living at the address if they (or the informant) consider the address to be their main residence. There are, however, certain rules which take priority over this criterion.

a   Children aged 16 or over who live away from home for the purposes of work or study and come home only for the holidays are not included at the parental address under any circumstances

b   Children of any age away from home in a temporary job and children under 16 at boarding school are always included in the parental household.

c   People who have been away from the address continuously for six months or longer are excluded.

d   People who have been living continuously at the address for six months or longer are included even if they have their main residence elsewhere.

e   Addresses used only as second homes are never counted as main residences.

Household type

The main classification of household type uses the following categories:

*   Married couple with no dependent children
    (includes married and cohabiting couples with no children or with non-dependent children only)

*   Married couple with dependent children
    (includes married and cohabiting couples with dependent children)

*   Lone parent family
    (includes one parent with dependent children)

*   Large adult household
    (includes lone parents with non-dependent children and households containing more than one couple or lone parent family)

*   One male

*   One female

The married couple and lone parent household types may include one-person family units in addition to the couple/lone parent family.

Income

Tables show the disposable weekly income of the tenancy group. Income includes earnings from employment, profit or loss from self employment, state benefits and pensions, income from investments and other receipts such as maintenance allowances and student grants. Tax, National Insurance, pension contributions, union subscriptions and regular maintenance payments have been deducted from earnings to arrive at disposable income.

Letting

Major changes were made by the Housing Act 1988 which took effect in January 1989 but lettings already in existence then were not affected. In this report the term "letting" is used for convenience for arrangements which in legal terms may be licences as well as for tenancies. Strictly a person who has been granted a letting is a "lessee" but the term "tenant" is used because it is more readily understood. The term will not always be legally accurate as it is used to cover licensees as well as tenants proper.

Regulated tenancies (with registered and unregistered rents)

Most private lettings with a starting date before January 1989 are Regulated tenancies which may be furnished or unfurnished. No new Regulated tenancies could be created after January 1989 but the status of Regulated tenancies in existence at that time remains unchanged. On first succession the tenancy remains regulated if the successor is the spouse. Any other qualifying members of the family succeed to an Assured tenancy. There is a right to a second succession but on the second succession the tenancy always becomes an Assured tenancy.

Either the landlord or the tenant can apply to the Rent Officer for registration of a fair rent. The fair rent as registered becomes the maximum that the landlord can legally charge. In fixing a fair rent the Rent Officer is required to have regard to all the circumstances other than the personal circumstances and to assume that the demand for accommodation in the area of the kind for which rent is being fixed does not exceed the supply. Fair rents can be reviewed at two-year intervals. Any increase takes effect immediately. The survey distinguishes between Regulated tenancies where a fair rent has been registered and those where one has not.

Tenants have full security with a right to two successions (see above). Possession can be granted to the landlord by the County Court only on one of the grounds specified by the Rent Act. They include misbehaviour by the tenant (for instance non-payment of the rent) and a number of mandatory grounds for possession for example when the owner let the dwelling to the tenant with an express statement (in writing) of his intention to return there or move there on retirement or on leaving the armed forces.

Resident landlord lettings

Lettings where the landlord lives in the same building are normally outside the rules governing Regulated or Assured tenancies and are subject to different provisions of the Housing Act 1988. They can be either furnished or unfurnished.

In practice, rent is agreed between landlord and tenant though for lettings whose rent was last agreed before 15 January 1989 with a right to apply to a Rent Tribunal for a reasonable rent to be fixed.

The landlord does not need any special grounds to apply to the County Court for a possession order. The court has to grant the order if satisfied that the letting was by a resident landlord but can suspend the order for not more than 6 weeks (3 months for lettings beginning before 16 January 1989).

Protected Shorthold and pre-1989 Assured tenancies

These two classes of letting were brought into being by the Housing Act 1980. Protected Shorthold lettings were a type of Regulated letting and like other Regulated lettings no new ones could be created after January 1989. Protected Shorthold lettings had to be for a period of at least one year and not more than five years. Assured tenancies prior to January 1989 could apply only to dwellings newly built or substantially renovated since the 1980 Act came into force and then only if owned by a body or person approved by the Secretary of State for the Environment.

The setting of rent for Protected Shorthold tenancies is as for other Regulated tenancies; for Assured tenancies rent is agreed between tenant and landlord.

Protected Shorthold tenancies have full security (as for other Regulated tenancies) for the term of the shorthold but none after that. For Assured tenancies, security is modelled on the law governing tenancies of business premises which provides a rather wider range of grounds for possession than did the Rent Acts.

Lettings with no security (accessible to the public)

In the surveys, lettings not accessible to the public are treated separately. Lettings accessible to the public that are outside the Rent Acts comprise lettings for the purpose of a holiday and lettings where the landlord provides meals and a substantial amount of attendance and lettings where a licence to occupy and not a tenancy was granted to the occupant. In the survey lettings are classified according to how the respondents described them to interviewers. Whether an arrangement that purports to be a licence really is such and not a tenancy can only be decided by a Court. One of the defining characteristics of a tenancy is exclusive possession whereas a licence to occupy does not confer exclusive possession. The distinction was the subject of a sequence of Court cases of which the leading case is Street v Mountford decided by the House of Lords in 1985. Rent is agreed between landlord and tenant and tenants have no security of tenure.

Lettings not accessible to the public

These comprise lettings of residential accommodation with business premises or farms lettings by employers to employees by virtue of their employment lettings by universities and colleges to their students and lettings at a low rent or rent free to relatives and friends of the owner. Being inaccessible to the public is not as such a legal category but all the groups listed are outside the Rent Acts as regards security of tenure. Residential accommodation rented with business premises and farms is governed by the law that applies to rented business premises and rented farms. Where accommodation is let by an employer by virtue of employment the Court must grant possession if (i) the tenant has left the employment and (ii) the employer can show that he needs the accommodation in order to fill the vacancy. Accommodation occupied rent free or at very low rents is excluded from the Rent Acts and the Housing Acts by the exclusion of lettings where the rent is less than two thirds of the rateable value or where there is no rateable value the rent is less than £1000 a year in London and £250 elsewhere.

Assured tenancies

All tenancies starting on 15 January 1989 or later are Assured or Assured Shorthold unless they are resident landlord lettings or fall into one of the other excluded categories described above. If there is no written notice that the tenancy is an Assured Shorthold it is a normal Assured tenancy.

Rent is agreed at the beginning of the tenancy by the tenant and landlord. At the end of the agreed term (if the letting is for a fixed term) or after at least one year (if it is a periodic tenancy) the rent may be reviewed. In the event of a dispute if there is no rent review mechanism in the tenancy agreement the tenant may apply to the Rent Assessment Committee to determine the rent which is required to be an open market rent.

The landlord can seek repossession only on one of the grounds specified.

Assured Shorthold tenancies
Tenancies starting from 15 January 1989 or later could be Assured Shorthold. The landlord has to give written notice at the outset that the tenancy is an Assured Shorthold. The letting is for a fixed term of at least 6 months.

Rent is agreed between landlord and tenant subject to the tenant having the right during the first term of the tenancy to apply to the Rent Assessment Committee for a determination of the rent on the grounds that the rent is "significantly higher than the rents payable under similar tenancies ... in the locality".

Security is the same as for Assured tenancies during the fixed term at the end of which the landlord is entitled to possession.

Letting classification
For the analysis in this report each group with a separate agreement with the landlord (tenancy group) has been allocated to a "subsector" defined in terms of broad legal status:

Resident landlord lettings were to tenants whose landlord was a private individual living in the same building or in the case of purpose-built flats in the same flat.

No security lettings are those described above as lettings with no security (accessible to the public). They include:

- non-exclusive occupancy agreements
- rental purchase agreements
- holiday lets
- lettings with meals provided.

Not accessible to the public lettings are those defined above as such. They include:

- accommodation that went with the job of someone in the tenancy group
- lettings by universities and colleges

- company licences
- lettings to friends and relatives of the landlord.

They are divided into:
- rented
- rent free.

Regulated lettings were all lettings starting before January 1989 except any that were: resident landlord lettings Protected Shorthold pre-1989 Assured lettings with no security and lettings not accessible to the public are as defined above. They were divided into:

- with registered rent rent registered at a rent office
- without registered rent rent not registered at a rent office.

Protected Shorthold and pre-1989 Assured lettings, Assured Shorthold lettings and Assured lettings are as defined above.

Marital status

Marital status is based on the informant's opinion and may differ from legal marital status.
Unrelated adults of the same or opposite sex are classed as cohabiting if they consider themselves to be living together as a couple. Cohabiting takes precedence over other categories.

Non self-contained accommodation

Households were classified as living in non self-contained accommodation if they shared a kitchen, bathroom or toilet with another household, or if they shared a hall or staircase which was needed in order to get from one part of the accommodation to another. Households which shared a common entrance hall, but otherwise had all their accommodation behind their own front door were not counted as living in non self-contained accommodation.

Rooms

These are defined as habitable rooms, including kitchens at least 2 metres wide, and excluding rooms which are used for business purposes and those not normally used for living in, such as bathrooms, toilets, storerooms, pantries, cellars and garages. Shared kitchens are not included in the room count.

Rent

Comparable weekly rent was defined as the charge for the accommodation minus any additional charges for services like telephone usage or electricity. Water rates were not included in rent.

Socio-economic group

The basic occupational classification used is the Registrar General's socio-economic grouping in Standard occupational classification, OPCS (HMSO,London,1990). A collapsed version of this classification has been used in the tables as follows:

Descriptive definition	SEG numbers
Professional	3,4
Employers and managers	1,2,13
Intermediate and junior non-manual	5,6
Skilled manual	8,9,12,14
Semi-skilled manual and personal services	7,10,15
Unskilled manual	11

Occupation details were collected for economically active and retired people. Unemployed people are coded according to their last occupation, and retired people are coded according to their previous main occupation.

Tenancy

The renting agreement whereby tenants rent the accommodation or occupy it free of charge (see letting above).

Head of tenancy

The head of tenancy is defined as the person in whose name the accommodation is rented unless that person is a married or co-habiting women. In such cases it is the women's husband or partner who is defined as the tenant in the same way that the definition of head of household, by statistical convention, to the male partner.

Tenancy group membership

Everyone covered by the same renting agreement who share the legal status conferred by the agreement and their accommodation is paid for by a single rent.

Tenancy group type

The main characteristics of tenancy group type use the following categories:

- One adult (aged 16-59)

- Two adults (aged 16-59)

- Couple with dependent child(ren)

- Lone parent with dependent child(ren)

- Large mainly adult (includes lone parents with non-dependent children and households containing more than one couple or lone parent family)

- Two adults (at least one 60 or over)

- One adult (60 or over)

Waiting list applicants

Waiting list applicants are families or individuals who are on a waiting list for council or housing association accommodation. They could be couple or lone parent families, one-person family units, or children aged 16 or over. Groups which contain the household head are referred to as *'existing households';* those which do not contain the household head are referred to as *'potential new households'.*

Appendix B
Survey design and response

1. Sample design

The SEH sample is selected from the small users version of the postcode address file (PAF). A two-stage sample design is used with postcode sectors, which are similar in size to wards, as the primary sampling units (PSUs). The design involves both stratification and clustering.

Initially, postcode sectors in England were allocated to major strata on the basis of region and area type. The sectors were distributed between 9 regions and a distinction was made between metropolitan and non-metropolitan areas resulting in 15 major strata.

Within each major stratum, postcode sectors were stratified according to selected housing and economic indicators from the 1981 Census. Sectors were initially ranked according to the proportion of households in privately rented accommodation, then divided into four bands containing approximately the same number of households . Within each band, sectors were re-ranked according to the proportion of households living in local authority accommodation and bands were subdivided to give eight bands of approximately equal size per major stratum (120 bands in all). Finally, within each band, sectors were re-ranked according to the proportion of household heads in socio-economic groups 1 to 5 or 13 (Professionals, Employers and Managers).

Major strata were divided into 780 minor strata of equal size, the number of minor strata being proportional to the size of the major stratum. One PSU was selected from each minor stratum and 65 selections were allocated to each month of the year so as to provide, as far as possible, a nationally representative sample each quarter. Within each PSU, 36 addresses were selected, representing one interviewer quota.

The total set sample size of the SEH was 28,080 addresses (36 addresses in 780 quotas). The delivery point count for England at the time of the PSU selection was 20,304,925. The sampling fraction is therefore 1/723.

Conversion of addresses to households

Most addresses contain just one household, a few contain no households (for example, institutions and addresses used solely for business purposes), while others contain more than one private household. On the SEH, interviews were carried out with all households at multi-household addresses.

Table B1 shows the number of private households identified at the 28,080 sampled addresses.

Table B1 The sample of addresses and households
England

Selected addresses	28 080
Ineligible addresses:	
Demolished or derelict	247
Used solely for business purposes	868
Temporary accommodation only	248
Empty	1 377
Address not traced	454
Other ineligible	196
Total ineligible	**3 390**
Addresses at which interviews were taken	24 690
Extra households identified at multi-household addresses	685
Total effective sample of households	**25 375**
Non contact	1 401
Refusal	3 509
Total number of households interviewed*	**20 307**

* 158 cases were lost in transmission

2. Data collection

Information for the SEH is collected week by week throughout the year by computer assisted personal interview (CAPI). The survey runs on a financial year and interviews took place between April 1993 and March 1994. Interviews are sought with household head or partner at each sampled household. In certain circumstances, an interview may be carried out with another household member if the head or partner is not available. This was necessary in only 2% of households.

Interviewers working on the SEH form part of the overall Social Survey field force. Before working on SEH, they attend a briefing session and new recruits are accompanied in the field by a training officer.

3. Response

Table B2 shows the response rate among eligible households for each region and England as a whole. Overall, interviews were achieved with 80% of eligible households, 6% were not contacted and 14% refused to take part. Response rates of at least 80% were achieved in all regions except the North (78%) and Greater London (73%). The relatively low rate in the North was attributable to a higher than average non-contact rate while, in London, the proportion of refusals and the proportion of non-contacts were both high.

Table B2 Response

	Interview	Non contact	Refusal	Total
England	80	6	14	100
North	78	7	14	100
Yorkshire and Humberside	83	4	13	100
North West	81	5	14	100
East Midlands	83	5	13	100
West Midlands	83	5	13	100
East Anglia	81	4	14	100
Greater London	73	10	16	100
Rest of South East	80	5	14	100
South West	83	4	12	100

Appendix C
Grossing

In this report results are presented as estimated total numbers of tenancies, and as percentages based on those numbers rather than directly on the sample numbers. This annex describes how the sample was grossed up to provide the estimated totals, and shows the effect on a number of key household measures: tenure, household size, household composition and economic status.

Outline of the grossing

The grossing method is similar to the method used for the predecessor to the SEH, the Housing Trailer to the 1991 Labour Force Survey (ref 1).

There are several stages. The first is to use the sampling fraction and response rate. Broadly, if the end result of sampling and non-response is that there is an interview for one in a thousand households, the grossing factor is one thousand. The initial grossing compensates for different response rates among households that were more or less difficult to find at home, measured by the number of calls needed to make contact.

The remaining stages adjust the factors so that there is an exact match with population estimates, separately for males and females and for broad age groups. An important feature of the SEH grossing is that this is done by adjusting the factors for whole households, not by adjusting the factors for individuals. The population figures being matched exclude people who are not covered by the SEH, that is those in bed-and-breakfast accommodation, hostels, residential care homes and other institutions. There is a final stage which applies only to private tenancy groups. This compensates for the small dropout between the main stage of the survey and the private renters module.

As mentioned in the Introduction to the report, a comparison of SEH results with those from other surveys, the Labour Force Survey in particular, suggested that the early phases of the SEH were under-representing private renters, particularly those in one-person households. It was important to provide comparability with previous estimates which were based on surveys linked to the LFS (ref 1). Factors were therefore calculated so that the SEH proportions in each tenure and proportions of one person households would match those in the corresponding LFS sample. This adjustment was carried out before the grossing described above.

The adjustment to the LFS is not ideal and it is not intended to repeat it in future years. Further study of the LFS has indicated that it overstates the number of one person households to some extent. Although the SEH, before adjustment, was undoubtedly understating such households, the proportions after adjustment are too high.

The effect of grossing

Tables C1 to C4 show the effects of grossing on a number of key household characteristics. The main points are:

Tenure (Table C1) - the proportion of households renting privately increases from 8.4% to 9.7% and the proportion of local authority tenants falls from 19.9% to 18.7%. Proportions of owner occupiers are little affected by the grossing. It is not just the adjustment to LFS proportions that boosts the proportion of private renters; the grossing proper adds 0.5 percentage points.

Household size (Table C2) - one person households increase from 24.8% to 28.7%. The adjustment to LFS proportions added 2.5 percentage points and the grossing proper a further 1.4.

Table C1 Tenure

Grossing	Owner occupiers		Rented				All
	Owned outright	With mortgage	Local authority	Housing Assoc	Private unfurn	Private furnished	
							percentage
Ungrossed	25.0	42.6	19.9	4.1	5.9	2.6	100.0
LFS adjustment	25.7	42.7	18.8	3.6	6.4	2.8	100.0
Grossed	25.2	42.7	18.7	3.7	6.6	3.1	100.0

Table C2 Household size

Grossing	One person	Two persons	Three persons	Four persons	Five persons	Six or more pers	All	Mean
							percentagenumber	
Ungrossed	24.8	34.8	16.8	15.7	5.7	2.2	100.0	2.503
LFS adjustment	27.3	33.7	16.2	15.2	5.5	2.1	100.0	2.454
Grossed	28.7	33.3	16.2	14.7	5.2	2.0	100.0	2.415

Table C3   Household type
All tenancies

Grossing	With dependent children		Non-dependent children only		No children			All
	Couple*	Lone parent	Couple*	Lone parent	Couple only	Other multi	One person	
	percentage							
Ungrossed	25.6	5.9	8.3	3.5	28.8	3.0	24.8	100.0
LFS adjustment	24.8	5.6	8.1	3.3	28.0	2.9	27.3	100.0
Grossed	23.5	5.4	8.4	3.5	27.4	3.1	28.7	100.0

* Including other with children

Table C4   Economic status of the head of household

Grossing	In employment		Unemployed or believe no work	Retired	Permanently sick or disabled	Othe rinactive	All
	Full time*	Part time					
							percentage
Ungrossed	49.7	5.1	7.0	28.0	4.1	6.1	100.0
LFS adjustment	49.6	5.1	6.9	28.5	4.0	5.9	100.0
Grossed	50.1	5.0	7.0	28.1	3.9	5.9	100.0

* Including unknown whether full or part time

Household type (Table C3) - apart from one person households, the largest effect was on couples with dependent children, reduced from 25.6% to 23.5%.

Employment status of the head of household (Table C4) - little affected.

Are the grossed estimates right?

Grossing has the largest effect on estimates of private renting and on household size. The question arises of whether the grossed estimate are right.

Private renters
Two lines of evidence from the Census support the estimate of private renters:

1. The design of the LFS in 1991 was very similar to that of the SEH. An OPCS study of response bias in the LFS using information from the 1991 Census showed that the response rate was significantly lower among privately renting households than for all tenures together, 80.6% compared with 85.4%. The grossing compensates for the resulting under-representation of private renters in the sample.

2. The grossing method used for the 1991 LFS Housing Trailer was also essentially the same as for the SEH. The proportion of private renters from the grossed 1991 LFS Housing Trailer, 9.4%, was in exact agreement with the proportion from the 1991 Census. Before grossing, the Housing Trailer proportion of private renters was only 8.6%. Although the exactness of the agreement of the grossed figure may owe something to chance - the LFS, like all sample surveys, is subject to sampling variability - it is nevertheless reassuring.

Household size
It is now known that the LFS data used for adjusting SEH proportions of one person households missed out an adult in a household if nothing was known about his or her employment circumstances. The LFS accepts information about a person given by other members of the household, so the loss is small. It does mean, however, that some households that appeared to be one person households were in reality two person households, and so on. This is most likely to happen in households of unrelated adults - a spouse usually knows enough about the partner to answer the survey questions, and the same is true for a parent answering for an adult child. Households of unrelated adults are mostly in the private rented sector, which is where the largest disagreement between the SEH and LFS samples was found. Comparison with other surveys indicated that one person households were under-represented in the early phases of the SEH, but the correction that has been applied is too large.

Household type
Comparison with population figures shows that children are over-represented in the sample. Since children are either in households consisting of a couple with children or a lone parent with children, this means that those two household types must also be over-represented. The grossing correctly compensates.

The stages of grossing

The outline above described the stages briefly. In order, they were as follows:

LFS adjustment

1. Apply factors so that the proportion of households in each broad tenure group is brought into agreement with the proportions from the LFS sample and, within each tenure, the proportion of one person households is in agreement. The broad tenures were: owner occupiers, council tenants, housing association tenants, and private tenants, so there were 8 factors in all. The LFS data used were for the spring, summer and autumn 1993 and winter 1994 quarters, using results from households being interviewed for the first time only (LFS is now a panel survey, in which households are interviewed in five successive quarters).

Sampling fraction and response rate

2. Calculate factors from the sampling fraction and response rates. Response rates were calculated separately according to the number of calls needed to make contact. Hard to contact households who do, eventually, give an interview tend to be different from those found more easily. In particular they are more likely to be private renters and to be small households - average household size falls from 2.6 persons for households interviewed on the first call to 1.6 for those interviewed only after 8 calls or more. Response rates fall as the number of calls needed to make contact (or the call number when the interviewer gives up) increases. The effect, therefore, is to give a higher grossing factor to the households interviewed only after many calls. To avoid random effects of small sample size, numbers of calls were grouped into four ranges: 1 or 2; 3; 4 or 5; 6 or more.

Age composition of the household

3. Calculate correction factors to achieve an exact match with OPCS figures for the population by age group. The figures include only people in the private household population, excluding those in institutions. The method employs household types defined in terms of the youngest person in the household. It starts with all households with children under 5. The correction factor for these households is simply the number of children in the population aged under 5 divided by the initial estimate from the previous stage of grossing. The next step is to deal with households with children aged 5 to 15 but none younger. Their correction factor gets the number of children aged 5 to 15 right, after allowing for those in households with younger children, whose numbers were fixed in the first step. The method proceeds up the age ranges in

similar fashion. A refinement from age 20 upward is to introduce a further division, into households that consist of people in the youngest age group only and those with older persons. The aim is to correct for the under-representation in the sample of young adults in households consisting only of young adults, relative to young adults still living in the parental home. From age 30 upwards, the age groups are broad (30 to 44, for example) as response does not vary rapidly with age at ages above 30. The method is described more fully in reference 1.

Age and sex

4. Calculate correction factors to get the numbers of each sex right within each age group. In the young adult and, to a lesser extent, the middle aged groups there are too few men and too many women, both in the sample and after the grossing up to this point. The method still keeps to household factors. Households are again allocated to types based on the age of the youngest person in the household but this time based also on whether the people in the youngest age group are all male, all female or there are members of both sexes. The method proceeds up the age ranges as for the previous stage. No adjustment is made to households with children up to age 15 (correction factor 1.0). No adjustment is made, either, to households with both males and females in the youngest age group. Factors are calculated for households with all males or all females in the youngest age group to give an exact match with the population figures for the age group by sex.

Region

5. Finally, calculate correction factors to give an exact match with the total population figures in each region, with the metropolitan areas treated as separate regions and Inner London treated separately from Outer London. The factors correct for response rates that are lower in some regions than in others. Response rates are lower in London, and especially in Inner London.

Private tenancy groups

6. Some 5% of the tenancy groups identified in the household interview did not provide a useable interview. A 5% uplift was therfore applied to the grossing factors used for tenancy group tables (but not for privately renting households).

Reference

1 Department of the Environment. *Housing in England: Housing Trailers to the 1988 and 1991 Labour Force Surveys.* HMSO, 1993.

Appendix D
Sampling errors

1. Sources of error in surveys

Like all estimates based on samples, the results of the SEH are subject to various possible sources of error. The total error in a survey estimate is the difference between the estimate derived from the data collected and the true value for the population. The total error can be divided into two main types: systematic error and random error.

Systematic error, or bias, covers those sources of error which will not average to zero over repeats of the survey. Bias may occur, for example, if certain sections of the population are omitted from the sampling frame, because non-respondents to the survey have different characteristics to respondents, or if interviewers systematically influence responses in one way or another. When carrying out a survey, substantial efforts are put into the avoidance of systematic errors but it is possible that some may still occur.

The most important component of random error is sampling error, which is the error that arises because the estimate is based on a sample survey rather than a full census of the population. The results obtained for any single sample may, by chance, vary from the true values for the population but the variation would be expected to average to zero over a number of repeats of the survey. The amount of variation depends on the size of the sample and the sample design and weighting method.

Random error may also arise from other sources, such as variation in the informant's interpretation of the questions, or interviewer variation. Efforts are made to minimise these effects through interviewer training and through pilot work.

2. Confidence intervals

Although the estimate produced from a sample survey will rarely be identical to the population value, statistical theory allows us to measure the accuracy of any survey result. The standard error can be estimated from the values obtained for the sample and this allows calculation of confidence intervals which give an indication of the range in which the true population value is likely to fall.

This report gives the 95% confidence intervals around selected survey estimates. The interval is calculated as 1.96 times the standard error on either side of the estimated percentage or mean since, under a normal distribution, 95% of values lie within 1.96 standard errors of the mean value. If it were possible to repeat the survey under the same conditions many times, 95% of these confidence intervals would contain the population value. This does not guarantee that the intervals calculated for any particular sample will contain the population values but, when assessing the results of a single survey, it is usual to assume that there is only a 5% chance that the true population value falls outside the 95% confidence interval calculated for the survey estimate.

3. Confidence intervals for percentages and means

The 95% confidence interval for a sample percentage estimate, p, is given by the formula:

$$p +/- 1.96 \times se(p)$$

where $se(p)$ represents the standard error of the percentage estimate.

For results based on a simple random sample (srs), which has no clustering or stratification or weighting, estimating standard errors is straightforward. In the case of a percentage, the standard error is based on the percentage itself (p) and the subsample size (n):

$$se(p) = \sqrt{p(100-p)}/n$$

When, as in the case of the SEH, the sample design is not simple random, the standard error needs to be multiplied by a design factor (deft). The design factor is the ratio of the standard error with a complex sample design to the standard error that would have been achieved with a simple random sample of the same size. The 95% confidence interval for a percentage from the SEH is therefore calculated as:

$$p +/- 1.96 \times deft \times \sqrt{p(100-p)}/n \quad .... 1$$

The 95% confidence interval for a mean (x) is given by:

$$x +/- 1.96 \times deft \times \sqrt{variance(x)/n} \quad .... 2$$

The standard errors, design factors and 95% confidence intervals for selected percentages and means estimated from the SEH are given in Tables D1 to D8. The errors shown are for weighted data.

Table D1 Standard errors by type of tenancy

Characteristic	Percentage (p)	Unweighted base	Standard error of p	Confidence interval	Design factor
Types of tenancy		1847			
Assured and Assured shorthold tenancies	55.6		1.59	52.48 - 58.72	1.37
Regulated	18.8		1.04	16.76 - 20.84	1.14
Tenancies not accessible to the public	17.3		1.11	15.12 - 19.48	1.25
Resident landlord and no security	8.3		0.76	6.81 - 9.79	1.18
Type of tenancy		1847			
Assured	17.5		1.04	15.46 - 19.54	1.17
Assured shorthold	38.1		1.42	35.32 - 40.88	1.25
Regulated, registered	11.3		0.79	9.75 - 12.85	1.08
Regulated non registered	7.5		0.69	6.15 - 8.85	1.12
Not accessible to the public, pays rent	6.7		0.74	5.25 - 8.15	1.27
Not accessible to the public, rent free	10.6		0.84	8.95 - 12.25	1.17
Resident landlord	7.3		0.71	5.91 - 8.69	1.17
No security	1.0		0.30	0.42 - 1.60	1.30

Table D2 Standard errors for types of property

Characteristic	Percentage (p)	Unweighted base	standard error of p	Confidence interval	Design factor
Assured and Assured shorthold tenancies		1011			
Detached house	7.8		0.99	5.86 - 9.74	1.18
Semi-detached house	14.0		1.36	11.35 - 16.69	1.25
Terraced house	30.5		2.02	26.54 - 34.46	1.39
Flat , purpose built	14.1		1.43	11.30 - 16.90	1.31
Flat, other	31.6		2.80	26.11 - 37.09	1.91
Other/ business	2.0		0.49	1.04 - 2.96	1.12
Regulated		336			
Detached house	7.7		1.45	4.86 - 10.54	1.00
Semi-detached house	26.1		2.43	21.34 - 30.86	1.01
Terraced house	35.7		2.72	30.37 - 41.03	1.04
Flat , purpose built	9.7		1.81	6.15 - 13.25	1.12
Flat, other	18.1		2.24	13.71 - 22.49	1.07
Other/ business	2.8		0.89	1.06 - 4.54	1.00
Tenancies not accessible to the public		347			
Detached house	22.0		2.34	17.41 - 26.59	1.05
Semi-detached house	24.6		2.47	19.76 - 29.44	1.07
Terraced house	19.7		2.73	14.36 - 25.06	1.28
Flat , purpose built	9.0		1.90	5.28 - 12.72	1.23
Flat, other	9.7		1.88	6.02 - 13.38	1.18
Other/ business	15.0		2.05	10.98 - 19.02	1.07
Resident landlord and no security		153			
Detached house	3.0		1.59	-0.12 - 6.12	1.15
Semi-detached house	12.8		3.12	6.68 - 18.92	1.15
Terraced house	32.6		5.17	22.51 - 42.77	1.36
Flat , purpose built	9.5		2.75	4.11 - 14.89	1.15
Flat, other	38.7		5.12	28.66 - 48.74	1.30
Other/ business	3.3		1.58	0.20 - 6.40	1.09

4. Confidence intervals for grossed estimates

Table D9 shows sampling errors for selected grossed estimates.

The grossed number of tenancies of a particular type (g) can be represented by:

$$g = \quad c/n \ \times N$$

where c = the number of tenancies of a particular type in the sample

n = the total sample size

N = the total number of households in England

As explained in Appendix C, the SEH sample was grossed to population totals so that there is no sampling error associated with N. The sampling error of the grossed estimate (g) can therefore be represented by the error associated with (c/n), that is, the proportion of such households in the sample. The standard errors and confidence intervals for the grossed estimate can therefore be calculated simply by multiplying the corresponding errors for the percentage estimates by the weighted sample total.

The above method has been used to derive the errors for grossed estimates based in the full sample. For estimates based on subsamples, a slight refinement has to be applied because the weighted number of tenancies in the subsample is not fixed by population figures. The characteristic has first to be expressed as a percentage of the total sample and then the method above can be applied.

5. How to estimate sampling errors for other characteristics

For percentages based on the sample of tenancies, standard errors can be estimated using formula 1. The sample size n is the unweighted sample total, 1958. The design factor should be the factor for a variable in Table D1 or D2 which is likely to be clustered in the same way. Errors for grossed estimates can be calculated using the method described above.

For estimates based on subsamples, Tables D1 to D8 show unweighted subsample sizes for selected characteristics or an approximation is given by the number of thousands in the corresponding cell in the tables. The design factor could be taken as the factor for a similar characteristic. However, design factors for characteristics based on subsamples are generally smaller than those for characteristics based on the total sample. Therefore, if the design factor for the characteristic is close to 1.0, it is probably sufficient to use the SRS standard error for estimates based on a subsample.

Table D3 Standard errors for the sharing of a kitchen or amenities by letting type

Characteristic	Percentage (p)	Unweighted base	standard error of p	Confidence interval	Design factor
Assured and Assured shorthold tenancies		1 011			
Shares at least one amenity	6.9		1.43	4.10 - 9.70	1.80
Missing at least one amenity	18.3		1.70	14.97 - 21.63	1.40
Regulated		336			
Share one or more amenities	1.0		0.58	-0.14 - 2.14	1.08
No access to one or more amenities	25.6		2.67	20.37 - 30.83	1.12
Tenancies not accessible to the public		347			
Share one or more amenities	1.3		0.68	-0.03 - 2.63	1.11
No access to one or more amenities	12.7		2.21	8.37 - 17.03	1.23
Resident landlord and no security		153			
Share one or more amenities	10.0		2.64	4.83 - 15.17	1.09
No access to one or more amenities	15.8		3.50	8.94 - 22.66	1.20

Table D4 Standard errors for family composition of the tenancy group by letting type

Characteristic	Percentage (p)	Unweighted base	standard error of p	Confidence interval	Design factor
Assured and Assured shorthold tenancies		1 011			
1 adult under 60	43.9		2.45	39.10 - 48.70	1.57
2 adults under 60	23.6		1.43	20.80 - 26.40	1.07
Family and dependent children	12.0		1.01	10.02 - 13.98	0.99
Lone parent and dependent children	8.0		0.78	6.47 - 9.53	0.91
Mainly adult tenancy	7.6		0.86	5.91 - 9.29	1.03
2 adults, 1 60 or over	1.9		0.42	1.08 - 2.72	0.99
1 adult 60 or over	2.9		0.57	1.78 - 4.02	1.08
Regulated		336			
1 adult under 60	13.4		2.08	9.32 - 17.48	1.12
2 adults under 60	4.5		1.03	2.46 - 6.50	0.91
Family and dependent children	7.2		1.30	4.65 - 9.75	0.92
Lone parent and dependent children	1.4		0.51	0.40 - 2.40	0.80
Mainly adult tenancy	8.0		1.24	5.57 - 10.43	0.84
2 adults, 1 60 or over	19.4		1.90	15.68 - 23.12	0.88
1 adult 60 or over	46.0		2.81	40.49 - 51.51	1.03
Tenancies not accessible to the public		347			
1 adult under 60	22.0		2.75	16.61 - 27.39	1.23
2 adults under 60	16.7		2.04	12.70 - 20.70	1.02
Family and dependent children	26.2		2.18	21.93 - 30.47	0.92
Lone parent and dependent children	2.0		0.69	0.65 - 3.35	0.93
Mainly adult tenancy	10.4		1.65	7.17 - 13.63	1.00
2 adults, 1 60 or over	7.2		1.39	4.48 - 9.92	1.00
1 adult 60 or over	15.4		2.34	10.81 - 19.99	1.20
Resident landlord and no security		153			
1 adult under 60	78.5		3.78	71.07 - 85.89	1.13
2 adults under 60	6.0		1.83	2.41 - 9.59	0.95
Family and dependent children	1.0		0.72	-0.41 - 2.41	0.89
Lone parent and dependent children	1.6		1.16	-0.67 - 3.87	1.15
Mainly adult tenancy	3.5		1.67	0.23 - 6.77	1.12
2 adults, 1 60 or over	0.9		0.63	-0.33 - 2.13	0.84
1 adult 60 or over	8.6		2.55	3.60 - 13.60	1.12

Table D5   Standard errors for tenant by age and sex

Characteristic	Percentage (p)	Unweighted base	standard error of p	Confidence interval	Design factor
Assured and assured shorthold tenancies		1 011			
Men under 30	36.0		1.86	32.35 - 39.65	1.23
Women under 30	19.0		1.71	15.65 - 22.35	1.39
Men 30-59	29.9		2.06	25.86 - 33.94	1.43
Women 30 -59	10.2		1.02	8.18 - 12.18	1.07
Men 60 or over	3.3		0.61	2.10 - 4.50	1.08
Women 60 or over	1.7		0.41	0.90 - 2.50	1.01
Regulated		336			
Men under 30	1.9		0.79	0.35 - 3.45	1.07
Women under 30	1.1		0.64	-0.18 - 2.32	1.14
Men 30-59	21.7		2.39	17.02 - 26.38	1.06
Women 30 -59	6.1		1.33	3.49 - 8.71	1.02
Men 60 or over	35.5		2.64	30.33 - 40.67	1.01
Women 60 or over	33.8		2.74	28.44 - 39.18	1.06
Tenancies not accessible to the public		347			
Men under 30	15.5		2.30	10.99 - 20.01	1.18
Women under 30	5.6		1.98	1.71 - 9.47	1.61
Men 30-59	46.9		3.01	41.00 - 52.80	1.12
Women 30 -59	6.7		1.39	4.00 - 9.44	1.03
Men 60 or over	15.4		2.05	11.38 - 19.42	1.05
Women 60 or over	9.9		1.92	6.14 - 13.66	1.19
Resident landlord and no security		153			
Men under 30	36.6		4.10	28.56 - 44.64	1.05
Women under 30	17.7		3.25	11.33 - 24.07	1.05
Men 30-59	29.8		4.04	21.88 - 37.72	1.09
Women 30 -59	6.0		2.09	1.90 - 10.10	1.09
Men 60 or over	3.7		1.55	0.63 - 6.71	1.02
Women 60 or over	6.3		2.11	2.16 - 10.44	1.07

Table D6   Standard errors for the employment status of the tenant

Characteristic	Percentage (p)	Unweighted base	standard error of p	Confidence interval	Design factor
Assured and assured shorthold tenancies		1 010			
Working full time	50.7		2.33	46.13 - 55.27	1.48
Working part time	5.2		0.77	3.72 - 6.74	1.10
Unemployed	18.7		1.54	15.68 - 21.72	1.26
Retired	2.7		0.52	1.72 - 3.76	1.00
Permanently sick or disabled	2.4		0.51	1.36 - 3.36	1.06
Other inactive	20.3		2.55	15.28 - 25.28	2.01
Regulated		336			
Working full time	20.9		2.35	16.32 - 25.54	1.06
Working part time	3.7		1.00	1.74 - 5.66	0.98
Unemployed	7.0		1.64	3.75 - 10.17	1.18
Retired	61.7		2.85	56.11 - 67.29	1.07
Permanently sick or disabled	3.3		0.96	1.40 - 5.16	0.98
Other inactive	3.4		1.04	1.38 - 5.46	1.04
Tenancies not accessible to the public		347			
Working full-time	66.8		3.33	60.27 - 73.33	1.31
Working part-time	5.2		1.25	2.75 - 7.65	1.04
Unemployed	2.8		0.96	0.92 - 4.68	1.09
Retired	17.8		2.30	13.29 - 22.31	1.12
Permanently sick or disabled	1.1		0.56	0.01 - 2.21	1.00
Other inactive	6.3		2.14	2.11 - 10.49	1.63
Resident landlord and no security		153			
Working full time	58.8		4.63	49.73 - 67.87	1.16
Working part time	4.3		1.75	0.84 - 7.70	1.06
Unemployed	13.9		3.44	7.16 - 20.64	1.23
Retired	6.4		2.08	2.32 - 10.48	1.04
Permanently sick or disabled	3.7		1.48	0.80 - 6.60	0.97
Other inactive	12.9		3.00	7.02 - 18.78	1.11

Table D7   Standard errors for tenant s getting or eligible for Housing Benefit, and the receipt of Housing Benefit by tenants

Characteristic	Percentage (p)	Unweighted base	standard error of p	Confidence interval	Design factor
Assured and assured shorthold tenancies					
Get/eligible for Housing Benefit	48.3	887	2.19	44.01 - 52.59	1.30
Receipt of Housing benefit	78.0	429	2.22	73.65 - 82.35	1.11
Regulated	1.96				
Get/eligible for Housing Benefit	60.3	293	3.10	54.22 - 66.38	1.08
Receipt of Housing Benefit	77.0	168	3.43	70.28 - 83.72	1.05
Tenancies not accessible to the public	1.96				
Get/eligible for Housing Benefit	12.2	293	2.16	7.97 - 16.43	1.13
Receipt of Housing Benefit	20.7	31	7.66	5.69 - 35.71	1.04
Resident landlord and no security	1.96				
Get/eligible for Housing Benefit	48.7	137	2.16	44.47 - 52.93	1.21
Receipt of Housing Benefit	68.5	67	5.62	57.48 - 79.52	0.98

Table D8   Standard errors for means

Characteristic	Mean	Unweighted base	Standard error	Confidence interval	Design factor
Rooms per person	2.4	1 603	0.05	2.30 - 2.50	1.36
Tenancy size	1.9	1 603	0.04	1.82 - 1.98	1.25
Comparable weekly rent (£)	59.9	1 527	1.46	56.99 - 62.7	1.28
Housing Benefit (weekly £)	16.4	1 406	1.04	14.39 - 18.47	1.24
Comparable weekly rent less Housing Benefit	42.9	1 352	1.55	39.86 - 45.94	1.20
Disposable weekly income (£)	188.4	1 409	6.14	176.39 - 200.45	1.30

Table D9   Sampling errors using weighted data: Grossed up figures

Characteristic	Estimate	Unweighted base	Standard error	95% confidence interval	Design factor
Type of letting		20 415			
Assured	378		28	322 - 434	1.31
Assured shorthold	826		46	736 - 918	1.60
Regulated	407		23	362 - 452	1.16
Not accessible to the public	376		24	328 - 422	1.24
Resident landlord and no security	180		18	146 - 214	1.18
Tenancy group composition		20 415			
One adult aged 16-59	809		61	690 - 928	1.81
Two adults aged 16-59	374		20	334 - 414	1.07
Couple with depedent child(ren)	274		15	244 - 304	0.95
Lone parent with dependent child(ren)	113		10	92 - 134	1.01
Large mainly adult	170		14	143 - 197	1.09
Two adults at least one 60 or over	130		11	109 - 151	0.96
One adult 60 or over	297		20	258 - 336	1.19
Income of tenancy group		20 415			
Under £60	303		35	235 - 371	1.83
£60-£79	224		19	186 - 282	1.31
£80-£119	300		21	259 - 341	1.2
£120-£179	287		22	254 - 340	1.27
£180-£249	258		21	217 - 299	1.27
£250 or more	512		26	460 - 564	1.19
Comparable weekly rent		20 415			
Under £25	284		27	231 - 337	1.46
£25, up to £50	654		45	585 -743	1.55
£50, up to £100	630		34	583 - 697	1.4
£100 or more	251		22	208 - 294	1.4

Appendix E
History of legislation for the private rented sector

(Contributed by the Department of the Environment)

The legislation reviewed relates to limitation on the rents that may be charged and to security of tenure provided by statute as distinct from by the terms of the lease. Other legislation relating to the obligations of landlords, for example, concerning repairs, is not referred to.

Rent control (with related security of tenure) began in 1915 as a wartime measure. Dwellings newly built or provided by conversion were excluded from control in 1919. All new lettings were excluded from control from 1923 to 1933 and some were excluded until 1939. In 1938 an estimated 2.75 million dwellings were let on Controlled tenancies out of a total 6.5 million privately rented dwellings. The maximum rents were normally the 1914 rents plus 40%. General rent control was reintroduced in 1939 by one of a batch of Acts passed rapidly by Parliament at the end of August in preparation for the outbreak of war, which could be seen to be imminent. Like the 1915 legislation, it applied to unfurnished accommodation. All such accommodation was covered, other than dwellings let by local authorities, unless the rateable values exceeded £100 in London and £75 elsewhere. These limits exempted less than 1% of all lettings. The rent was restricted to what it had been when the Act became law (1 September 1939). For about three fifths of the stock, that was a rent agreed between landlord and tenant; for the other two fifths, the controlled rent. The security of tenure was in substance the same as provided for Controlled tenancies by the earlier legislation. The tenant would not be dispossessed except by order of the Court and then only for fairly narrowly defined reasons (for example, non-payment of rent, wilful damage, allowing the property to be used for immoral purposes, or, for a dwelling occupied by virtue of employment, that the accommodation was needed for a new employee). Accommodation rented furnished was outside the scope of the Act, as with the 1915 Act and the inter-war amending legislation.

Limited increases in controlled rents were permitted by the Housing Repairs and Rents Act 1954 on proof of expenditure of specified amounts on repair. But otherwise controlled rents remained at the levels set by the 1939 Act until 1957, by which time the value of money had fallen by more than one half. The Rent Act 1957 raised controlled rents to twice the gross rateable value (on the 1956 revaluation, which valued domestic properties at their 1939 rental values) in the normal case where the landlord was responsible for repair and exterior decoration. The same Act withdrew control from lettings where the gross rateable value exceeded £40 in London and £30 elsewhere (which proved to be the top 10% of the market, approximately). This was termed 'block decontrol': there were precedents for this in the inter-war legislation, and the Act contained a power (in the event never used) to extend 'block decontrol' to lower tranches of rateable values by Statutory Instrument. Control ceased to apply to lettings where there was a change of tenant (termed 'de-control by movement'). Under the law as it stood in 1957, and indeed had done since 1915, the tenants' rights were all or nothing: either full security, including a right of succession for a widow or other member of the family living with the tenant, and a rent fixed in money terms or neither of these rights. Tenants of lettings not subject to control had no protection under the Act against eviction other than the statutory requirement of a minimum of one month's notice.

The next major reform for unfurnished tenancies was the introduction by the Rent Act 1965 of the 'Regulated tenancy'. This applied to unfurnished tenancies other than those subject to control under the Rent Act 1957 or with rateable values (1963 valuations) of over £400 in London and £200 elsewhere or part of farm or business premises. The same security of tenure was provided as for Controlled tenancies, plus a second succession (extended by the 1965 Act to controlled tenancies also). New procedures were introduced for setting rents with new administrative machinery, the Rent Officers and Rent Assessment Committees. Either the landlord or the tenant could apply to the Rent Officer for determination of a fair rent, which became the maximum that could legally be charged. In determining a fair rent, regard was to be had to all the circumstances other than the personal circumstances, with an assumption of balance between demand and supply in the area for accommodation of the kind in question. An appeal lay to the Rent Assessment Committee. Re-registration of a fair rent could be applied for after a minimum of three years.

Controlled rents were not directly affected by the 1965 Act and, as before, the controlled rent ceased to apply when there was a change of tenant. But from 1965 onwards a change of tenant caused a transfer to rent regulation, not exclusion from the Rent Acts altogether. The Housing Act 1969 provided for transfer from Controlled to Regulated tenancies of dwellings in satisfactory repair and with all the basic amenities (in order to give landlords an incentive to improve the dwellings in this way). The Housing Finance Act 1972 provided for the transfer of the remainder, unless formally represented as unfit, to Regulated tenancies in six blocks, defined by rateable value, at half-yearly intervals. The first three blocks (above £70 rateable value in London and £35 elsewhere) were transferred; transfer of the others was suspended in 1974. Both the 1969 and 1972 Acts required a fair rent to be registered in order to transfer the tenancy to regulation and provided for resulting increase in rent to be phased over five years. This precedent was followed when the Housing Act 1980 abolished the remaining Controlled tenancies (about 0.2 million).

Until 1974 furnished lettings were differently treated. Furnished accommodation was excluded from the 1915 and 1939 Acts, as mentioned above. Legislation in 1946 and 1949 provided for Rent Tribunals that would, on application, fix 'reasonable' rents for accommodation let furnished and at that time grant up to six months security of tenure. This difference from the security for tenants renting unfurnished inevitably led to a considerable amount of litigation about the distinction. A major change was made by the Rent Act 1974, which replaced the distinction between unfurnished and furnished lettings by the distinction between non-resident and resident landlord. Tenancies of furnished accommodation rented from a non-resident landlord became Regulated tenancies. Tenants of resident landlords, whether renting furnished or unfurnished accommodation, had 'restricted contracts' with broadly the same rights as tenants of furnished accommodation previously, to apply to Rent Tribunals for a reasonable rent to be fixed and for up to six months security of tenure. The Housing Act 1980 transferred security of tenure from Rent Tribunals to the Courts, which were obliged to grant possession on application by a resident landlord, with a delay not to exceed 3 months.

Two new forms of tenure were introduced by the Housing Act 1980: Protected Shorthold tenancies (Shorthold) and Assured tenancies. Shortholds were tenancies for a fixed term of not less than one year or more than five years. During the term, the tenant had the same security of tenure as with a Regulated tenancy but, at the end, there was no obligation on the landlord to renew the tenancy, with the Court obliged to grant possession should the landlord apply. Rents were to be according to the same rules as for Regulated tenancies. Assured tenancies were lettings

on terms modelled on the law relating to tenancies of business premises (Landlord and Tenant Act 1954) and could apply only to properties newly built or substantially renovated after the Act came into force, and then only if owned by a body approved by the Secretary of State for the Environment. Rents were agreed between landlord and tenant, with a right to extension of the tenancy at the end of the period originally agreed, at a market rent (to be determined by the County Court in the event of dispute) unless the landlord could succeed in Court in resisting an extension on one of the grounds specified.

The Rent Acts always applied only to tenancies and did not extend to licences to occupy. One of the defining characteristics of a tenancy is exclusive possession, for the term of the tenancy. Where exclusive possession is not conferred, usually because the owner has reserved the right to allow someone else to occupy the premises, what is granted is usually a licence to occupy (residential licences). The distinction was the subject of litigation, with the judgements of the Court of Appeal tending to widen the scope of the arrangements that legally were residential licences and not tenancies. The most prominent of these judgements, Somma v Hazelhurst, was overruled by the House of Lords in 1985 in Street v Mountford, the leading case on the subject. This judgement narrowed the scope of residential licences and has been confirmed by later House of Lords judgements (A.G. Securities v Vaughan and Antoniades v Villiers and Another, both 1988).

Major changes were made by the Housing Act 1988 which came into force in January 1989. Regulated tenancies in being at that date continue but no new Regulated tenancies can be brought into being, except through transfer from one letting to another when both belong to the same landlord. On first succession, the successor's tenancy is a Regulated tenancy. The right to a second succession remains but the tenancy becomes an Assured tenancy. New tenancies, other than lettings by resident landlords, will normally be either Assured tenancies or Assured Shorthold tenancies. In an Assured tenancy the rent is agreed at the beginning of the tenancy between landlord and tenant. At the end of the agreed term (if the letting is for a fixed term) or after at least one year (if it is a periodic tenancy) the rent may be reviewed and, in the event of dispute, the tenant may apply to the Rent Assessment Committee to determine the rent, which is required to be an open market rent. The landlord can seek re-possession only on one or more of the grounds specified. An Assured Shorthold tenancy is a letting for a term of at least six months, at the end of which term the landlord is entitled to possession. Rents are agreed between landlord and tenant, subject to the tenant having the right to apply for determination of rent to the Rent Assessment Committee on the grounds that the rent is 'significantly higher than the rents payable under similar tenancies ... in the locality'. For lettings by resident landlords, the maximum period for which the Court can suspend an order for possession was reduced to six weeks if the letting began after 15 January 1989. The right to apply to a Rent Tribunal for a reasonable rent was confined to lettings that began before that date and no new rent was agreed.

Appendix F
The questionnaire

The survey was carried out using computer assisted interviewing. This is a copy of the questions.

SEH HOUSEHOLD INTERVIEW

COMPLETE FOR EACH HOUSEHOLD AT ADDRESS

HOUSEHOLD DATA

ALL HOUSEHOLDS

ArNum   Area Number

AdNum   Address Number

HHNum   Household Number

IntNum   Interviewer Number

Date   ENTER DATE LAST SUNDAY

Adult   First of all, I need to know some details about all members of your household. (By 'household' I mean people who use the same living room or share at least one meal a day) First, how many people aged 16 or over are there living regularly in this household?

NumChil   How many children aged under 16 are there living regularly in this household?

HOUSEHOLD BOX

Table HHBox **INFORMATION COLLECTED FOR EACH ADULT IN HOUSEHOLD**

Name   Name or other identifier

Sex   1 Male
            2 Female

Age   What was ....'s age last birthday?

RelHOH   1 HOH (must be person 1)
            2 Spouse/partner of HOH (must be person 2)
            3 Son/daughter (including adopted/step-child)
            4 Foster child
            5 Son-in-law/daughter-in-law
            6 Parent/step-parent
            7 Parent-in-law
            8 Brother/sister (including adopted/step)
            9 Brother-in-law/sister-in-law
            10 Grandchild
            11 Grandparent
            12 Other (related)
            13 Other (not related)

MarCon   1 Married (spouse in household)
            2 Married (spouse not in household)
            3 Living as couple (cohabiting/living together)
            4 Single - never been married
            5 Widowed
            6 Separated
            7 Divorced

IF MARRIED (SPOUSE IN OR NOT IN HOUSEHOLD) AT MARCON

Marr2   As I told you, this interview is about housing. The way people are housed can be affected if one marriage comes to an end and they marry again so, may I just check, you said .... is married - is this ....'s first marriage or has .... been married before?

            1 First marriage
            2 Subsequent marriage
            3 Not actually married

EthGrp   SHOW CARD A
            To which of these groups do you consider .... belongs? INFORMANT'S OPINION

            1 White
            2 Black - Carribean
            3 Black - African
            4 Black - Other
            5 Indian
            6 Pakistani
            7 Bangladeshi
            8 Chinese
            9 Other

FamUnit   FAMILY UNIT ENTER NUMBER NOW OR LATER

IF FAMILY UNIT NUMBER IS NOT ONE

FRel   ASK OR CODE RELATIONSHIP TO HEAD OF FAMILY UNIT
            Head of family unit

            1 Spouse/partner of head of family unit
            2 Child (in-law) of head of family unit

FUNo   INTERVIEWER: HAVE YOU FILLED IN ALL FAMILY UNIT NUMBERS? IF NOT, GO BACK AND COMPLETE THEM NOW

Inf   INTERVIEWER CODE: IS INFORMANT:

            1 HOH
            2 Spouse/partner of HOH
            3 Another adult member of household?

IF ANOTHER ADULT MEMBER AT INF

OthRel   ASK OR CODE: Is informant:

            1 Related to HOH
            2 Not related to HOH?

IF OTHER AT INF

OthPNo   CODE PERSON NUMBER OF INFORMANT

INFORMATION COLLECTED FOR EACH CHILD IN HOUSEHOLD

CName — Name or other identifier

CSex
1 Male
2 Female

CAge — What was ....'s age last birthday?

CFamUn — FAMILY UNIT ENTER NUMBER

CRel — ASK OR CODE RELATIONSHIP TO HOH

1 Child of HOH/spouse (including adopted + step-child)
2 Foster child of HOH/spouse
3 Grandchild of HOH/spouse
4 Other relation
5 Other (not related)

NumFam — HOW MANY FAMILY UNITS ARE THERE IN THIS HOUSEHOLD?

IF MORE THAN ONE FAMILY UNIT IN HOUSEHOLD

SubLet — Does anyone in your household pay rent to .... (HOH/spouse)?

1 Yes, pays rent
2 No-one pays rent/someone contributes to expenses but no-one pays formal rent

If PAYS RENT AT SUBLET

WhoLet — Is that someone who is related to ....(HOH/spouse) or not?
CODE ALL THAT APPLY

1 Parent/child/brother/sister (include step- and in-law)
2 Other relation
3 Not related

ACCOMMODATION DATA

ALL

HAccom — INTERVIEWER CODE IS THE HOUSEHOLD'S AC-COMMODATION:

1 A house or bungalow
2 A flat or maisonette
3 A room/rooms
4 Other?

HseTyp — **IF HOUSE OR BUNGALOW AT HACCOM**

INTERVIEWER CODE IS IT:

1 Detached
2 Semi-detached
3 Or terraced/end of terrace?

IF FLAT OR MAISONETTE AT HACCOM

Flttyp — INTERVIEWER CODE IS IT IN:

1 A purpose-built block
2 A converted house/some other kind of building?

IF OTHER AT HACCOM

AccOth — INTERVIEWER CODE IS IT:

1 A caravan, mobile home or houseboat
2 Or some other kind of accommodation?

IF HOUSE/BUNGALOW, FLAT/MAISONETTE OR OTHER AT HACCOM

Busnes — INTERVIEWER CODE OR ASK:

Is this an address with business premises?

1 Yes
2 No

IF YES AT BUSNES

Access — Can you get from the business premises to any part of the private area inside the building?

1 Yes
2 No

IF YES AT ACCESS

HhAcc — Can you get from the business premises to your house-hold's accommodation?

1 Yes
2 No

ALL

YrBult — When was this property built?
PROMPT AS NECESSARY

1 Before 1919
2 1919-1944
3 1945-1964
4 1965-1984
5 1985 or later

TENURE

HHolder — In whose name is the accommodation owned or rented?

1 HOH (alone or with other apart from spouse/partner)
2 Both HOH and spouse/partner (alone or with other)
3 Spouse/partner (alone or with other apart from HOH)

Ten1 — In which of these ways do you (....) occupy this accommodation? SHOW CARD B

1 Own it outright
2 Buying it with the help of a mortgage or loan
3 Pay part rent and part mortgage (shared ownership)
4 Rent it
5 Live here rent-free (not squatting)
6 Have it in some other way
7 Squatting

IF OWN OUTRIGHT/WITH MORTGAGE/SHARED OWN-ERSHIP AT TEN1

Lease   May I just check, do you own the house/bungalow (flat/maisonette) freehold or on a lease?

    1 Freehold
    2 On a long lease

IF ON A LONG LEASE AT LEASE AND FLAT OR MAISON-ETTE AT HACCOM

LngthL   When you first bought the flat/maisonette, how long did the lease have to run?

    1 Less than 22 years
    2 22 - 29 years
    3 30 - 39 years
    4 40 - 59 years
    5 60 - 79 years
    6 80 years or longer

LgthLN   And how long does the lease have to run now?

    1 Less than 22 years
    2 22 -29 years
    3 30 - 39 years
    4 40 - 59 years
    5 60 - 79 years
    6 80 years or longer

Freehld   You said that the flat/maisonette is on a long lease but, may I just check, do you own the freehold of   the whole building, either as an individual or along with the other leaseholders collectively?

    1 Owns freehold of whole building
    2 Does not own freehold

IF OWNS FREEHOLD OF WHOLE BUILDING AT FREEHLD

SoleCol   Do you have the sole ownership of the freehold of the whole building or do you own it along with the   other leaseholders collectively?

    1 Sole ownership
    2 With other leaseholders collectively

IF DOES NOT OWN FREEHOLD AT FREEHLD

FrHlder   Is the freehold owned by:

    1 A private individual
    2 A company
    3 A housing association
    4 A charity or charitable trust (not a housing association)
    5 A local authority or council
    6 The Church Commissioners
    7 Or some other organisation?

IF RENT, RENT-FREE OR OTHER AT TEN1

Ten2   May I just check, were you (....) ever buying this accommodation with the help of a mortgage or loan?

    1 Yes
    2 No

IF SHARED OWNERSHIP AT TEN1

Share1   May I just check, did you (....) have a shared ownership arrangement when you (....) first began to buy this accommodation or were you (....) just buying it with a mortgage at first?

    1 Shared ownership
    2 Just a mortgage at first

IF YES AT TEN2 OR JUST A MORTGAGE AT SHARE1

Chnge1   When did you (....) change to renting/shared ownership?

    Year

Chnge2   Month

IF OWN OUTRIGHT AT TEN1

PaidM   May I just check, have you (....):

    1 Paid off a mortgage or loan,
    2 Or have you never had a mortgage or loan on this property?

IF RENT, RENT-FREE OR OTHER AT TEN1

Tied   Does the accommodation go with the job of anyone in the household?

    1 Yes
    2 No
    3 Used to go with job but does not now

IF RENT, RENT-FREE, SHARED OWNERSHIP, OTHER OR DK AT TEN1

LLord   Who is your landlord:
CODE FIRST THAT APPLIES

    1 The local authority or council
    2 A housing association or co-operative or charitable trust
    3 A property company
    4 Your (HOH's/spouse's) employer (organisation)
    5 Another organisation
    6 Someone who is related to you (HOH/spouse)
    7 Someone who was already a friend before you (....) lived here
    8 Your (HOH's/spouse's employer (individual)
    9 Another individual private landlord?

IF HOUSING ASSOCIATION AT LLORD

TransHA   Has the tenancy been transferred from a local authority to a housing association?

    1 Yes
    2 No

IF YES AT TRANSHA

YrHA   When did you (....) first become the tenant(s) of your (... present housing association?

IF 1989 AT YRHA

Jan15 Was this after 15 January 1989?

1 Yes
2 No

IF YES AT TIED (BUT NOT YOUR EMPLOYER - ORG. OR INDIV. AT LLORD)

LEmp May I just check, you said that your accommodation goes with the job of someone in your household, so is the landlord your (HOH's/spouse's) employer?

1 Yes
2 No

IF RENT, RENT-FREE OR OTHER AT TEN1

urn Is the accommodation provided

1 Furnished
2 Partly furnished
3 Or unfurnished?

IF SOMEONE RELATED, SOMEONE ALREADY A FRIEND, INDIVIDUAL EMPLOYER OR OTHER INDIVIDUAL PRIVATE LANDLORD AT LLORD

esLL Does the landlord live in the building?

1 Yes
2 No

IF YES AT RESLL AND PURPOSE-BUILT AT FLTTYP

esLL2 Does the landlord live in the same flat as you or not?

1 Lives in same flat
2 Does not live in same flat

ALL HOUSEHOLDS

Sblet Is there any part of your household's accommodation that is usually sublet but which is not sublet at the moment?

1 Yes
2 No

IF HOUSE AT HACCOM OR OTHER AT ACCOTH OR CONVERTED HOUSE AT FLTTYP

hareH INTERVIEWER ASK OR CODE
May I just check, does anyone else live in this building apart from the people in your household?

1 Yes
2 No

IF HOUSE AT HACCOM OR OTHER AT ACCOTH OR CONVERTED HOUSE AT FLTTYP

hareE Is there any empty living accommodation in this building outside your household's accommodation?

1 Yes
2 No

IF YES AT SHAREH OR YES AT SHAREE

NumRm I want to ask you about all the rooms you have in your accommodation; please include any rooms you sublet to other people and any rooms you share with people who are not in your household (or would share If someone moved into the empty accommodation). How many bedrooms do you have, including bed-sitting rooms and spare bedrooms?

IF NO/DK/NA AT SHAREH AND SHAREE

NumRm2 I want to ask you about all the rooms you have in your accommodation. How many bedrooms do you have, including bed-sitting rooms and spare bedrooms?

ALL

Kit Apart from the rooms you have mentioned, do you have (the use of) a kitchen, that is, a separate room in which you cook?

1 Yes
2 No

IF YES AT KIT

NumKit How many kitchens have you (the use of)?

FOR EACH KITCHEN

KitSiz Is the narrowest side of the kitchen at least six and a half feet from wall to wall?

1 6 and a half feet or more
2 Less than 6 and a half feet

ALL

Bath Apart from the rooms you have mentioned, do you have (the use of) a bathroom with a bath or shower that is plumbed in?

1 Yes
2 No

IF YES AT BATH

NumBth How many bathrooms (with plumbed-in bath or shower) do you have (the use of)?

ALL

NumWC How many inside flush toilets do you have (the use of)?

IF 1 AT NUMWC AND YES AT BATH

WCBath Is this in the bathroom (one of the bathrooms) you have just mentioned?

1 Yes
2 No

IF MORE THAN 1 AT NUMWC AND YES AT BATH

WCBat2 Are any of these in the bathroom(s) you have just mentioned?

1 None in bathroom
2 One in bathroom
3 More than one in bathrooms

IF MORE THAN ONE AT WCBAT2

NumWCB   ENTER NUMBER

ALL

NumRmO   How many other rooms do you have, not counting bedrooms, kitchens, bathrooms or toilets?

CHeat   Is there central heating (even if it is not used or not working in:

1 All your living rooms and bedrooms
2 Some of these rooms but not all
3 Or is there no central heating in these rooms?

Floor   On what floor of this building is your main living accommodation?
CODE LOWEST FLOOR WITH LIVING ACCOMMODATION

1 Basement/semi-basement
2 Ground floor/street level
3 1st floor
4 2nd floor
5 3rd floor
6 4th-9th floor
7 10th floor or higher

FlBld   How many floors are there in the whole building?
1 One (bungalow)
2 Two
3 Three
4 Four
5 Five - nine
6 Ten or more

CTax   Could you please tell me which Council Tax band this accommodation is in?
THIS MUST BE THE BAND GIVEN BY THE COUNCIL DO NOT ACCEPT INFORMANT'S OWN ESTIMATE OF VALUE OF PROPERTY

1 A Up to £40,001
2 B £40,001 - £52,000
3 C £52,001 - £68,000
4 D £68,001 - £88,000
5 E £88,001 - £120,000
6 F £120,001 - £160,000
7 G £160,001 - £320,000
8 H £320,001 or more
9 Household accommodation not valued separately

IF HOUSEHOLD ACCOMMODATION NOT VALUED SEPARATELY AT CTax

CTax2   Could you tell me which council tax band the whole address is in?
ANSWER CODES AS ABOVE

SHARING

IF YES AT SHAREH OR YES AT RESLL OR FLAT A⁻ HACCOM OR ROOM AT HACCOM

Share2   (You said earlier that there are other people living in th⁻ building apart from your household) Does your househol⁻ (Do you) have the whole of your accomodation to you⁻ selves (yourself) or do you share any of it with someon⁻ outside your household?

1 Have whole accommodation
2 Share with someone outside household

IF YES AT SHAREE AND WHOLE ACCOMMODATION DK/NA AT SHARE2

Share3   If all the empty accommodation in this building wer⁻ occupied, would your household (you) have to share an⁻ part of your accommodation with anyone who had move⁻ in?

1 Yes
2 No

IF WHOLE ACCOMMODATION AT SHARE2

ShCirc   In getting from one part of your accommodation to anothe⁻ do you have to use any hall, landing or staircase which⁻ open to someone outside your household?

1 Yes
2 No

IF YES AT SHCIRC AND YES AT RESLL

CircLL   You said that the landlord lives in the building. May I ju⁻ check, do you share the use of this hall, landing ⁻ staircase with:

1 The landlord
2 With someone else outside your household
3 Or with both the landlord and someone else?

IF NO AT SHARE3

Circ2   In getting from one part of your accommodation to anothe⁻ do you have to use any hall, landing or staircase whic⁻ would be open to someone who moved into the emp⁻ accommodation?

1 Yes
2 No

Table of shared rooms

IF SHARE AT SHARE2

ShRm   Do you share a kitchen with someone outside your hous⁻ hold?

1 Yes
2 No

IF YES AT SHRM AND YES AT RESLL

WhoSh   Do you share a kitchen with:

1 The landlord only
2 The landlord and someone else outside your househo⁻
3 Just with someone else outside your household?

IF YES AT SHARE3

ShRmE   If someone moved into the empty accommodation in this building, would you have to share a kitchen with them?

1 Yes
2 No

SHRM, WHOSH AND SHRME ARE REPEATED FOR "A BATHROOM", "A TOILET" AND "ANOTHER ROOM"

IF SHARE AT SHARE2 OR YES AT SHARE 3 OR YES AT SHCIRC OR YES AT CIRC2

ShareP   How do you feel about having completely self-contained accommodation which you would not have to share in any way with people in another household? Would you:

1 Strongly prefer self-contained accommodation
2 Prefer it but not strongly
3 Or would you prefer to share in some way?

MOVES AND HOUSING HISTORY

ALL

HLong   We are interested in how often people move so, may I just check, how long have you (HOH) been living at this address? **(MUST GIVE INFORMATION ABOUT HOH)**

1 Under 6 months
2 6 months but not 1 year
3 1 year but not 2 years
4 2 years but not 3 years
5 3 years but not 5 years
6 5 years but not 10 years
7 10 years but not 20 years
8 20 years but not 30 years
9 30 years but not 40 years
10 40 years or longer

IF HOH IS MARRIED (SPOUSE IN HOUSEHOLD) OR COHABITING

MovTog   May I just check, did you (HOH) and .... (spouse) move into this accommodation at the same time or was one here before the other?

1 Moved in at same time
2 One moved in before the other

IF ONE MOVED IN BEFORE THE OTHER AT MOVTOG

First   Which of you (....) moved in first?

1 HOH
2 Spouse/partner

IF SPOUSE AT FIRST

HLong1   How long has .... (spouse) been living at this address?

1 Under 6 months
2 6 months but not 1 year
3 1 year but not 2 years
4 2 years but not 3 years
5 3 years but not 5 years

6 5 years but not 10 years
7 10 years but not 20 years
8 20 years but not 30 years
9 30 years but not 40 years
10 40 years or longer

QUESTION APPLIES TO HOH UNLESS SPOUSE AT FIRST IF UNDER 3 YEARS AT HLONG (OR HLONG1)

PrevAc   Thinking about the accommodation you (HOH/spouse) lived in immediately before you moved here, will you please tell me in which of the ways on this card you occupied the accommodation? SHOW CARD D

1 Owned it in own name/jointly
2 Spouse/partner owned it
3 Rented it in own name/jointly
4 Spouse/partner rented it
5 Had it rent-free in own name (or spouse's/partner's name)
6 Did not have accommodation in own name or spouse's/partner's name

IF OWNED AT PREVAC

PreOO   At the time when you (HOH/spouse) moved, did you:

1 Own it outright
2 Or were you buying it with the help of a mortgage or loan?

IF OWNED AT PREVAC AND RENT, RENT-FREE OR OTHER AT TEN1

Prev1   May I just check, what happened to the house/flat which you (HOH/spouse) owned previously?

1 Sold it
2 On the market
3 Still owns but not on the market
4 Previous spouse/partner lives there
5 Repossessed/taken over by building society/ mortgage lender
7 Other (e.g. demolished)

IF RENTED OR RENT-FREE AT PREVAC

PrevR   Did you rent it (have it rent-free) from

1 A local authority or council
2 A housing association or co-operative or housing charitable trust
3 Or some other individual or organisation?

IF OWNED, RENTED OR RENT-FREE AT PREVAC (OWN NAME)

Miles   How many miles from here was the place where you lived before moving here?

1 Under 1 mile
2 1 mile but not 2 miles
3 2 miles but not 5 miles
4 5 miles but not 10 miles
5 10 miles but not 20 miles
6 20 miles but not 50 miles
7 50 miles or more
8 Northern Ireland
9 Abroad

IF NOT NORTHERN IRELAND OR ABROAD AT MILES

Region   **REGION IS CODED FROM COUNTY AND, WHERE NECESSARY, LOCAL AUTHORITY**

Where   What county was it in?

IF COUNTY DOES NOT DEFINE REGION, A FURTHER QUESTION IS ASKED ABOUT LOCAL AUTHORITY

IF NOT NORTHERN IRELAND OR ABROAD AT MILES

HLong2   How long did you live in that accommodation?

1 Under 6 months
2 6 months but not 1 year
3 1 year but not 2 years
4 2 years but not 3 years
5 3 years but not 5 years
6 5 years but not 10 years
7 10 years but not 20 years
8 20 years but not 30 years
9 30 years but not 40 years
10 40 years or longer

WhyM   SHOW CARD E

Here are some reasons why people move; can you tell me why you (HOH/spouse) moved last time?
CODE ALL THAT APPLY

1 To move to better neighbourhood/pleasanter area
2 To be near a new job
3 To be nearer existing job
4 Wanted larger house/flat or one which was better in some other way
5 Wanted smaller/cheaper house/flat
6 Had to leave tied accommodation/took job with tied accommodation
7 Could not afford mortgage payments on previous house/flat
8 Could not afford rent on previous house/flat
9 Divorce/separation
10 Marriage/began cohabiting
11 Other family/personal reasons
12 Wanted to buy
13 Wanted independent accommodation/own home not shared
14 To go to/finished college/university
15 Previous accommodation no longer available
16 Other reason

IF MORE THAN ONE ANSWER AT WHYM

MainR   Could you tell me what was the main reason why you moved?

CODES AS AT WHYM

IF LOCAL AUTHORITY OR HOUSING ASSOCIATION AT LLORD

HowRen   May I just check, how did you (HOH/spouse) come to rent this house/flat? Please choose your answer from this card. SHOW CARD F

1 From local authority or housing association waiting list or transfer list
2 Arranged by local authority or housing association without being on waiting list

3 Exchanging with previous tenant by arrangement with local authority
4 By private agreement with previous tenant
5 Inheriting the tenancy on death of previous tenant by agreement with local authority
6 By private agreement on death of previous tenant
7 Accepted as homeless
8 In some other way

ALL

AgeLft   May I just check, how old were you (HOH) when you first left home and had a home of your own, I mean, when you stopped living with your parents or stopped living in a college hostel or university hall?

IF HOH IS COHABITING

MarChk   And may I just check, have you (HOH) ever been legally married?

1 Yes
2 No

IF HOH HAS BEEN LEGALLY MARRIED (MARRIED WIDOWED/SEPARATED/DIVORCED AT MARCON OF YES AT MARCHK)

BefMar   Did you first leave home:

1 Before you (HOH) were first married
2 At the time when you were first married
3 Or after you were first married?

IF INFORMANT IS SPOUSE OF HOH (ASKED FOR PUBLIC RELATIONS PURPOSES)

SpAge   And what about you. How old were you when you first left home and had a home of your own?

SATISFACTION WITH PRESENT ACCOMMODATION

ALL

HSatis   How satisfied are with this accommodation?
SHOW CARD G

1 Very satisfied
2 Fairly satisfied
3 Neither satisfied nor dissatisfied
4 Slightly dissatisfied
5 Very dissatisfied

PUBLIC SECTOR HOUSING WAITING LISTS

ALL

WList   May I just check, do you (HOH) (or your wife/partner) have your name on a council house or housing association waiting list (or transfer list)?

1 Yes
2 No

IF MORE THAN ONE ADULT (APART FROM HOH'S SPOUSE) IN HOUSEHOLD

WList2   Is anyone else in your household on a council house or housing association waiting list or transfer list and trying to get separate accommodation?

1 Yes
2 No

IF YES AT WLIST OR WLIST2

NoList   CODE OR ASK

So how many separate houses/flats are people in your household looking for?

FOR EACH SEPARATE WAITING LIST GROUP

NameL   Whose name is actually down for the first (2nd etc.) house/flat? (CODE ALL THAT APPLY -PERSON NO OR CODE "NON-HOUSEHOLD MEMBER")

TimeW   How long has .... been on the waiting list? IF MORE THAN ONE APPLICATION, GIVE LONGEST PERIOD ON ANY LIST

1 Under 6 months
2 6 months, less than 1 year
3 1 year, less than 2 years
4 2 years, less than 3 years
5 3 years, less than 5 years
6 5 years, less than 10 years
7 10 years or longer

Typew   May I just check, is it a local authority list or a housing association list?
IF ON BOTH LISTS GIVE PRIORITY TO LOCAL AUTHORITY

1 Local authority
2 Housing association

OWNER OCCUPATION

IF NEVER HAD MORTGAGE AT PAIDM

Buy   You said earlier that you (HOH/spouse) never had a mortgage on this accommodation; did you:

1 Buy this house/flat
2 Inherit it
3 Or acquire it in some other way?

IF OWN WITH MORTGAGE OR SHARED OWNERSHIP AT TEN1, OR PAID OFF MORTGAGE AT PAIDM OR YES AT TEN2

Lender   When you (HOH/spouse) first started to buy this accommodation, who did you get the mortgage from; was it:

1 Building society (including Abbey National)
2 A bank
3 A local authority
4 An insurance company
5 Or someone else?

IF OWN WITH MORTGAGE OR SHARED OWNERSHIP AT TEN1, OR PAID OFF MORTGAGE AT PAIDM OR YES AT TEN2 OR BUY AT BUY

Source   (Apart from the mortgage) How did you finance the purchase of the accommodation? SHOW CARD H
CODE ALL THAT APPLY

1 Savings
2 Proceeds from sale of previous home
3 Money paid by local authority/housing association to encourage move from council/housing association accommodation
4 Money paid by private landlord to encourage move
5 Gift or loan from family or friend
6 Loan to cover deposit/bridging loan from elsewhere e.g. bank, employer
7 Inherited money
8 Windfall
9 Other
10 No other source - 100% mortgage

Seller   Who did you buy this accommodation from? SHOW CARD I

1 Private individual or a builder
2 A local authority, council or New Town Corporation
3 A housing association
4 A bank or building society or agent on their behalf (repossession sale)
5 Someone else

YrBuy   In which year did you buy/start to buy this accommodation?

RentPr   Before you bought/began buying this accommodation, were you renting it?

1 Yes
2 No

IF YES AT RENTPR

RtFrm   Did you rent it from:

1 A local authority or New Town Corporation
2 A housing association
3 Or some other landlord?

IF OWN OUTRIGHT, OWN WITH MORTGAGE OR SHARED OWNERSHIP AT TEN1 AND HOH DID NOT OWN PREVIOUS ACCOMMODATION AT PREVAC

OwnPr   You may have told me this already but, may I just check, have you (HOH) owned any other accommodation before this house/flat?
CODE FIRST THAT APPLIES

1 HOH has owned previously (not jointly with present spouse)
2 HOH has owned previously (only jointly with present spouse)
3 HOH has not owned previously

IF OWNED PREVIOUSLY (NOT JOINTLY OR JOINTLY) AT OWNPR OR HOH OWNED PREVIOUS ACCOMMODATION AT PREVAC

YrFst   In which year did you (HOH) become the owner of the first accommodation you ever owned?

SitTn   Thinking about the first accommodation you (HOH) ever owned, were you renting it before you became the owner?

1 Yes
2 No

IF YES AT SITTN

StLa   Did you rent it from:

1 A local authority or New Town Corporation
2 A housing association
3 Or some other landlord?

IF HOH IS MARRIED/COHABITING AND OWN OUTRIGHT, OWN WITH MORTGAGE OR SHARED OWNERSHIP AT TEN1

SpOwn   You may have told me this already but, may I just check, has ....(spouse/partner) owned any accommodation apart from this house/flat?
CODE FIRST THAT APPLIES

1 Spouse/partner has owned previously (not jointly with present HOH)
2 Spouse/partner has owned previously (only jointly with present HOH)
3 Spouse/partner has not owned previously

IF SPOUSE/PARTNER HAS OWNED PREVIOUSLY (NOT JOINTLY WITH PRESENT HOH AT SPOWN

SpYFst   In which year did she become the owner of the first accommodation she ever owned?

SpStTn   Thinking about the first accommodation she (spouse) ever owned, was she renting it before she became the owner?

1 Yes
2 No

IF YES AT SPSTTN

SpStLA   Did she rent it from:

1 A local authority or New Town Corporation
2 A housing association
3 Or some other landlord?

IF OWN WITH MORTGAGE OR SHARED OWNERSHIP AT TEN1 OR BUY AT BUY OR PAID OFF MORTGAGE AT PAIDM AND IF HOH/SPOUSE/PARTNER HAS OWNED PREVIOUSLY JOINTLY OR NOT JOINTLY (OWNPR, PREVAC, SPOWN)

SellOt   Did you (HOH/spouse) sell a house or flat at the time when you bought this one?
(INCLUDE SELLING SOON AFTERWARDS WITH HELP OF BRIDGING LOAN)

1 Yes
2 No

IF YES AT SELLOT

NumSel   May I just check, was that just one house or flat that you sold or more than one?

1 One
2 More than one

ShOwn   May I just check, did anyone else apart from you (HOH and present spouse/partner) have a share in the ownership of the place(s) you sold or not?

1 Share with someone else apart from HOH (spouse/partner)
2 Just in name(s) of HOH (spouse/partner)

THERE ARE DIFFERENT VERSIONS OF THE FOLLOWING QUESTIONS ACCORDING TO (1) WHETHER OR NOT MORE THAN ONE PROPERTY WAS SOLD AND (2) WHETHER OR NOT ANYONE APART FROM HOH AND PRESENT SPOUSE/PARTNER HAD A SHARE IN THE OWNERSHIP

Price
Price2
Price3
Price4   How did the price paid for this place compare with the price(s) (share of the price) at which the previous place(s) was sold; was the price paid for this place:

1 Higher
2 About the same
3 Or lower than the price for which the previous place was sold?

IF OWN WITH MORTGAGE OR SHARED OWNERSHIP AT TEN1

MortSz
MrtSz2
MrtSz3
MrtSz4   And how did the size of the mortgage for this place compare with that of the previous mortgage (the total amount (share of the amount) borrowed on the previous property(ies); was the new mortgage:

larger
about the same
or smaller than the previous mortgage?

No mortgage on previous property

Lend2   Is your (HOH's/spouse's) present mortgage still with a ....(ANSWER AT LEND)

Yes
No

IF YES AT LEND2

Lend3   Is it still with the same ....(ANSWER AT LEND) that provided the original mortgage or with a different one?

Same
Different

IF NO AT LEND2

Lend4   Who did you get the present mortgage from:
a building society (including Abbey National)
a bank
a local authority
an insurance company
or someone else?

IF NO AT LEND2 OR DIFFERENT AT LEND3

YrMort   When did your present mortgage begin?

IF OWNED WITH MORTGAGE OR SHARED OWNER-SHIP AT TEN1

WPay   How often are payments due on the mortgage?

One week
Two weeks
Three weeks
Four weeks
Calendar month
Other

IF OTHER AT WPAY

WPayO   Will you please give me that in weeks?

IF OWNED WITH MORTGAGE OR SHARED OWNER-SHIP AT TEN1

AMort   What was the amount of the last payment due on your (HOH's/spouse's) mortgage?
ENTER AMOUNT TO NEAREST £1
ENTER AMOUNT DUE EVEN IF PAYMENTS ARE MADE, IN PART OR IN FULL, BY THE DSS

PInt   Do the mortgage payments cover:

interest only - like an endowment mortgage
or interest and principal - like a repayment mortgage?

TaxRlf   Has standard rate tax relief on the mortgage already been deducted from the payment you just mentioned?

Yes
No

IF INFORMANT IS HOH OR SPOUSE/PARTNER OF HOH

MrgArr   As you know, many people have been falling behind with their mortgage payments recently. Will you please look at this card and tell me what your position is?
SHOW CARD J

Up-to-date with payments
Less than 3 months behind
3 months but not 6 months behind
6 months or more behind

IF UP-TO-DATE WITH PAYMENTS AT MRGARR

MrgAr2   How easy are you finding it to keep up with your mortgage payments. Would you say you:

have no difficulty in keeping up
find it rather difficult
or find it very difficult to keep up

PUBLIC SECTOR RENTING

IF INFORMANT IS HOH OR SPOUSE/PARTNER AND IF LOCAL AUTHORITY/HOUSING ASSOCIATION AT LLORD AND NOT YES AT TIED AND IF RENT OR RENT-FREE AT TEN1

LABuy   Do you think you (HOH/spouse/partner) will eventually buy somewhere or not?

Yes
No

IF YES AT LABUY

LASiT   Do you think you will buy this place or not?

Yes
No

IF YES AT LASIT

LALong   How long do you think it will be before you buy this place?

Less than 3 months
3 months but less than 6 months
6 months but less than 1 year
1 year but less than 2 years
2 years but less than 5 years
5 years or more

IF YES AT LASIT OR NO/DON'T KNOW AT LABUY

LAMove   Do you think you will move from here some time in the future or not?

Yes
No

IF LOCAL AUTHORITY/HOUSING ASSOCIATION AT LLORD AND NOT YES AT TIED AND IF YES AT LAMOVE OR NO/DON'T KNOW AT LASITT

Long1   How much longer do you think you will be in this accommodation?

Less than 3 months
3 months but less than 6 months
6 months but less than 1 year
1 year but less than 2 years
2 years but less than 5 years
5 years or more

IF LOCAL AUTHORITY/HOUSING ASSOCIATION AT LLORD AND NOT YES AT TIED AND IF RENT/RENT-FREE AT TEN1 AND IF YES AT LABUY AND NO/DON'T KNOW AT LASITT

RtLABuy   Do you think that you will rent again (straight away) or buy somewhere?

Rent
Buy

IF RENT/DON'T KNOW AT RTLABUY

Long2   How long do you think it will be before you buy somewhere?

Less than 3 months
3 months but less than 6 months
6 months but less than 1 year
1 year but less than 2 years
2 years but less than 5 years
5 years or more

IF YES AT LABUY

Fince   When people buy their homes they may finance themselves in a number of different ways. Here is a list. Please tell me which of these ways you would use if you bought this/a house or flat?
SHOW CARD K

Mortgage or loan
Savings
Money paid by local authority/housing association to encourage move from this accommodation
Gift or loan from family or friend
Loan to cover deposit/bridging loan from elsewhere e.g. bank, employer
Proceeds from sale of previous home
Inherited money
Windfall
Other

IF NO/DON'T KNOW AT LABUY

Like   Even if you don't expect to buy anywhere in the future, would you like to if you could?

Yes
No

IF YES/DON'T KNOW AT LIKE

Offer   In some parts of the country where council (Housing Association) housing is scarce, local authorities (housing associations) sometimes give their tenants cash to buy new homes so as to let someone else move into their rented accommodation. Do you think you might buy a house or flat if you were offered a contribution to the purchase price of another home by the local authority (housing association)?

IF LOCAL AUTHORITY/HOUSING ASSOCIATION AT LLORD AND NOT YES AT TIED

LARnt   How often does your rent become due?

One week
Two weeks
Three weeks
Four weeks
Calendar month
Other

IF OTHER AT LARNT

LARntO   Will you please give me that in weeks?

IF LOCAL AUTHORITY/HOUSING ASSOCIATION AT LLORD AND NOT YES AT TIED

LAAmt   After any Housing Benefit or rent rebate you get, how much rent was due last time?
ENTER TO NEAREST £1 AFTER HOUSING BENEFIT

IF AN AMOUNT ABOVE £0 IS GIVEN AT LAAMT

PTax   May I just check, does this rent include Council Tax (the tax that has taken the place of Poll Tax)?

Yes
No

IF YES AT PTAX

PTaxA   You said that the amount due in rent last time was .... (ANSWER AT LAAMT); how much of this was for Council Tax (or Poll Tax)?
ENTER AMOUNT TO NEAREST £1

IF AN AMOUNT ABOVE £0 IS GIVE AT LAAMT

LAHol   Do you have a rent holiday?

Yes
No

IF YES AT LAHOL

HolWk   For how many weeks a year do you have a rent holiday?

IF LOCAL AUTHORITY/HOUSING ASSOCIATION AT LLORD AND NOT YES AT TIED AND RENT/RENT-FREE AT TEN1

LAHB   Was any Housing Benefit (Rent Rebate/Rent Allowance) allowed in connection with the last rent that was due?

Yes
No

IF NO AT LAHB

HBWait   Are you awaiting the outcome of a claim for Housing Benefit (Rent Rebate/Rent Allowance)?

Yes
No

IF YES AT LAHB

AmtHB   How much Housing Benefit was allowed for the last rent?

PerHB   How long did this cover?

IF OTHER AT PERHB

PerHBO   Will you please give me that in weeks?

IF YES AT LAHB

HBReb   Is Housing Benefit normally deducted from the rent or are you supposed to pay the rent in full and get the money back later?

Housing Benefit deducted from rent
Paid in full and got money back later

IF AN AMOUNT OVER £0 IS GIVEN AT LAAMT AND YES AT LAHB

HBRnt   May I just check, you said that the amount due in rent last time was ....(ANSWER AT LAAMT). Is that before or after deduction of Housing Benefit (rebate)?

Before
After

IF LOCAL AUTHORITY/HOUSING ASSOCIATION AT LLORD AND NOT YES AT TIED AND IF THE INFORMANT IS THE HOH OR WIFE/PARTNER OF THE HOH

Arr   May I just check, is your rent paid up-to-date at present or is any rent owing (I mean, owing for a fortnight or longer)?

Paid up-to-date
Rent owing for a fortnight or longer

IF PAID UP-TO-DATE AT ARR

PrArr   Have you been up-to-date with the rent for the whole of the last 12 months or has any rent ever been owing for a fortnight or longer during that time?

Up-to-date during the last 12 months
Rent owing fortnight or longer

IF RENT OWING AT ARR OR RENT OWING AT PRARR

ArrRea   Did you have difficulty paying the rent on time because of any of the things on this card?
SHOW CARD L CODE ALL THAT APPLY

Increase in the rent
Unemployment
Illness
Reduction in working hours
Loss of overtime
Other debts or responsibilities
Problems in connection with Housing Benefit
Domestic problems
None of these

IF PROBLEMS IN CONNECTION WITH HOUSING BENEFIT AT ARRREA

HBProb   What was the problem?

Delay in getting reply to application for Housing Benefit/still waiting
Delay in payment of Housing Benefit/still waiting
Paid less than expected
Application turned down
Other

EMPLOYMENT AND OCCUPATION

COMPLETE FOR EACH MEMBER OF THE HOUSEHOLD AGED 16 OR OVER

EPerNo   Person number entered automatically

IF MALE AND AGED 16-64 OR FEMALE AND AGED 16-59

Scheme   Last week, that is, in the seven days ending Sunday ...., were you on any of the following schemes:
CODE ONE ONLY

Youth Training (YT) (AGES 16-20 ONLY)
Community Industry
Employment Training (ET)
Employment Action
Any other kind of scheme?

None of these

IF YT/ET AT SCHEME

YTEtmp   In the week ending Sunday ...., on that government scheme, were you:
CODE FIRST THAT APPLIES

with an employer who was providing work experience or practical training
at a college or training centre
temporarily away from an employer or project
temporarily away from a college or training centre

IF MALE AND AGED 65 OR OVER OR FEMALE AND AGED 60 OR OVER OR IF (YOUNGER AND) NONE OF THESE AT SCHEME

Wrking   Did you do any paid work last week, either as an employee or self-employed?

Yes
No

IF NO AT WRKING

JBAway   Even though you were not doing paid work, did you have a job or business that you were away from last week?

Yes
No
Waiting to take up new job/business already obtained

IF NO OR WAITING TO TAKE UP NEW JOB AT JBAWAY

IF YES AT WRKING OR YES AT JBAWAY

FtPtWk   In your present job do you work:

full time
or part time?

IF WORKING PART-TIME

YPtJob   Why did you take a part-time rather than a full-time job?
Was it because: CODE FIRST THAT APPLIES
you were a student/you were at school?
you were ill or disabled?
you could not find a full-time job?
you did not want a full-time job?
None of these.

IF COMMUNITY INDUSTRY AT SCHEME OR NO AT JBAWAY

Look1   Last week (ending Sunday ....), were you looking for any kind of paid work?

Yes
No

IF MALE AND AGED 16-64 OR FEMALE AND AGED 16-59 AND IF NO AT LOOK1

LstWk   Last week ending Sunday ...., were you:
CODE FIRST THAT APPLIES

waiting to take up a job that you had already obtained
waiting for the results of an application for a job
not looking for work because you were
temporarily sick or injured
not looking for work because you were on holiday?

None of these

IF MALE AND AGED 65 OR OVER OR FEMALE AND AGED 60 OR OVER OR IF YOUNGER AND NONE OF THESE AT LSTWK

NoLook   May I just check, what was the main reason why you were not looking for work last week?

On YTS/ET
Student
Long-term sick or disabled
Looking after family or home
Retired from work
Doesn't want/need employment
Believes no jobs available
Not yet started looking
Any other reason

IF AT COLLEGE/TEMPORARILY AWAY FROM COLLEGE AT YTETMP OR WAITING TO TAKE UP NEW JOB AT JBAWAY OR WAITING TO TAKE UP JOB/ WAITING FOR RESULTS/SICK/ ON HOLIDAY AT LSTWK OR YTS (OR ET)/STUDENT/SICK/LOOKING AFTER FAMILY/RETIRED/BELIEVES NO JOBS/OTHER AT NOLOOK

WLkJob   Even though you were not looking for work last week, would you like to have a regular paid job at the moment, either a full-time or a part-time job?

Yes
No

IF YES AT WLKJOB OR YES AT LOOK1

Start   If a job (or a place on a government scheme) had been available last week, would you have been available to start within two weeks?

Yes
No

IF WAITING TO TAKE UP JOB/WAITING FOR RESULTS/SICK/ON HOLIDAY AT LSTWK OR YES AT WLKJOB

Start4   Thinking about the four weeks ending last Sunday .... (DATE), were you looking for paid work (or a Youth Training/ET place) at any time in those four weeks?

Yes
No

Occupation and industry

ASKED FOR HEAD OF HOUSEHOLD ONLY

IF LONG-TERM SICK/LOOKING AFTER FAMILY/ DOESN'T WANT EMPLOYMENT/BELIEVES NO JOB AVAILABLE/NOT YET STARTED LOOKING/OTHER REASON AT NOLOOK

EverWk   Have you ever had a paid job or a place on a government scheme, apart from casual or holiday work?

Yes
No

IF YES AT EVERWK

LeftYr   In which year did you leave your last paid job (or government scheme)?

IF YT/COMMUNITY INDUSTRY/ET/EMPLOYMENT ACTION/OTHER SCHEME AT SCHEME OR FULL-TIME/ PART/TIME AT FTPTWK AND IF NOT STUDENT AT NOLOOK

OInd1   ASK ABOUT CURRENT JOB OF HEAD OF HOUSEHOLD
What is HOH's job?
What does HOH mainly do in his/her job?
CHECK SPECIAL QUALIFICATIONS
JOB TITLE

IF RETIRED AT NOLOOK

OInd3   ASK ABOUT JOB WHICH HEAD OF HOUSEHOLD HAS DONE THROUGH MOST OF WORKING LIFE

JOB TITLE

IF NOT STUDENT AT NOLOOK AND YES AT LOOK1 OR WAITING TO TAKE UP JOB/WAITING FOR RESULTS/TEMPORARILY SICK/ON HOLIDAY AT LSTWK OR IF DATE AT LEFTYR IS LESS THAN 8 YEARS BEFORE THE DATE OF THE INTERVIEW

OInd2   ASK ABOUT LAST JOB OF HEAD OF HOUSEHOLD

JOB TITLE

IF ANY ANSWER AT OIND1, OIND2 OR OIND3

OcInd2   JOB DESCRIPTION

Employee
Self-employed

IF EMPLOYEE AT OCIND2

Ocind3   STATUS

Manager
Foreman/supervisor
Other employee

SizeEst   How many employees work(ed) in the establishment?

1 - 24
25 - 499
500 or more

OInd5   Are/were you working for a public sector employer, for example, for central of local government or for the health service?

Yes, public sector
No, not public sector

IF SELF-EMPLOYED AT OCIND2

OInd4   Do/did you employ other people
DO NOT COUNT SELF, BUSINESS PARTNER OR RELATIVES IN HOUSEHOLD

Yes
No

IF YES AT OIND4

NoEmpee   How many people do/did you employ?
DO NOT COUNT SELF, BUSINESS PARTNER OR RELATIVES IN HOUSEHOLD

1 - 24
25 - 499
500 or more

IF ANY ANSWER AT OIND1, OIND2 OR OIND3

SOC1   IS OCCUPATIONAL CODING TO BE DONE NOW OR LATER?

Now
Later

SOC   ENTER OCCUPATION CODE

IF HOH IS MARRIED OR COHABITING

SpOcc   (ASK IF APPROPRIATE)
CHECK DETAILS OF SPOUSE/PARTNER'S CURRENT OR LAST JOB

INCOME

IF INFORMANT IS HOH/SPOUSE/PARTNER OF HOH AND OWN OUTRIGHT/WITH MORTGAGE OR SHARED OWNERSHIP AT TEN1 OR IF LOCAL AUTHORITY/HOUSING ASSOCIATION AT LLORD AND NOT YES AT TIED

SrcInc   This card shows various possible sources of income. Can you please tell me which kinds of income you (HOH) (and spouse/partner) receive? SHOW CARD M

Earnings from employment or self-employment
Pension from former employer
Child Benefit
Mobility Allowance
Income Support
Other state benefits
Interest from savings etc.
Other kinds of regular allowance from outside the household
Other sources, e.g. rent
No source of income

IF ANY ANSWER EXCEPT NO SOURCE AT SRCINC

Per   I'd like to ask you about your total income from all these sources. I don't mind whether you give it as a weekly amount, a monthly amount or an annual amount; which of these would be easiest for you:

weekly
monthly
or annually?

IF NOT YES AT LAHB

Gross   (I've just been asking you about where you both get your income from but can I ask first about ....'s (HOH's) income.) Will you please look at this card and tell me which group represents your (HOH's) total weekly/monthly/annual income from all these sources before deductions for income tax, National Insurance etc.?
SHOW CARD S AND EXPLAIN ENTER BAND NUMBER

IF 90 AT GROSS

Gross3   Could you please give me that as a monthly amount?
ENTER BAND NUMBER

IF YES AT LAHB

Gross2   (I've just been asking you about where you both get   .....)
Will you please look at this card and tell me which group represents your (HOH's) total weekly/monthly/annual income from all these sources before deductions for income tax, National Insurance etc.?   Please do not include Housing Benefit.
SHOW CARD S AND EXPLAIN ENTER BAND NUMBER

IF 90 AT GROSS

Gross4   Could you please give me that as a monthly amount?
ENTER BAND NUMBER

IF HOH IS MARRIED/COHABITING AND NOT YES AT LAHB

JntInc   And will you please look at the card again and tell me which group represents your total income and ....'s (spouse/partner's) total income taken together, before any deductions?
SHOW CARD S ENTER BAND NUMBER

IF 90 AT JNTINC

Gross5   Could you please give me that as a monthly amount?
ENTER BAND NUMBER

IF HOH IS MARRIED/COHABITING AND YES AT LAHB

JntInc2   And will you please look at the card again and tell me which group represents your total income and ....'s (spouse/partner's) total income taken together, before any deductions. Please do not include Housing Benefit.
SHOW CARD S ENTER BAND NUMBER

IF 90 AT JNTINC2

Gross6   Could you please give me that as a monthly amount?
ENTER BAND NUMBER

IF OWN WITH MORTGAGE/SHARED OWNERSHIP AT TEN1 AND INCOME SUPPORT AT SRCINC

DSSMort   People who get Income Support may get help with their mortgage repayments from the Department of Social Security, either by getting the money themselves or by having it paid direct to the building society or lender; may I just check, are your mortgage payments paid for you by the DSS:

in full
in part
or not at all?

LANDLORD SECTION

EVERPL   **To All**
INTRODUCE LANDLORD SECTION; ASK QUESTIONS ABOUT HOH
The Department of Environment is interested in people who let accommodation in return for rent.
May I check, have you (HOH) ever let a room, flat or house in return for rent?
INCLUDE LETTING PART OF OWN ACCOMMODATION/ SUBLETTING A ROOM TO OTHER HOUSEHOLD MEMBER

Yes
No

STILPL   **IF EVERPL = YES**
Are you (HOH) letting any accommodation now?
Yes
No

LAST(IF STILPL = NO)
In what year did you (HOH) last let accommodation in return for rent?
ENTER YEAR

POSSPL (IF EVERPL= NO)
Have you (HOH) ever considered letting a room, flat o house in return for rent?

Yes
No

CONNOW (IF POSSPL = YES)
Are you still considering letting or have you decided against?

Still considering
Decided against

CONPLY (IF CONNOW = DECIDED AGAINST)
In what year did you (HOH) decide against letting accommodation?
ENTER YEAR

WHYNPL (IF CONNOW = DECIDED AGAINST)
Why did you decide against letting the accommodation?
PROBE ALL REASONS

VACANT (TO ALL)
Do you have a house or flat that is vacant now?

Yes
No

WHYVAC (IF VACANT=YES)
Why is the house/flat vacant?
PROBE ALL REASONS

IFSELL (IF VACANT=YES)

(May I just check,) do you expect ...

to let the house/flat
to sell it
or do you have other plans for it?

VACPLN (IF IFSELL = other)
What do you expect to do with the house/flat?

PLFUP1 (IF EVERPL = YES OR POSSPL = YES)
The Department of Environment will be carrying out a survey later in the year among people who have experience of / have considered letting accommodation. Would you mind if we passed them your (HOH's) name and address as someone who might be willing to be interviewed by an independent research agency?

Willing: COMPLETE DOE CARD
Refused

PLFUP2 (IF VACANT = YES AND PLFUP1 NOT ASKED)
The Department of Environment will be carrying out a survey later in the year among people who have vacant accommodation. Would you mind if we passed them your (HOH's) name and address as someone who might be willing to be interviewed by an independent research agency?

Willing: COMPLETE DOE CARD
Refused

PRIVATE RENTING TENURE GROUPS

IF MORE THAN 1 FAMILY UNIT IN HOUSEHOLD AND IF ANY ANSWER EXCEPT LOCAL AUTHORITY OR HOUSING ASSOCIATION AT LLORD OR IF YES AT TIED

SmAg   Thinking about all the people in your household, I mean (.... .... etc.), are you all covered by the same renting agreement with your landlord or does any of you have a separate agreement with the landlord?

All covered by same agreement
Some member(s) of household covered by separate agreement(s)

IF OTHER RELATION/NOT RELATED AT WHOLET

SmAg1   CODE OR ASK
Thinking about the people you sublet to, are they all covered by the same rental agreement or do any of them have separate agreements with you?

All covered by same agreement
Some covered by separate agreement(s)

IF ALL COVERED BY SAME AGREEMENT/SOME COVERED BY SEPARATE AGREEMENT(S) AT SMAG OR OTHER RELATION/ NOT RELATED AT WHOLET

SbLet2   May I just check, does anyone in your household except you (HOH/spouse/partner) sublet or have rent from anyone else in the household?

Yes
No

IF ANY ANSWER EXCEPT LOCAL AUTHORITY/HOUSING ASSOCIATION AT LLORD OR YES AT TIED OR IF OTHER RELATION/NOT RELATED AT WHOLET

NumAgr   ENTER NUMBER OF SEPARATE TENANCY AGREEMENTS (I.E. GROUPS OF PEOPLE COVERED BY SEPARATE AGREEMENTS)
1. PUT ALL COUPLES IN THE SAME TENANCY GROUP
2. PUT CLOSE RELATIONS, I.E. PARENTS, CHILDREN, SIBLINGS (IN-LAW) IN THE SAME TENANCY GROUP, UNLESS COVERED BY DIFFERENT RENTING AGREEMENTS

ASK FOR EACH TENANCY GROUP

Agre   Which adults are covered by the first (second etc.) agreement?
ENTER PERSON NUMBERS

IF ANY ANSWER EXCEPT LOCAL AUTHORITY/HOUSING ASSOCIATION AT LLORD OR YES AT TIED OR IF YES, PAYS RENT AT SUBLET

PRIVATE RENTERS INTERVIEW
COMPLETE FOR EACH TENANCY GROUP

All

ArNum   AREA NUMBER   ENTERED AUTOMATICALLY

AdNum   ADDRESS NUMBER   ENTERED AUTOMATICALLY

HHNum   HOUSEHOLD NUMBER   ENTERED AUTOMATICALLY

TenNo   TENANCY GROUP NUMBER   ENTER NUMBER OF FIRST GROUP TO BE INTERVIEWED

IntNo   INTERVIEWER NUMBER   ENTER

TenMem   THE MEMBERS OF THIS TENANCY GROUP ARE ....
(ENTERED AUTOMATICALLY)
HAVE YOU SELECTED THE CORRECT TENANCY GROUP NUMBER?
IF NOT, GO BACK AND CHANGE TENANCY GROUP NUMBER
ENTER 1 TO CONTINUE

PRDate   ENTER DATE OF LAST SUNDAY

PRAdult ENTER NUMBER OF PEOPLE AGED 16 OR OVER IN THIS TENANCY GROUP

PRChild ENTER NUMBER OF CHILDREN AGED UNDER 16 IN THIS TENANCY GROUP

Tenancy Group table

PNo   ENTER PERSON NUMBER
ENTER HEAD OF TENANCY GROUP FIRST
ENTER SPOUSE/PARTNER (IF ANY) SECOND

Name   NAME OR IDENTIFIER ENTERED AUTOMATICALLY

SexP   Sex

Male
Female

Rel   Relationship to head of tenancy group

Head of tenancy group
Spouse/partner
Child of head of tenancy group/spouse
Other relation
Other

Child table

CNo   ENTER PERSON NUMBER OF CHILD

CRel   Relationship to head of tenancy group

Child of head of tenancy group/spouse
Other relation
Other

PRInf   INFORMANT IS:

Head of tenancy group
Spouse/partner of head of tenancy group
Child/stepchild of head of tenancy group
Other

Inf2   IS HEAD OF THE TENANCY GROUP HEAD OF THE HOUSEHOLD?

Yes
No

Renter   CODE OR ASK

In whose name or names is the acccommodation rented?
READ OUT CODES IF NECESSARY

Head of tenancy group's only
Head of tenancy group's and spouse's/partner's jointly
Spouse's/partner's only
Head of tenancy group's jointly with someone else
Spouse's/partner's jointly with someone else
Head of tenancy group's and spouse's/partner's jointly with someone else

IF THE INFORMANT IS NOT THE HEAD OF THE TENANCY GROUP/SPOUSE PARTNER AND THE ACCOMMODATION IS IN THE NAME OF SOMEONE ELSE APART FROM HEAD OF GROUP/SPOUSE/PARTNER (LAST 3 CODES AT RENTER)

Oth   Is the accommodation rented jointly in your name o not?

Yes
No

IF TENANCY GROUP INCLUDES SPOUSE/PARTNER OF HEAD OF GROUP

Whofst   May I just check, did .... (HEAD OF TENANCY GROUP) and .... (SPOUSE/PARTNER) move in here together or did one of you/them move in first?

Moved in together
Head of group moved in first
Spouse/partner moved in first

IF YES AT OTH

Othfst   Did you move in here at the same time as .... (HEAD OF GROUP) or did one of you move in first?

Moved in at same time
Head of group moved in first
Informant moved in first
IF SPOUSE FIRST AT WHOFST AND INFORMANT FIRST AT OTHFST OR IF SPOUSE'S JOINTLY WITH SOMEONE ELSE AT RENTER AND SPOUSE FIRST AT WHOFST AND YES AT OTH

OFst1   Did you move in at the same time as .... (SPOUSE/PARTNER) or did one of you move in first?

Moved in at same time
Spouse/partner moved in first
Informant moved in first

TYPE AND CONDITIONS OF TENANCY
"YOU" REFERS TO HOH/SPOUSE/PARTNER OR OTHER FORMAL TENANT OR TO THE TENANT WHO MOVED IN FIRST, WHERE THIS IS APPROPRIATE

PLLord   INTERVIEWER CODE OR ASK
May I just check, is the landlord:

an individual
or an organisation?

IF INDIVIDUAL AT PLLORD OR IF HEAD OF TENANCY GROUP IS HEAD OF HOUSEHOLD AND SOMEONE RELATED/SOMEONE ALREADY A FRIEND/INDIVIDUAL EMPLOYER/ANOTHER INDIVIDUAL LANDLORD AT LLORD (IN HOUSEHOLD INTERVIEW)

LlHh CODE OR ASK
Is the landlord a member of your household?

Yes
No

ALL

RDir Do you (HEAD OF GROUP/SPOUSE/PARTNER) rent directly
from the landlord or do you rent through an estate or letting agency?

Directly from the landlord
Through a professional agent
Through someone else on behalf of the owner

NOT ASKED IF HEAD OF TENANCY GROUP IS HEAD OF HOUSEHOLD - INFORMATION ALREADY COLLECTED

FurnPr Is your accommodation provided:

furnished
partly furnished
or unfurnished?

ALL

YStart In which year did .... (HEAD OF GROUP/SPOUSE/PARTNER - WHICHEVER MOVED IN FIRST) first become tenant(s) of this accommodation - I mean when it was first in your name?

IF 1989 AT YSTART

MStart In which month was that?

Ctract (THIS QUESTION REFERS TO THE TIME WHEN THE FIRST OF THE PRESENT TENANTS BECAME A TENANT (BEFORE THE INFORMANT MOVED IN))

When .... first started to rent this accommodation:

did .... and the landlord sign a written agreement
did .... have a written agreement which you didn't sign
or did .... just have an unwritten agreement?

IF UNWRITTEN OR DK/REFUSAL/NA AT CTRACT

Written Did .... have a notice in writing saying what kind of agreement it was?

Yes
No

IF SIGNED WRITTED/HAD WRITTEN AGREEMENT AT CTRACT

Copy Was .... given a copy of the contract/agreement or not?

Given a copy
Not given a copy

IF GIVEN A COPY AT COPY OR YES AT WRITTEN

ConChk ASK INFORMANT TO GET THE CONTRACT OR AGREEMENT/NOTICE FOR REFERENCE IN THE FOLLOWING QUESTIONS AND CODE WHETHER YOU HAVE BEEN ABLE TO CHECK IT OR NOT

Contract/notice checked
Contract/notice not checked

IF SIGNED WRITTEN/HAD WRITTEN AGREEMENT AT CTRACT OR YES AT WRITTEN AND IF NOT YES AT LLHH

Short I'd like to ask you a few questions to make sure what kind of agreement it is.
There is a form of tenancy called a shorthold. It is for a fixed period and you must be given a notice in writing by the landlord that tells you that it is a shorthold tenancy agreement. Since January 1989, new shorthold agreements have been Assured Shortholds; before that date, they were Protected Shortholds. Here is an example of a notice to a tenant saying that the agreement is an Assured Shorthold. SHOW EXAMPLE OF NOTICE
Does the agreement or notice state that it is:

an Assured Shorthold
a Shorthold (not Assured)
or does it not say that it is a Shorthold at all?
Shorthold but not sure if Assured or not

IF DOES NOT SAY SHORTHOLD/DK/NA AT SHORT OR YES AT LLHH

OthWay There are various other ways in which landlords can let accommodation.
Will you please look at this card and tell me if the letting is one of these? SHOW CARD N
ENTER FIRST THAT APPLIES

Company licence
College licence
Non-exclusive occupancy agreement
Holiday let
Low season let
None of these

IF COMPANY LICENCE AT OTHWAY

Empa CHECK: DOES ANYONE IN THE TENANCY GROUP WORK FOR THE COMPANY?

Yes
No

IF NONE OF THESE/DK/NA/DNA AT OTHWAY AND NOT YES AT LLHH

Mrtge Some tenants have a rental-purchase agreement which is rather like hire purchase; they pay a mortgage but don't own the property until the final payment has been made. Is the agreement like this?

Yes
No

IF AFTER 1980 AND BEFORE 1989 AT YSTART AND IF DOES NOT SAY SHORTHOLD/DK/NA AT SHORT AND IF NONE OF THESE/DK/NA AT OTHWAY AND NO/DK/ NO AT MRTGE AND IF NOT YES AT LLHH

Assure   At the time when .... (HEAD OF GROUP/SPOUSE/PART-NER) began to rent this accommodation, some lettings were called Assured tenancies. Was .... notified at that time that it was an Assured tenancy or not?

IF INFORMANT IS HEAD OF GROUP/SPOUSE/PART-NER OR IF INFORMANT IS SOMEONE ELSE AND YES AT OTH

Advice   Have you ever had any professional advice about a rental contract or rights as a tenant from any of the people or organisations on this card? SHOW CARD N2

Solicitor (private)
Citizens' Advice Bureau
Local Authority
Law centre
Company lawyer
Housing Advice Centre
Other Official Organisation

None of these
IF DATE AT YSTART 2 YEARS AGO OR MORE RECENT

PR2y   Was this accommodation rented privately before .... (FIRST TO MOVE IN) moved in here?

Yes
No

IF YES AT PR2y AND DATE AT YSTART 1 YEAR AGO OR MORE RECENT

PR1Y   Was it rented privately 1 year ago?
IF INFORMANT DOES NOT KNOW, TRY TO FIND OUT FROM SOMEONE ELSE AT THE ADDRESS, IF APPRO-PRIATE

Yes
No

IF YES AT PR2y AND DATE AT YSTART MORE THAN 1 YEAR AGO OR IF YES AT PR1Y

PR2Y2   Was it rented privately 2 years ago?
IF INFORMANT DOES NOT KNOW, TRY TO FIND OUT FROM SOMEONE ELSE AT THE ADDRESS, IF APPRO-PRIATE

Yes
No

ALL

TFix   When .... started ....'s first rental agreement here, was it taken on for a fixed length of time or not ?

Fixed time
Not

IF FIXED TIME AT TFIX

LFix   How long a period was that?

Under 6 months
6 months, less than 12
1 year, less than 2
2 years, less than 3
3 years, less than 5
5 years or over

EFix   Has that first period expired or not?

Yes
No

IF YES AT EFIX

NAgre1   Since the first rental agreement with the landlord, have y signed another agreement?

Yes
No

IF NO AT NAGRE1

NAgre2   Have you had a new agreement in writing?

Yes
No

IF NO AT NAGRE2

NAgre3   Have you agreed in discussion with the landlord that you continue renting or not?

Have agreed
Have not agreed/has not been discussed

IF YES AT NAGRE1 OR YES AT NAGRE2 OR HA AGREED AT NAGRE3

YNew   In which year did you agree formally to continue renting h or sign another contract?

IF 1989 AT YNEW

MNew   In which month was that?

IF YES AT NAGRE1 OR YES AT NAGRE2 OR HA AGREED AT NAGRE3

NFix   Was this new agreement for a fixed length of time or no

Fixed time
Not for fixed time

IF FIXED TIME AT NFIX

LNew   How long a period was this agreement for?

Under 6 months
6 months, less than 12
1 year, less than 2
2 years, less than 3
3 years, less than 5
5 years or over

ALL

Move   Do you have the right to stay here for as long as you like or might you have to move some time, even if you wanted to stay?

Right to stay as long as like
Doesn't have the right to stay but thinks will be able to stay
Might have to move

IF MIGHT HAVE TO MOVE/DK AT MOVE

MMove   Under what circumstances might you have to move even if you wanted to stay?

If the landlord wanted to sell the accommodation/ renovate/redevelop it
If the landlord needed accommodation for self or own family
If left job - accommodation goes with job
When rental contract comes to an end
If did not pay rent
Other, for example, if landlord dies

ALL

WJob   Does this accommodation go with your present job or the job of anyone covered by this tenancy agreement (that is ....)?

Goes with someone's job
Does not go with anyone's job
Used to go with job but does not now
Goes with job of someone not at present in household

IF GOES WITH SOMEONE'S JOB AT WJOB

JWho   Whose job does it go with?
ENTER PERSON NUMBER

IF GOES WITH SOMEONE'S JOB/JOB OF SOMEONE NOT AT PRESENT IN HOUSEHOLD

RLeave   Do you (....) have to live here as long as you (....) the job or would you (....) be allowed to live somewhere else if you (....) wanted to?

Has to live here
Allowed to live somewhere else

RStay   If you (....) gave up the job, would you (....) have the right to stay on in this accommodation or would you (....) have to move out?

Would have the right to stay on
Might be able to stay on
Would have to move

ALL

LandR   May I just check, do you rent this accommodation from someone who normally lives here and expects to come back after you move out?

Yes
No

IF NOT YES AT LLHH

TSuc   People sometimes take over a tenancy from their parents or someone else already living in the accommodation. Did you do this?

Yes
No

IF YES AT TSUC

TWho   Who was that?
CODE FIRST THAT APPLIES

Husband/wife/partner
Father/mother
Brother/sister
Son/daughter
Father-in-law/mother-in-law
Son-in-law/daughter-in-law
Brother-in-law/sister-in-law
Grandparent
Other

NTen   Had you been living here before you took over the tenancy?

Had been living here
Had not been living here

TenD   Did you take over the tenancy on the death of the previous tenant?

Yes
No

RENT
QUESTIONS REFER TO OVERALL RENT FOR WHOLE OF TENANCY GROUP'S ACCOMMODATION

RFree   May I just check, are you charged rent or is the accommodation rent-free?

Charged rent
Rent-free
Pays part of rent, employer pays part (accommodation goes with job)

IF RENT-FREE AT RFREE

PFree   You said that you have the accommodation rent-free. Does anyone outside your household pay rent on your behalf?

Yes
No

IF RENT-FREE AT RFREE AND GOES WITH SOMEONE'S JOB AT WJOB

Wage   Is anything deducted from your (....'s) salary/wages for rent?

Yes
No

IF YES AT WAGE

WagePer   How often is rent deducted from your (....'s) salary/wages?

Week
Two weeks
Three weeks
Four weeks
Calendar month
Three months
Six months
Year
Other

IF OTHER AT WAGEPER

SWPer   Please specify
ENTER NUMBER OF WEEKS

IF YES AT WAGE

WageAmt   How much is deducted from your (....'s) salary/wages for rent?
ENTER AMOUNT TO NEAREST £1

IF CHARGED RENT/PAYS PART OF RENT AT RFREE OR YES AT PFREE

RPer   How often do you pay the rent? (How often is the rent paid?)

Week
Two weeks
Three weeks
Four weeks
Calendar month
Three months
Six months
Year
Other

IF OTHER AT RPER

SRPer   Please specify
ENTER NUMBER OF WEEKS

IF CHARGED RENT/PAYS PART OF RENT AT RFREE OR YES AT PFREE

PRent   How much is the rent each (..../time you pay) before any Housing Benefit or rent rebate?
ENTER AMOUNT TO NEAREST £1
GIVE TOTAL RENT CHARGED FOR TENANT'S AC-COMMODATION BEFORE HOUSING BENEFIT

IF CHARGED RENT/PAYS PART OF RENT AT RFREE OR YES AT PFREE OR YES AT WAGE

BusP   INTERVIEWER CODE OR ASK
Does the accommodation include business premises?

Yes
No

IF YES AT BUSP

NBuSP   Does the rent you mentioned include rent for the business part of the accommodation or not?

Includes rent for business accommodation
Does not include it

IF INCLUDES RENT FOR BUSINESS ACCOMMODA-TION AT NBUSP

BusPR   How much is the rent for the accommodation without the business premises?
ENTER AMOUNT TO NEAREST £1

IF CHARGED RENT/PAYS PART OF RENT AT RFREE OR YES AT PFREE OR YES AT WAGE

PRSbLet   May I just check, do you sublet to any other member of your household?
DO NOT INCLUDE CLOSE RELATIONS (PARENTS, CHILDREN, SIBLINGS OR CLOSE IN-LAWS)

Yes
No

IF YES AT PRSBLET

SubRen   How much rent do you get (altogether) from sub-letting?
ENTER AMOUNT TO NEAREST £1
GIVE TOTAL RENT PAID BY SUB-TENANTS APART FROM CLOSE RELATIONS

SubPer   How long a period does that cover?

Week
Two weeks
Three weeks
Four weeks
Calendar month
Three months
Six months
Year
Other

IF OTHER AT SUBPER

SpSub   Please specify
ENTER NUMBER OF WEEKS

IF BEFORE 1989 AT YSTART

FairR   Most rents are agreed privately between the landlord and tenant. Sometimes the tenant can apply to the local rent officer or rent assessment committee to decide on a 'fair' rent which is then registered. Has your rent for this accommodation been registered as a fair rent in this way or not?

Fair rent registered
Not registered

IF FAIR RENT REGISTERED AT FAIRR

FLast   In what year was the rent last registered?

FFirst   In what year was the rent first registered?

IF 1989 OR LATER AT YSTART

P1989   Most rents are agreed privately between the landlord and tenant. Sometimes the tenant can apply to the local rent officer or rent assessment committee to decide on a reasonable market rent. Has your rent for this accommodation been set as a reasonable market rent in this way or not?

Set as reasonable market rent
Not set as reasonable market rent

IF CHARGED RENT/PAYS PART OF RENT AT RFREE OR YES AT PFREE OR YES AT WAGE

Meals   May I just check, does the landlord provide any regular meals which are paid for either as part of the rent or separately?

Yes
No

IF YES AT MEALS

InRent   Is the cost of meals included in the rent or is there a separate charge for them?

Included in rent
Separate charge

IF INCLUDED IN RENT AT INRENT

RMeal   How much of the rent is for meals?
ENTER TO NEAREST £1

MPer   What period does this cover?

Week
Two weeks
Three weeks
Four weeks
Calendar month
Three months
Six months
Year
Other

IF OTHER AT MPER

SMPer   Please specify
ENTER NUMBER OF WEEKS

IF SEPARATE CHARGE AT INRENT

PMeal   How much does the landlord charge for these meals on top of the rent?
ENTER TO NEAREST £1

MPerP   What period does this cover?

Week
Two weeks
Three weeks
Four weeks
Calendar month
Three months
Six months
Year
Other

IF OTHER AT MPERP

SMPerP   Please specify
ENTER NUMBER OF WEEKS

IF CHARGED RENT/PAYS PART OF RENT AT RFREE OR YES AT PFREE OR YES AT WAGE

Incr   In some rental agreements, the rent covers things like heating and lighting; in others the landlord makes an extra charge for things of this sort.
SHOW CARD O Will you please look at this card and tell me if any of the items listed are included in the rent? CODE ALL THAT APPLY

Heating (including central heating)
Lighting inside the accommodation
Hot water
Gas
Electricity
Telephone rental (line and/or instrument)
Garage
Cleaning services
Laundry services
Care of the garden
Porter or caretaker services
Lighting outside the accommodation
Any other service
None of these

FOR EACH ITEM INCLUDED IN RENT

SerPay   How much of the rent each week (....) is for (....)?
ENTER TO NEAREST £1

IF CHARGED RENT/PAYS PART OF RENT AT RFREE OR YES AT PFREE OR YES AT WAGE

AddCh   Do you pay an additional charge to the landlord for any of the services on this card?

Codes as at Incr
FOR EACH ITEM FOR WHICH THERE IS AN ADDITIONAL CHARGE

AddPay   How much did you pay for (....) last time?
ENTER TO NEAREST £1

AddPer   What time period did this cover?

Week
Two weeks
Three weeks
Four weeks
Calendar month
Three months
Six months
Year
Other

IF OTHER AT ADDPER

SAdPer   Please specify
ENTER NUMBER OF WEEKS

IF CHARGED RENT/PAYS PART OF RENT AT RFREE OR YES AT PFREE OR YES AT WAGE

WRates   Do you pay water and sewerage rates on top of the rent, either direct to the water company or to the landlord?

Yes
No

IF YES AT WRATES

WAmt   How much was the last water and sewerage bill for?
ENTER AMOUNT DUE TO NEAREST £1
IF NO BILL SO FAR AT THIS ADDRESS, ENTER [FOR DON'T KNOW

WPer   How many times a year is this amount paid?

IF CHARGED RENT/PAYS PART OF RENT AT RFREE OR YES AT PFREE OR YES AT WAGE AND IF BEFORE APRIL 1990 AT YSTART (AND MSTART)

Rates   Before the Community Charge or Poll Tax came in, in April 1990, were domestic rates included in the rent or did you pay rates separately?

Included in rent
Paid separately

IF INCLUDED IN RENT AT RATES

Rfund   When the Community Charge came in and the landlord no longer paid rates on your behalf, was the rent adjusted to take account of this, for example, through a rent reduction or a smaller increase than there would have been otherwise?

Yes
No

IF YES AT RFUND

Action   How was the rent adjusted?

Rent reduced
Rent not increased
Rent increased less than it would have been
Refund give
Other financial benefit
Non-financial benefit

IF NO AT REFUND

Refuse   Had you asked the landlord to make an adjustment to the rent or not?

Had asked
Had not asked

IF CHARGED RENT/PAYS PART OF RENT AT RFREE OR YES AT PFREE OR YES AT WAGE

RChnge   In the last two years (Since you moved here IF MORE RECENTLY) has the total rent for the accommodation:

gone up
gone down
gone both up and down

IF GONE UP/BOTH UP AND DOWN AT RCHNGE

YInc   In which year did it last go up?

LRent   How much was the rent each (....) before it went up last time?
ENTER AMOUNT TO NEAREST £1

IF CHARGED RENT/PAYS PART OF RENT AT RFREE OR YES AT PFREE OR YES AT WAGE AND IF DATE AT YSTART IS NOT MORE THAN 5 YEARS BEFORE DATE OF INTERVIEW

Bond   To get this accommodation did you have to pay:

a returnable deposit to cover damage,
a non-returnable premium or fee,
or did you not have to pay a deposit or premium?

IF DEPOSIT TO COVER DAMAGE OR NON-RETURN-ABLE PREMIUM AT BOND

BondP   How much was that?
ENTER AMOUNT TO NEAREST £1

IF CHARGED RENT/PAYS PART OF RENT AT RFREE OR YES AT PFREE OR YES AT WAGE

ERent   You said that you pay the rent every (....); when you first began to rent this accommodation, did you just make:

one payment in advance
or did you have to pay more in advance than for just one rent period?

Rent paid in arrears

IF MORE THAN FOR JUST ONE RENT PERIOD AT ERENT

EPer   What period did that cover?

Week
Two weeks
Three weeks
Four weeks
Calendar month
Three months
Six months
Year
Other

IF OTHER AT EPER

SEPer   Please specify
ENTER NUMBER OF WEEKS

IF MORE THAN FOR JUST ONE RENT PERIOD AT ERENT

ERentP   How much did you have to pay in advance?
ENTER AMOUNT TO NEAREST £1

IF CHARGED RENT/PAYS PART OF RENT AT RFREE OR YES AT PFREE OR YES AT WAGE

Ford When you were looking for somewhere to rent, did you have to turn down any suitable place because you couldn't afford the deposit or the rent in advance, even though you would have been able to afford the normal rent?

Yes
No

Level What do you think of the level of the present rent for your accommodation; do you think it is:

very high for what you get
slightly high
about right
slightly low
very low for what you get?

IF INFORMANT IS HEAD OF GROUP/SPOUSE/PART-NER/CHILD OF INFORMANT OR IS SOMEONE ELSE AND YES AT OTH

rrPr May I just check, is the rent paid up-to-date at present or is any rent owing, I mean, owing for a fortnight or longer?

Paid up-to-date
Rent owing for a fortnight or longer

IF PAID UP-TO-DATE AT ARRPR

rrPrP Have you been up-to-date with the rent for the whole of the last 12 months or has any rent ever been owing for a fortnight or longer during that time?

Up-to-date during the last 12 months
Rent owing for fortnight or longer

IF RENT OWING AT ARRPR OR RENT OWING AT ARRPRP

rrReP Did you have difficulty in paying the rent on time because of any of the things on this card?
SHOW CARD P
CODE ALL THAT APPLY

Increase in the rent
Unemployment
Reduction in working hours
Loss of overtime
Illness
Other debts or responsibilities
Problems in connection with Housing Benefit
Domestic problems
None of these

IF PROBLEMS IN CONNECTION WITH HOUSING BEN-EFIT AT ARRREP

BPrbP You said that you have had problems with Housing Benefit; what was the problem? SHOW CARD Q

Delay in getting reply to application for Housing Benefit/still waiting
Delay in payment of Housing Benefit/still waiting
Housing Benefit paid was less than expected
Application turned down
Other

REPAIRS AND RELATIONS WITH LANDLORD

ALL

RepRes Now a few questions about repairs. First, thinking about structural and external repairs, including gutters, pipes, drains and outside painting; are repairs of this kind the landlord's responsibility or your responsibility?

Landlord's responsibility
Tenant's responsibility
Joint responsibility of landlord and tenant(DO NOT PROMPT)
Other

RepWGE And thinking of repairs to the water, gas and electricity supply, heating and water heating; are repairs of this kind the landlord's responsibility or your responsibility?

Codes as at RepRes

RepDec And what about internal decoration; is that the landlord's responsibility or your responsibility?

Codes as at RepRes

RepNS And thinking about other non-structural repairs, such as repairing or replacing door handles or electrical fittings; are repairs of this kind the landlord's responsibility or your responsibility?

Codes as at RepRes

IF LANDLORD'S RESPONSIBILITY OR JOINT RE-SPONSIBILITY AT REPRES

SelfR You said that the landlord is responsible for structural external repairs but have you ever had any repairs of this kind done yourself instead of getting the landlord to do them?

Yes
No

IF LANDLORD'S RESPONSIBILITY OR JOINT RE-SPONSIBILITY AT REPWGE

SelfWG You said that the landlord is responsible for repairs to the water, gas and electricity supply but have you ever had any repairs of this kind done yourself instead of getting the landlord to do them?

Yes
No

IF LANDLORD'S RESPONSIBILITY OR JOINT RE-SPONSIBILITY AT REPDEC

SelfD You said that the landlord is responsible for internal decoration but have you ever had this done yourself instead of getting the landlord to do it?

Yes
No

IF LANDLORD'S RESPONSIBILITY OR JOINT RESPONSIBILITY AT REPNS

SelfNS   You said that the landlord is responsible for other non-structural repairs such as door handles but have you ever had any repairs of this kind done yourself instead of getting the landlord to do them?

Yes
No

ALL

AskRep   May I just check, since you have been here have you asked the landlord to carry out any repairs or not?

Have asked for repairs
Have not asked for repairs

IF HAS ASKED FOR REPAIRS AT ASKREP

AllRep   Has the landlord carried out all the repairs you asked for or not? Please choose your answer from this card.
SHOW CARD R
CHOOSE MOST APPROPRIATE CODE

Has carried out all repairs asked for
Repairs asked for only recently
Repairs being done but not completed
Has carried out some repairs but not all
Has not carried out any repairs asked for

SortDf   Have you had any difficulties of the kind shown on this card in getting the landlord to do the repairs?

Repairs never done
Landlord reluctant but did them
Repairs not finished/badly done
Tenant had to pay for repairs
Tenant had to do repairs
Difficult to get hold of/communicate with landlord
Repairs took too long
Any other kind of difficulty
None of these

IF HAS NOT ASKED AT ASKREP AND LANDLORD'S RESPONSIBILITY OR JOINT RESPONSIBILITY AT REPRES, REPWGE, REPDEC OR REPNS

ExpRep   If you were to ask the landlord to carry out repairs, do you think you would have any difficulty in getting them carried out or not?

Expect to have difficulty
Do not expect to have difficulty
Other answer, e.g. depends on kind of repair

CRep   If you needed to get repairs carried out by the landlord, who would you get in touch with first?

Landlord
The landlord's agent
Other named person or builder

ALL

NRep   Could you look at this card and tell me whether the accommodation is in need of any repairs of the kinds we have been talking about at present.
SHOW CARD T2
CODE ALL THAT APPLY

structural or external repairs
repairs to water, gas or electricity
internal decoration
other non-structural repairs
other structural repairs
none of these

TermsL   On the whole, how would you describe your relationship with the landlord (and the agent); would you say you are on:

good terms
poor or sometimes poor terms
neither good nor poor terms

IF POOR OR SOMETIMES POOR AT TERMSL

TBadR   Why is that? CODE ALL THAT APPLY

Conflict about repairs
Landlord wants to get tenant out/taking action to evict
Landlord making financial demands
Landlord entering premises without permission
Landlord using threats/intimidating behaviour
Landlord hard to contact
Landlord unpleasant/untrustworthy/difficult
Other

ALL

WTen2   Has the landlord ever tried to get you to sign a new tenancy agreement which you felt to be worse than the existing agreement?

Yes
No

IF GOOD TERMS OR NEITHER GOOD NOR POOR TERMS AT TERMSL

WTen1   Although you are not on poor terms with the landlord, has he/she ever tried to get you to sign a new tenancy agreement which you felt to be worse than the existing agreement?

Yes
No

IF YES AT WTEN2 OR YES AT WTEN1

STen   Did you sign the new agreement?

Yes
No

ALL

MakeL   Has the landlord ever done any of the things on this card? SHOW CARD U CODE ALL THAT APPLY

Offered you money to leave
Tried to get you out in other ways
Done anything which made you want to leave
Done anything which made you feel uncomfortable in any way
None of these

IF TRIED TO GET OUT, DONE ANYTHING WHICH MADE WANT TO LEAVE OR MADE FEEL UNCOMFORTABLE AT MAKEL

How   In what ways has the landlord tried to get you out or done things that made you want to leave or feel uncomfortable?

Slow or poor quality repairs
Has taken legal proceedings to evict
Has entered property without permission
Has made financial demands
Has used intimidating or threatening behaviour
Other

SATISFACTION WITH ACCOMMODATION

NOT ASKED IF HEAD OF TENANCY GROUP IS HEAD OF HOUSEHOLD (ASKED IN HOUSEHOLD INTERVIEW)

Satis   How satisfied are you with this accommodation? SHOW CARD V

Very satisfied
Fairly satisfied
Neither satisfied nor dissatisfied
Slightly dissatisfied
Very dissatisfied

FINDING PRIVATELY RENTED ACCOMMODATION

IF DATE AT YSTART IS NOT MORE THAN 5 YEARS BEFORE DATE OF INTERVIEW

Find   When you were trying to find somewhere to rent, how did you first find out about this accommodation? SHOW CARD W

Through a friend or relative
Through someone at work
Knew someone already living here
Card in shop window
Notice board at work/college
Through a newspaper or magazine
Through an estate or letting agent
Sign outside the property
Other

Easy   How easy was it to find somewhere to rent:

very easy
fairly easy
slightly difficult
very difficult?

IF SLIGHTLY/VERY DIFFICULT AT EASY

Suit   Did you have difficulty in finding somewhere suitable which you could afford?

Yes
No

DiffO   Did you have any other difficulties?

Yes
No

IF YES AT DIFFO

Diffs   What sorts of difficulty did you have? CODE ALL THAT APPLY

Finding somewhere in the right area
Finding somewhere in good condition
Finding somewhere large enough
Finding somewhere small enough
Finding somewhere which took children
Finding somewhere which took pets
Finding somewhere suitable in other ways
Finding somewhere quickly
Providing references
Finding somewhere which accepted DSS claimants
Other

HOUSING HISTORY IN LAST 10 YEARS THE QUESTIONS APPLY TO THE HEAD OF THE TENANCY GROUP UNLESS THE SPOUSE/PARTNER IS A TENANT AND MOVED IN BEFORE HER HUSBAND/PARTNER

ALL

PrevAP   I want to ask you about all the places you (....) lived in in the last ten years (or since you (....) were 16 if that is more recent). Please tell me by looking at this card about all the kinds of accommodation you (....) lived in, apart from the present accommodation, during that period. SHOW CARD X
CODE ALL THAT APPLY
IF A PLACE FALLS INTO MORE THAN ONE CATEGORY, CODE THE FIRST ON THE LIST

Only at this address
Lived abroad
At home with parents/in-laws/close family
With distant relatives or friends
In a college, student hostel or hall of residence
In some other type of hostel (including women's refuge)
In accommodation that went with job
As the owner of a house or flat
As the tenant of a council house or flat
As the tenant of a housing association, co-operative As the tenant of a privately rented house or flat
As a sharer in a privately rented house or flat
As a lodger/boarder in bed and breakfast or other accommodation
Sleeping rough
Some other arrangement

IF ANY ANSWER EXCEPT ONLY AT THIS ADDRESS/ LIVED ABROAD AT PREVAP

MoveYN   Have you (....) moved in the last three years?

Yes
No

IF YES AT MOVEYN

NoMove   In the last three years, that is since (DATE), how many times have you moved in all, including the time when you moved here?
IF MORE THAN 10 TIMES, ENTER 10

LastAc   Which of the following best describes your last accommodation? SHOW CARD X AND EXPLAIN THAT THE FIRST 2 CODES WILL NOT APPLY

CODES AS AT PREVAP

DMOVE, DMONTH AND RMOVE ARE NOT ASKED IF THE HEAD OF THE TENANCY GROUP IS THE HEAD OF HOUSEHOLD (ASKED IN HOUSEHOLD INTERVIEW)

DMove   When did you (....) start living there?
ENTER YEAR

DMonth   In which month did you (....) start living there?

RMove   Here are some reasons why people move; can you tell me why you (....) moved last time? SHOW CARD Y

To move to a better neighbourhood/pleasanter area
To be near a new job
To be nearer existing job
Wanted larger house/flat or one which was better in some other way
Wanted smaller/cheaper house/flat
Had to leave tied accommodation/took job with tied accommodation
Could not afford mortgage payments on previous house/flat
Could not afford rent on previous house/flat
Divorce/separation
Marriage/began living together
Other family/personal reasons
Wanted independent accommodation/own home not shared To go to/finished college/university
Previous accommodation no longer available
Other reason

Miles   How many miles from here was the last place you (....) lived?

Abroad
Under 1 mile
1 mile but not 2 miles
2 miles but not 5 miles
5 miles but not 10 miles
10 miles but not 20 miles
20 miles but not 50 miles
50 miles or more

FUTURE EXPECTATIONS
ASKED ONLY IF INFORMANT IS HEAD OF TENANCY GROUP OR SPOUSE/PARTNER OF HEAD

PRBuy   Do you think you will always go on renting or do you think you will buy somewhere in the future?

Go on renting
Buy somewhere
Other

IF BUY SOMEWHERE AT PRBUY

PThis   Do you think you will buy this place or not?

Yes
No

IF YES AT PTHIS

PLong   How long do you think it will be before you buy this place?

In the process of buying
Within 12 months
1 but not 2 years
2 but not 3 years
3 but not 6 years
5 but not 10 years
10 years or more

IF BUY SOMEWHERE AT PRBUY AND YES AT PTHIS OR IF RENT/DK AT PRBUY

PMove   Do you think you will move from here at some time in the future or not?

Yes
No

IF YES AT PMOVE OR NO/DK AT PTHIS

PLong1   How much longer do you think you will be in this accommodation? SHOW CARD Z

Less than 3 months
3 months but less than 6 months
6 months but less than one year
1 year but less than 2 years
2 years but less than 5 years
5 years or longer

IF BUY SOMEWHERE AT PRBUY AND NO/DK AT PTHIS

PRtBuy   If you move, do you expect to rent again straight away or to buy somewhere?

Rent
Buy

IF BUY SOMEWHERE AT PRBUY AND NO/DK AT PTHIS AND RENT/DK AT PRtBuy

PLong2   How long do you think it will be before you buy somewhere?

In the process of buying
Within 12 months/year
1 but not 2 years
2 but not 3 years
3 but not 6 years
6 but not 10 years
10 years or more

EMPLOYMENT OF HEAD OF TENANCY GROUP NOT ASKED IF HEAD OF TENANCY GROUP IS HEAD OF HOUSEHOLD (INFORMATION COLLECTED ELSEWHERE)

EmpHT   ASK OR RECORD
CODE MAIN ACTIVITY OF HEAD OF TENANCY GROUP

Are you (....) at present:

in full-time paid work
in part-time paid work
on Employment Training or a Youth Training scheme
unemployed and actively seeking work
retired from paid work
in full-time education
or doing something else?

IF DOING SOMETHING ELSE AT EMPHT

EverWk   Have you ever had a paid job or a place on a government scheme, apart from casual or holiday work?

Yes
No

IF YES AT EVERWK

LeftYr   In which year did you leave your last paid job (or government scheme)?

IF FULL-TIME/PART-TIME PAID WORK OR EMPLOYMENT/YOUTH TRAINING AT EMPHT

POIn1   ASK ABOUT CURRENT JOB OF HEAD OF TENANCY GROUP

JOB TITLE

IF UNEMPLOYED AT EMPHT OR IF DATE AT LEFTYR IS LESS THAN 8 YEARS BEFORE THE DATE OF THE INTERVIEW

POIn2   ASK ABOUT LAST JOB OF HEAD OF TENANCY GROUP

JOB TITLE

IF RETIRED AT EMPHT

POIn3   ASK ABOUT JOB WHICH HEAD OF TENANCY GROUP HAS DONE THROUGH MOST OF WORKING LIFE

JOB TITLE

IF NOT FULL-TIME EDUCATION AT EMPHT AND IF ANY ANSWER AT POIN1, POIN2 OR POIN3

POInd2   JOB DESCRIPTION OF HEAD OF TENANCY GROUP
Employee
Self-employed

IF EMPLOYEE AT POIND2

POInd3   STATUS OF HEAD OF TENANCY GROUP

Manager
Foreman
Other employee

SizeEst   How many employees work(ed) in the establishment?

1 - 24
25 - 499
500 or more

POInd5   Are/were you working for a public sector employer, for example, for central or local government or for the health service?

Yes, public sector
No, not public sector

IF SELF-EMPLOYED AT POIND2

POInd4   Do/did you employ other people?
DO NOT COUNT SELF, BUSINESS PARTNER OR RELATIVES IN HOUSEHOLD

Yes
No

IF YES AT POIND4

NoEmpee   How many people do/did you employ?
DO NOT COUNT SELF, BUSINESS PARTNER OR RELATIVES IN HOUSEHOLD

1 - 24
25 - 499
500 or more

IF ANY ANSWER AT POIN1, POIN2 OR POIN3

SOC1   IS OCCUPATIONAL CODING TO BE DONE NOW OR LATER?

Now
Later

SOC   ENTER OCCUPATION CODE

PRIVATE RENTERS INCOME SECTION

INFORMATION COLLECTED FOR EACH ADULT IN TENANCY GROUP, BEGINNING WITH INFORMANT

Intro   INTRODUCE INCOME SECTION
IF POSSIBLE, GET INCOME DATA FROM EACH ADULT MEMBER OF TENANCY GROUP IN TURN; IF NOT, TRY TO GET INCOME DATA FOR EACH ADULT BY PROXY
CODE OUTCOME

Willing to give (some) income data
Refused income section altogether

IPerNo   ENTER PERSON NUMBER
START WITH INFORMANT

PerNam — **NAME/IDENTIFIER SHOWN ON SCREEN AUTOMATI-CALLY**

EmpAct — ASK OR RECORD
CODE MAIN ACTIVITY

Are you (....) at present:

in full-time paid work
in part-time paid work
on Employment Training or a Youth Training scheme
unemployed and actively seeking work
retired from paid work
in full-time education
or doing something else?

IF WILLING TO GIVE (SOME) DATA AT INTRO

Pergiv — INTERVIEWER RECORD: IS INCOME INFORMATION GIVEN BY:

the person to whom it refers (1st OPTION)
or someone else (proxy) (2nd OPTION)?

1st AND 2nd OPTIONS NOT POSSIBLE

IF INCOME INFORMATION CANNOT BE OBTAINED FROM THE PERSON TO WHOM IT APPLIES OR BY PROXY, THE INTERVIEWER FIRST ATTEMPTS TO GET AN OVERALL ESTIMATE OF TOTAL TENANCY GROUP INCOME (SEE BELOW) OR MAY TRY TO ARRANGE A FURTHER VISIT AFTER CONSULTING HEADQUARTERS

IF INFORMATION GIVEN BY PERSON/BY PROXY AT PERGIV AND EMPLOYMENT TRAINING/YOUTH TRAINING AT EMPACT

PerET — What period does your pay from your government scheme usually cover?

One week
Two weeks
Three weeks
Four weeks
Calendar month
One quarter (three months)
Six months
One year

PayET — How much in total do you receive from your government scheme each .... after deductions for tax and National Insurance?
IF RECEIVES £10 PLUS BENEFIT, ENTER ONLY £10 HERE AND THE REMAINDER AS INCOME FROM BENEFITS
ENTER TO NEAREST £1

IF DK AT PAYET

EstET — Will you please look at this card and estimate how much your receive each .... after deductions for tax and National Insurance? SHOW CARD S AND EXPLAIN
ENTER BAND NUMBER

IF INFORMATION GIVEN BY PERSON/PROXY AT PERGIV AND UNEMPLOYED/RETIRED/FULL-TIME EDUCATION/SOMETHING ELSE AT EMPACT

PdWk — (You may have told me this already) May I just check, are you doing any kind of paid work at present?

Yes
No

IF INFORMATION GIVEN BY PERSON/PROXY AT PERGIV AND FULL-TIME/PART-TIME WORK AT EMPACT OR YES AT PDWK

ESemp — CODE OR ASK
Are you working as an employee or are you self-employed?

Employee
Self-employed

IF SELF-EMPLOYED AT ESEMP

SEarn — How much did you earn from self-employment after tax, National Insurance, expenses and wages during the most recent 12 months or other period for which you have the figures?
ENTER TO NEAREST £1 ENTER 0 IF NOTHING OR MADE A LOSS

IF DK AT SEARN

EstSE — Will you please look at this card and estimate the amount you earned from self-employment after tax, National Insurance, expenses and wages during the most recent 12 months or other period for which you have the figures?
SHOW CARD S AND EXPLAIN IF FIRST TIME
ENTER BAND NUMBER

IF ANY AMOUNT OVER 0 GIVEN AT SEARN OR ESTSE

PerSE — Are these earnings for a twelve-month period or for a different period of time?

Twelve months
Different period

IF DIFFERENT PERIOD AT PERSE

PerSEE — How many months do the earnings cover?
ENTER TO THE NEAREST NUMBER OF MONTHS

IF 90 AT ESTSE (TOP BAND CHOSEN)

Top1 — You said that you earned £36,000 or more after tax, National Insurance, expenses and wages; can you please tell me what that would be each calendar month or average?
SHOW CARD S ENTER BAND NUMBER

ENTER TO NEAREST NUMBER OF MONTHS

IF SELF-EMPLOYED AT ESEMP

NI — Do you pay a National Insurance contribution?

Yes
No

IF YES AT NI

NIAmt   How much National Insurance did you pay for the period which the earnings covered?
ENTER AMOUNT TO NEAREST £1

IF DK AT NIAMT

EstNI   Will you please look at this card and estimate how much you paid in National Insurance for the period which the earnings covered?
SHOW CARD S AND EXPLAIN IF FIRST TIME
ENTER BAND NUMBER

IF SELF-EMPLOYED AT ESEMP

TaxSE   Have you paid any income tax direct to the Inland Revenue for the period which the earnings covered?

Yes
No

IF YES AT TAXSE

TaxAmt   How much income tax did you pay direct to the Inland Revenue for that period?
ENTER AMOUNT TO NEAREST £1

IF DK AT TAXAMT

EstTax   Will you please look at this card and estimate how much income tax you paid direct for that period?
SHOW CARD S ENTER BAND NUMBER

IF SELF-EMPLOYED AT ESEMP

SEPen   Do you make any payments into a personal or private pension plan?

Yes
No
IF YES AT SEPEN
PerSEP   How often do you make the payments?

One week
Two weeks
Three weeks
Four weeks
One Calendar month
One Quarter (three months)
Six months
One year

SEPpay   How much was the last payment you made?
ENTER TO NEAREST £1

IF DK AT SEPPAY

EPen1   Will you please look at this card and estimate how much you paid for your personal pension last time?
SHOW CARD S AND EXPLAIN IF FIRST TIME ENTER BAND NUMBER

IF INFORMATION GIVEN BY PERSON/PROXY AT PERGIV AND SELF-EMPLOYED AT ESEMP AND YES AT SEPEN AND ANY AMOUNT OVER 0 GIVEN AT SEARN OR ESTSE

DedPen   You've just told me your most recent earnings from self-employment after deductions for tax, National Insurance,

expenses and wages; is that before or after deducting any pension payments you made?

Before deducting payments
After deducting payments

IF INFORMATION GIVEN BY PERSON/PROXY AT PERGIV AND SELF-EMPLOYED AT ESEMP AND 0 AT SEARN OR DK AT ESTSE

RegP   Do you receive any regular payment from your work in a similar way to an employee?

Yes
No

IF INFORMATION GIVEN BY PERSON/PROXY AT PERGIV AND EMPLOYEE AT ESEMP OR YES AT REGP

PerWag   How often are you paid?

One week
Two weeks
Three weeks
Four weeks
One Calendar month
One Quarter (three months)
Six months
One year

THPay   How much is your usual take-home pay per ...., including overtime, bonuses, tips and commission but after deductions for tax, National Insurance and any contribution to your employer's pension scheme?
ENTER TO NEAREST £1

IF DK AT THPAY

EstTHP   Will you please look at this card and estimate your usual take-home pay per ...., including overtime, bonuses, tips and commission but after deductions for tax, National Insurance and pension contribution?
SHOW CARD S AND EXPLAIN IF FIRST TIME
ENTER BAND NUMBER

IF 90 AT ESTTHP

Top2   Can you please tell me what that would be each calendar month?
ENTER BAND NUMBER

TDed   How much is usually deducted for income tax and National Insurance per ....
ENTER TO NEAREST £1

IF DK AT TDED

EWag   Will you please look at this card and estimate how much is usually deducted for income tax and Nationa Insurance per .... SHOW CARD S AND EXPLAIN IF FIRST TIME
ENTER BAND NUMBER

Pens   May I just check, do you pay contributions into your employer's pension scheme which are deducted from your pay?
DO NOT INCLUDE PAYMENTS INTO PERSONAL PENSION PLAN ALREADY GIVEN EARLIER

Yes
No

IF YES AT PENS

ConPen   How much is deducted per .... altogether as contributions to pension funds?
ENTER TO NEAREST £1

IF DK AT CONPEN

EstCon   Will you please look at this card and estimate how much is deducted per .... altogether as contributions to pension funds?
SHOW CARD S AND EXPLAIN IF FIRST TIME ENTER BAND NUMBER

IF INFORMATION GIVEN BY PERSON/PROXY AT PERGIV AND EMPLOYEE AT ESEMP OR YES AT REGP

PSlip   INTERVIEWER CODE
Was pay slip consulted?

Not consulted
Consulted by informant only
Consulted by interviewer

IF FULL-TIME/PART-TIME WORK OR EMPLOYMENT/ YOUTH TRAINING AT EMPACT AND INFORMATION GIVEN BY PERSON/ PROXY AT PERGIV

OthJb   Do you earn any money from any other jobs or work you do?

Yes
No

IF YES AT OTHJB

PayOth   How much did you take home from your second job or jobs last month, after deductions for tax, National Insurance and pension contributions, if any?
ENTER TO NEAREST £1

IF DK AT PAYOTH

EstOth   Will you please look at this card and estimate how much you took home from your second job or jobs last month, after deductions for tax, National Insurance and pension contributions, if any?
SHOW CARD S AND EXPLAIN IF FIRST TIME ENTER BAND NUMBER

IF YES AT OTHJB

PaySec   Before any deductions, how much did you earn from your second job or jobs last month?
ENTER TO NEAREST £1

IF DK AT PAYSEC

EstSec   Will you please look at this card and estimate how much you earned from your second job or jobs last month, before any deductions?
SHOW CARD S AND EXPLAIN IF FIRST TIME ENTER BAND NUMBER

IF INFORMATION GIVEN BY PERSON/PROXY AT PERGIV AND NOT SELF-EMPLOYED AT ESEMP

PrP   May I just check, do you make any payments into a personal or private pension plan?

Yes
No

IF YES AT PRP

FrqP   How often do you make the payments?

One week
Two weeks
Three weeks
Four weeks
One Calendar month
One Quarter (three months)
Six months
One year

PrPPay   How much do you pay each .... in contributions to pension funds?
ENTER TO NEAREST £1

IF DK AT PRPPAY

SPrPay   Will you please look at this card and estimate how much you pay per .... in contributions to pension funds?
SHOW CARD S AND EXPLAIN IF FIRST TIME ENTER BAND NUMBER

IF INFORMATION GIVEN BY PERSON/PROXY AT PERGIV

OthSrc   Will you please look at this card and tell me if you are receiving any regular payments of the kinds listed on it?
SHOW CARD AA
     CODE ALL THAT APPLY

     Occupational pensions from former employer(s)
     Occupational pensions from spouse's/partner's former employer(s)
     Private pensions or annuities
     Regular redundancy payments from former employer(s)   None of these

IF ANY ANSWER EXCEPT NONE OF THESE AT OTHSRC

TotOS   How much do you receive in total each month from .... after tax is deducted?
ENTER TO NEAREST £1

IF DK AT TOTOS

EstOS   Will you please look at this card and estimate how much you receive in total each month from .... after tax is deducted?
SHOW CARD S AND EXPLAIN IF FIRST TIME ENTER BAND NUMBER

IF ANY ANSWER EXCEPT NONE OF THESE AT OTHSRC

TaxOS   How much tax is deducted from these payments each month?
ENTER TO NEAREST £1

IF DK AT TAXOS

EstTOS — Will you please look at this card and estimate how much tax is deducted from these payments each month?
SHOW CARD S AND EXPLAIN IF FIRST TIME
ENTER BAND NUMBER

IF INFORMATION GIVEN BY PERSON/PROXY AT PERGIV

OSrc2 — Will you please look at this card and tell me if you are receiving any regular payments of the kinds listed on it? SHOW CARD BB
CODE ALL THAT APPLY

Education grant
Regular payments from relatives or friends outside the household
Rent from property or subletting
Maintenance or separation allowance
None of these

IF ANY ANSWER EXCEPT NONE OF THESE AT OSRC2

TotOS2 — How much do you receive in total each month from ...., after tax is deducted?
ENTER TO NEAREST £1

IF DK AT TOTOS2

EstOS2 — Will you please look at this card and estimate how much you receive each month from ...., after tax is deducted?
SHOW CARD S AND EXPLAIN IF FIRST TIME
ENTER BAND NUMBER

IF ANY ANSWER EXCEPT NONE OF THESE AT OSRC2

TaxOS2 — How much tax is deducted from these payments each month? ENTER TO NEAREST £1

IF DK AT TAXOS2

EstTOS2 — Will you please look at this card and estimate how much tax is deducted from these payments each month?
SHOW CARD S AND EXPLAIN IF FIRST TIME ENTER BAND NUMBER

IF INFORMATION GIVEN BY PERSON/PROXY AT PERGIV

Saving — At present do you have over £3,000 in cash or savings, including bank and building society deposits, National Savings certificates, bonds, stocks and shares?
IF SAVINGS ARE HELD JOINTLY, ENTER IN ONE RECORD ONLY

All savings held jointly with another household member and given elsewhere
Yes, over £3,000
£3,000 or less in savings
No savings

IF ALL SAVINGS HELD JOINTLY AT SAVING

JtSav — ENTER PERSON NUMBER OF RECORD IN WHICH JOINT SAVINGS ARE GIVEN

IF YES, OVER £3,000 AT SAVING

MorSav — Do you have over £16,000 in cash or savings?

Yes, over £16,000
£16,000 or less in savings

IF £16,000 OR LESS AT MORSAV

TotSav — How much do you have in savings to the nearest £500?
ENTER TO NEAREST £500

IF YES, OVER £3,000/£3,000 LESS AT SAVING

IntSav — Do your savings/investments earn you interest?

Yes
No

IF YES AT INTSAV

TotInt — How much did you receive altogether in interest from your savings in the last 12 months?
ENTER TO NEAREST £1

IF DK AT TOTINT

EstInt — Will you please look at this card and estimate how much you received altogether in interest from your savings in the last 12 months?
SHOW CARD S AND EXPLAIN IF FIRST TIME
ENTER BAND NUMBER

IF INFORMATION GIVEN BY PERSON/PROXY AT PERGIV

Alout — At present do you make any regular payments to someone outside the household as maintenance or separation allowance?

Yes
No

IF YES AT ALOUT

PayAl — How much was the last payment?
ENTER TO NEAREST £1

IF DK AT PAYAL

EstAl — Will you please look at this card and estimate how much the last payment was?
SHOW CARD S AND EXPLAIN IF FIRST TIME ENTER BAND NUMBER

IF ANY ANSWER GIVEN AT PAYAL OR ESTAL

PerAl — What period did that cover?

One week
Two weeks
Three weeks
Four weeks
One Calendar month
One Quarter (three months)
Six months
One year

IF INFORMATION GIVEN BY PERSON/PROXY AT PERGIV

HBen   Some people qualify for Housing Benefit, that is, a rent rebate or allowance. Are you receiving Housing Benefit either directly or by having it paid to your landlord on your behalf?

Yes
No

IF YES AT HBEN

NHBen   Is it paid in your name?

Yes
No

IF YES AT NHBEN

FulHB   Is the benefit based on the full rent or on a reduced figure determined by the Rent Officer?

Full rent
Reduced figure

IF REDUCED FIGURE AT FULHB

RedHB   What was the reduced figure for rent?
ENTER TO NEAREST £1

IF ANY ANSWER GIVEN AT REDHB

PerRen   What period does that rent cover?

One week
Two weeks
Three weeks
Four weeks
One Calendar month
One Quarter (three months)
Six months
One year

IF YES AT HBEN

TotHB   How much did you get last time you received Housing Benefit?
ENTER TO NEAREST £1

IF DK AT TOTHB

EstHB   Will you please look at this card and estimate how much you received in Housing Benefit last time?
SHOW CARD S AND EXPLAIN IF FIRST TIME
ENTER BAND NUMBER

IF ANY ANSWER AT TOTHB OR ESTHB

PerHBP   How long a period did the Housing Benefit cover?

One week
Two weeks
Three weeks
Four weeks
One Calendar month
One Quarter (three months)
Six months
One year

IF INFORMATION GIVEN BY PERSON/PROXY AT PERGIV

BenA   Will you please look at this card and tell me if you are receiving any of the state benefits listed on it?
SHOW CARD CC
CODE ALL THAT APPLY
N.B. ENTER CHILD BENEFIT ON WOMAN'S RECORD UNLESS PAID TO LONE MALE PARENT

Child benefit (including one-parent benefit)
Income Support
State retirement pension or old age pension
Unemployment benefit
National Insurance sickness benefit (not employer's statutory sick pay)
Family Credit
Invalidity pension, invalidity benefit or allowance
Severe disablement allowance
None of them

BenB   Here is another list of benefits; are you receiving any of the benefits on this card?
SHOW CARD DD
CODE ALL THAT APPLY

Widow's pension or war widow's pension
Any other state widow's benefit (e.g. widowed mother's allowance)
War disablement pension
Industrial disablement benefit
Attendance allowance
Invalid care allowance
Disability working allowance
Disability living allowance
Any other type of state benefit
None of them

IF ANY ANSWER EXCEPT NONE OF THEM AT BENA OR BENB

PerBen   Thinking about all the benefits you receive, from both lists can you please tell me how often they are paid; are any of the benefits paid:
CODE ALL THAT APPLY

once a week
once a fortnight
once every three weeks
once every four weeks
once every calendar month
at any other periods?

IF AT ANY OTHER PERIODS AT PERBEN

SPerBn   How often is it/are they paid?
SPECIFY IN WEEKS

FOR EACH PERIOD MENTIONED AT PERBEN

TotBn1   Thinking of the benefit/all the benefits that is/are
TotBn2   paid once a week (....), how much do you receive (in etc total) from that/those benefit(s) each week?
ENTER TO NEAREST £1

IF DK AT TOTBN1 ETC.

EstBn1   Will you please look at this card and estimate how
etc.   much you receive (in total) each week from benefits that are paid once a week?
SHOW CARD S AND EXPLAIN IF FIRST TIME
ENTER BAND NUMBER

IF ANY ANSWER EXCEPT NONE OF THEM AT BENA OR BENB AND ANY AMOUNT GIVEN AT TOTBN1 ETC. OR TOTBN2 ETC.

TelBn   Thinking about all the benefits we have mentioned, it looks as though you receive about £.... per week in benefits altogether; does that seem about right or do you receive more than that or less than that?

About right
More
Less

IF MORE/LESS AT TELBN

EstBnT   Will you please look at this card and estimate how much you receive per week from benefits altogether?
SHOW CARD S AND EXPLAIN IF FIRST TIME
ENTER BAND NUMBER

IF INFORMATION GIVEN BY PERSON/PROXY AT PERGIV

RegInc   Do you have any regular income from any other source(s) which I haven't asked you about?

Yes
No

IF YES AT REGINC

TotRI   How much do you receive each month from sources not mentioned so far?
ENTER TO NEAREST £1

IF DK AT TOTRI

EstRI   Will you please look at this card and estimate how much you receive each month from sources not mentioned so far?
SHOW CARD S AND EXPLAIN IF FIRST TIME
ENTER BAND NUMBER

IF INFORMATION GIVEN BY PERSON/PROXY AT PERGIV

ETax   Have you paid any income tax direct to the Inland Revenue in the last 12 months, apart from any you may have told me about already?

Yes
No

IF YES AT ETAX

TaxP   How much tax have you paid direct to the Inland Revenue in the last 12 months, apart from any tax you have already told me about?
ENTER TO NEAREST £1

IF DK AT TAXP

EstTx   Will you please look at this card and estimate how much tax you have paid directly to the Inland Revenue in the last 12 months, apart from any tax you have already told me about?
SHOW CARD S AND EXPLAIN IF FIRST TIME
ENTER BAND NUMBER

IF INFORMATION GIVEN BY PERSON/PROXY AT PERGIV

TelNet   I've been asking you about your income from many different possible sources and, from what you have told me, it looks as though your total income from all sources after deductions for income tax and National Insurance is about £.... per week; that is, £.... per month or £.... per year. Does that look about right or is your total net income more than that or less than that?

About right
More
Less

IF MORE/LESS AT TELNET

EstNet   Will you please look at this card and estimate how much your total income from all sources is after deductions for income tax and National Insurance? Please give it weekly, monthly or annually, whichever you prefer.
SHOW CARD S AND EXPLAIN IF FIRST TIME
ENTER BAND NUMBER

IF ANY BAND CHOSEN AT ESTNET

PerNet   Is that:

weekly
monthly
or annually?

IF 90 AT ESTNET AND ANNUALLY AT PERNET

TopNet   Can you please tell me what that would be each calendar month?
SHOW CARD S AND ENTER BAND NUMBER

IF INFORMATION GIVEN BY PERSON/PROXY AT PERGIV

TelGrs   It looks as though your total income from all sources before deductions for income tax and National Insurance is about £.... per week; that is, £.... per month or £.... per year. Does that look about right or is your total gross income more than that or less than that?

About right
More
Less

IF MORE/LESS AT TELGRS

EstGrs   Will you please look at this card and estimate how much your total income from all sources is before deductions for income tax and National Insurance? Please give it weekly, monthly or annually, whichever you prefer.
SHOW CARD S AND EXPLAIN IF FIRST TIME
ENTER BAND NUMBER

IF ANY BAND CHOSEN AT ESTGRS

PerGrs   Is that:

weekly
monthly
or annually?

IF 90 AT ESTGRS AND ANNUALLY AT PERGRS

TopGrs   Can you please tell me what that would be each calendar month?
SHOW CARD S AND ENTER BAND NUMBER

IF OPTION 1 AND OPTION 2 NOT POSSIBLE AT PERGIV

NtEst   ASK OF MAIN INFORMANT
We need to have an idea of the total income of the people who are covered by your tenancy agreement, that is, ...
.... You are in a better position to make a guess at this than we are, so would you mind looking at this card and telling me where you think your total income added together falls, after deductions for tax and National Insurance? Please give it as a weekly amount, a monthly amount or an annual amount, whichever you find easiest.
SHOW CARD S AND ENTER BAND NUMBER

IF ANY BAND CHOSEN AT NTEST

PerE   May I just check, is that a weekly, monthly or

Weekly
Monthly
Annual

IF ANY BAND EXCEPT 90 CHOSEN AT NTEST OR IF 90 CHOSEN AND ANNUAL AT PERE

GsEst   And would you mind looking at the card again and telling me where you think your total weekly/monthly/annual income added together falls, before deductions for tax and National Insurance?
SHOW CARD S AND ENTER BAND NUMBER

IF 90 AT GSEST

GsEs1   Can you please tell me what that would be each calendar month?
SHOW CARD S AND ENTER BAND NUMBER

IF 90 AT NTEST AND ANNUAL AT PERE

NtEstM   Can you please tell me what that would be each calendar month on average?
SHOW CARD S AND ENTER BAND NUMBER

GsEstM   And would you mind looking at the card again and telling me where you think your total income added together falls, before deductions for tax and National Insurance? Can you please give it to me as a monthly amount.
SHOW CARD S AND ENTER BAND NUMBER.

List of figures and tables

List of figures and tables

Chapter 3

Figures

Annex tables

Chapter 4

Figures

Chapter 5

Chapter 6

Printed in the United Kingdom for HMSO.
Dd.0301078, C9, 6/95, 3400, 5673, 326010.